INSIGHTS

SOCIAL

PSYCHOLOGY

A Customized Psychology Reader

General Editor
Marianne Miserandino
Arcadia University

Compiled by
Dr. Mary Inman
Hope College
Social Psychology
Spring 2008

Pearson Learning Solutions

New York   Boston   San Francisco
London   Toronto   Sydney   Tokyo   Singapore   Madrid
Mexico City   Munich   Paris   Cape Town   Hong Kong   Montreal

Senior Vice President, Editorial and Marketing: Patrick F. Boles
Senior Sponsoring Editor: Natalie Danner
Development Editor: Mary Kate Paris
Editorial Assistant: Jill Johnson
Marketing Manager: Brian T. Berkeley
Operations Manager: Eric M. Kenney
Production Manager: Jennifer Berry
Rights Manager: Jillian Santos
Art Director: Renée Sartell
Cover Designer: Seamus Culligan

Cover Art: "Vine Pattern," courtesy of Photo Disc, Inc.

Please visit our website at *www.pearson custom .com.*

· Attention bookstores: For permission to return any unsold stock, contact us at *pe-customreturns@pearson.com.*

Pearson Learning Solutions, 501 Boylston Street, Suite 900, Boston, MA 02116
A Pearson Education Company
www.pearsoned.com

10 11 12 13 14 V3NL 17 16 15 14 13

ISBN 10: 0-536-77598-2
ISBN 13: 978-0-536-77598-6

PREFACE

Insight is not one moment of revelation. The self is not a book to be read; its pages are constantly turning in a high wind and only a word can be glimpsed here, a line there, from which, with persistence, some idea of the whole can be pieced together.

Jo Coubert

Pearson Custom Publishing and our General Editor for social psychology, Marianne Miserandino, arc proud to bring you *Insights: Readings in Social Psychology.*

Our goal in the creation of *Insights* is that it does, in fact, assist you in providing your students with the richest possible learning experience—one that goes beyond just the basic facts, dates, definitions and so on of a survey text to one that also exposes students to the key central ideas of social psychology *and* gives key examples of that theory in practice through applied examples. In doing this, we hope that the learning experience will help impart a fascination with the subject not only during the undergraduate course, but for many years to come.

With *Insights*, we have provided you with a rich and diverse archive of high quality, carefully edited readings in such a way that both professors and students will have easy and cost-effective access to the minds and ideas that reveal and help explain some of the central ideas and issues of social psychology. Within *Insights*, you will find over 130 readings and 15 topical introductions—both of which we will be updated and expanded yearly—from which you can choose *only* those readings and introductions that are germane to your particular course. No longer will you and your students have to be dependent on the standard 'one-size-fits-all' college reader, which often includes more material than will be covered in the course, yet often also lacks those particular pieces that are viewed as essential by individual instructors.

Our ultimate hope that you will find *Insights* to be an essential source of readings in social psychology—a source noted for its depth, breadth, *and* flexibility—that meets the highest scholarly and pedagogical standards.

We welcome your feedback and suggestions on *Insights* at any time. Please simply send comments and suggestions to customlibrary@pearson.com.

Contents

WHAT IS SOCIAL PSYCHOLOGY?

"Imagine you are a skin cell. . . . [Y]our job is to toss out bundles of chemicals when told to, to shrivel up tight when told to, to stand your ground when bumped, and generally to keep up your borders. Food and water gets (*sic*) delivered when you need it. . . . If you thought about yourself at all you would be unlikely to think of yourself as an independent cell, doing your own thing. . . . [Y]ou would know that you are part of a body. If you left, you would die. If you quit and the others around you quit, the body would die" (Aron & Aron, 1981, p. 21).

That we are a part of a social system, much like the skin cell described above, is at the heart of social psychology. Social psychology is that branch of psychology which studies how people interact with other people in social situations. Social psychology "attempts to understand and explain how the thoughts, feelings, and behavior of individuals are influenced by the actual, imagined, or implied presence of other human beings" (Allport, 1954, p. 5). In contrast to personality psychology, which focuses on those factors *inside* a person that may cause an individual to think or act in certain ways, social psychology studies those factors *outside* a person which cause people to think or act in certain ways.

The idea that people may behave in certain ways is probably not new to you. However, the idea that external situations may cause or elicit certain thoughts or behaviors from people may be new or unusual. This is the basic assumption of social psychology. According to Aron and Aron (1981), the goal of social psychology is to make people aware that, just as the cell described above is part of a body, we are each part of a social organism.

The tricky thing is that we are often not aware that we are part of a larger social world. We tend to think of ourselves and others as separate individuals. One way to illustrate this basic assumption of social psychology is to imagine that understanding another person is like a figure-ground problem (see Figure 1). When you look at this picture, can you see the vase? We see people acting and interacting in the world, and often we assume that their behavior stems from the kind of people they are on the inside. A driver lets us go first at a stop sign, a stranger smiles at us, a mother takes the hand of her toddler to cross the street. In trying to explain behavior, social psychology focuses not on the person, but on the background, or social situation, that may be influencing that person—much as the vase in Figure 1 makes a silhouette of two faces when pushed to the background. How might the social situation explain the above behaviors? The other person at the stop sign is a cop waiting to ticket stop-sign violators, the stranger thinks you are attractive, the mother is guiding the toddler away from a strange dog.

Social psychology encompasses three major areas: social influence, attitudes and attitude change, and our perception and interaction with others. Social influence includes topics such as culture, conformity, obedience, compliance, and group influences. Attitudes and attitude change include persuasion and advertising. Perception and interaction include forming impressions, making social judgments, understanding ourselves, attraction, liking, loving, prejudice, aggression, altruism, gender, and conflict and peace-making. Finally, social psychology also includes a number of applied areas, such as environmental psychology, psychology and the law, and health psychology.

Figure 1 *Social Psychology as a Figure-Ground Problem*

With this description of the field in mind, let's now explore five major themes in social psychology. We'll then consider some questions that are the focus of current research. Finally, we'll take a look at the various career opportunities open to social psychologists today.

ᓬ FIVE THEMES IN SOCIAL PSYCHOLOGY

There are five themes, or guiding principles, of human social behavior that can help you to organize and understand the many and diverse topics that make up the field of social psychology. Though social psychologists might argue about exactly which themes best summarize the field (for examples, see Fiske & Stevens, 1999; Aronson, Wilson, & Akert, 1997; Smith & Mackie, 1995; and Zimbardo, 1992), all would agree that these five are among the most important. Let's consider each of these in turn (see Table 1).

Table 1 *Five Themes in Social Psychology*

Theme 1:	People construct their social worlds.
Theme 2:	People tend to underestimate the impact of the social situation.
Theme 3:	People need to view themselves in a positive light.
Theme 4:	People need to feel connected to other people.
Theme 5:	People process information about their social world in the most efficient way possible.

Theme 1: People construct their social worlds. This first theme suggests that, if we want to understand a person's behavior, reality is not nearly as important as the person's *understanding,* or *construal,* of reality. That is, to understand how a person is influenced by others—from the definition of social psychology—it is more important to understand how that person perceives or interprets the social environment than it is to understand the environment itself (Lewin, 1943). Further, people often create their own realities by their expectations and their actions. To understand how this principle works, try the following thought experiment: Imagine that as you are walking to your next class, you smile at every person you pass. How do you think people would react to your behavior? In a college or university community, most people would probably smile back at you. How would you feel by the time you reached your destination? You would probably feel pretty good about yourself and your community. You might think, "Wow, what a friendly place! I like going to school here." But now imagine scowling at every person you passed. How would others react to you? They would probably express displeasure or confusion and avoid you. How would you feel, and what would you think about your community? You might mutter to yourself, "What a bunch of snobs. I can't stand this place." Now compare these two experiences. Despite the fact that each "social world" involves the exact same individual and setting, you would probably prefer to live in the first one.

This example reveals what is meant by construal. Despite the same "reality" in both scenarios, the campus would feel different depending on your interpretation of the events in each case. Yet, you were the one who caused the campus to appear different in these two situations. Similar social "experiments" like this happen all the time. The amazing thing is that often we don't even know that we are interpreting or construing things or that we have actually caused or constructed our social situations.

Sometimes we share that construal with other people; for example, when you and a friend agree on an interpretation of another friend's behavior. Sometimes an entire society shares a construction; for example, perpetuating different salaries for men and women who are doing the same job equally well. In such cases, the only "reality" that exists is the one that people have constructed. It does a woman no good to tell herself that she is just as competent as the man working next to her if their salary differences tell her that she's not. To an amazing extent, the "social reality"—what others say or what society says—is more powerful than "objective reality."

In trying to understand how someone is influenced by other people, we need to understand that person's interpretation of his or her social world. At the same time, however, we would need to remind ourselves that people's perceptions are highly subjective. Social psychologists believe that people strive to make sense out of their social worlds. This sense-making involves interpreting the raw data that the world presents. As a result, different people may arrive at very different conclusions while interpreting the same data. But because each person has his or her own perspective, we can't say that one interpretation is wrong and another one is right.

2

Theme 2: *People tend to underestimate the impact of the social situation*. This second principle follows directly from the first one (see Ross & Nisbett, 1991). One way that people consistently construe their social world is to *overestimate* the internal personality factors of the people involved and to *underestimate* the impact of the situation. This tendency is so pervasive that it is called the fundamental attribution error (Ross, 1977), the correspondence bias (Jones & Harris, 1967), or lay dispositionism (Ross & Nisbett, 1991). For example, many people come to believe that actors are like the characters they play, even though the actors are merely playing a role. In a newspaper article, Tom Hanks reported that after he played Forrest Gump, a simple character who reflected that "life is like a box of chocolates" in a popular movie, fans sent the actor hundreds of boxes of chocolates (*Newsday*, 1995). The believability of Hank's acting may have caused these fans to forget that the situation—getting paid to play a role—was what had shaped his behavior in the movie, not his personality.

Similarly, the fundamental attribution error can lead us to assume that people who hurt one another in the name of obedience are crazy or sadistic (Milgram, 1965), that bystanders who fail to intervene in a crime are apathetic (Latané & Darley, 1969), that people who conform are weak-willed (Asch, 1955), that people who are in prison are less than human (Zimbardo, 1975), or that people who behave aggressively are aggressive by nature (Berkowitz & LePage, 1967). *All of these assumptions are wrong!* In each of these experiments, as we will see, the situation had a much greater effect on the results than did the personalities of the participants. This second theme—that we underestimate the impact of the social situation—explains why we find so many results of social psychology experiments counterintuitive, interesting, and even shocking.

Theme 3: *People need to view themselves in a positive light*. We all have a strong need to view ourselves "as decent, competent, likable, honorable, human beings" (Aronson, Wilson, & Akert, 1997, p. 19). In order to achieve a positive view of ourselves, we may interpret events in a favorable or self-flattering way. This tendency to construe events so as to maintain a high or positive view of ourselves leads to many interesting social phenomena. For example, we tend to present ourselves in the best possible light (Jones & Pittman, 1982), justify or rationalize our behavior and change our attitudes (Festinger, 1957), make excuses for our social *faux pas* (Miller & Ross, 1975), see ourselves as better than average (Alicke et al., 1995), remember our successes more than our failures (Kunda, 1990), see good things as more likely and bad things as less likely to happen to us than to others (Weinstein, 1980), give ourselves but not others the benefit of the doubt (Pettigrew, 1979), act favorably toward people in our own social group and act in a prejudicial manner toward outsiders (Tajfel, Billig, & Bundy, 1971), and believe that we have control in uncontrollable situations (Langer, 1975). We

also strive to maintain our self-esteem by choosing certain friends (Tesser, 1988) or rooting for winning sports teams (Cialdini et al., 1976).

Theme 4: *People need to feel connected to other people*. We are inherently social beings. From the time we are born, we not only want to feel close to others but also need other people in order to survive physically and emotionally (Bowlby, 1969). We naturally form bonds with our family and friends, and with larger social groups. We also seek the support and acceptance of others. How we become attracted to or attached to others through friendship and kinship constitutes a major area of research in social psychology. There are many theories about how and why we form bonds with others through attraction, liking, and loving, and how we dissolve bonds through separation, divorce, or death. This basic theme of connectedness to others even informs theories about why we help some people, why we act aggressively toward others, and how we maintain our health or design and decorate our living space. Remember that the definition of social psychology starts with the premise that we are influenced by the "actual, imagined, or implied *presence of other human beings*" (Allport, 1954, p. 5). Without other people, there would be no *social* psychology.

Theme 5: *People process information about their social world in the most efficient way possible*. We are constantly perceiving, thinking, and making decisions about our social worlds. How do we process all of this information? We do it by taking shortcuts, applying rules of thumb, reducing complex problems into simple ones, and using our preconceptions or biases. In short, we act as "cognitive misers" when thinking about and responding to our social worlds (Taylor, 1981).

Some early models of how people think about their social worlds were prescriptive; that is, they described ways in which people *ought to* process information. The many variations of what we call attribution theory are examples of such prescriptive models (see Kelly, 1967). But more recently, social psychologists have discovered that people are not nearly so thoughtful or rational as these models suggested. Instead, we seem to prefer efficiency over accuracy, searching for fast, adequate interpretations and decisions rather than taking the time to arrive at slower, more accurate ones (Fiske & Taylor, 1991). In understanding others in order to get along with them, we seem to strive for a practical or pragmatic accuracy rather than a psychological understanding of their entire personalities (Swann, 1984).

This realization has led to the metaphor of the social thinker as a "motivated tactician" (Fiske & Taylor, 1991). In other words, we each have many ways of thinking about and making decisions, and we choose which strategy to use depending on our goals, needs, and motives of the moment. Sometimes we choose for accuracy, as in deciding whether a potential mate is "the one." More often, we choose the cognitively easy way out, as in selecting a potential date because he or she is attractive—without thinking about how little we have in common or what we will talk about on the date. This tendency can help explain stereotyping and prejudice, approaches to conflict resolution, patterns in eyewitness identification, and responses to advertising and persuasion.

❧ CURRENT RESEARCH AND PHILOSOPHICAL QUESTIONS

The field of social psychology is particularly prone to self-reflection (Taylor, 1998). As a result, social psychologists are continually debating various issues. Some of these issues can be explored through research; others are broader, more philosophical questions. Let's turn to some current research questions and then consider the larger philosophical issues that the field is grappling with today (see Table 2).

Table 2 *Current Research and Philosophical Questions*

Are people more like intuitive scientists or motivated tacticians?

What is the relative influence of personality and social situations on behavior?

What motivates people to help others, altruism or egoism?

Is social psychology progressing as a science?

Which is more valuable, basic or applied research?

How can social psychology help solve the social problems facing the world today?

Are people more like intuitive scientists or motivated tacticians? Recall that people tend to process information about their social worlds in the most efficient way possible. Even though social psychologists agree with this basic premise, they still debate the meaning of "efficiency." This is an exciting time in cognitive social psychology, and theories about how people think about their social worlds are shifting dramatically. For example, some researchers are asking whether the earlier view of people as "intuitive psychologists" (Kelley, 1967) ought to be abandoned in favor of the newer "motivated tactician" view. Others are questioning whether the metaphor "motivated tactician" truly describes how people think about their social worlds (Fiske & Taylor, 1991).

What is the relative influence of personality and social situations on behavior? For the last 30 years or so, the field of social psychology has emphasized the role of the situation in human behavior. As a result of the emphasis on how people think about social situations, there is now a renewed interest in the role of personality in behavior (Baumeister, 1998). Many researchers believe that an integration of our knowl-edge of the situation *and* of the person can greatly enrich our understanding of social behavior.

What motivates people to help others, altruism or egoism? This is a very old question for social psychologists who study prosocial, or helping, behavior (see Batson, 1987). For a long time, some researchers assumed that all helping was altruistic; that is, people helped others without any thought of personal gain. Others have pointed out that there is nearly always a personal gain or a benefit through helping, and that helping is therefore motivated not by altruism but by egoism. This question—Is there such a thing as true altruism—continues to stimulate lively debate within the field.

Is social psychology progressing as a science? A recent paper in the *Journal of Personality and Social Psychology* that summarized publication trends led to a symposium on what these trends might mean. Reis and Stiller (1992) found that research based on multiple studies, large numbers of subjects, and complicated statistical techniques had increased over the previous 20 years. These two authors argued that the trend towards increasing complexity in research methods suggested progress and maturation in the field. Others wondered whether this trend meant that research was simply becoming more sophisticated or esoteric (Funder, 1992; West, Newsom, & Fenaughty, 1992; Zanna, 1992). Still others worried that this trend toward complexity was an indication that the field had come to value the avoidance of mistakes. Such meticulousness might mean that some interesting, creative, and "cutting-edge" research was not being published (Higgins, 1992). Indeed, one researcher, only half-kidding, lamented "the premature demise of the solo experiment" (Wegner, 1992).

Which is more valuable, basic or applied research? In social psychology, basic research is concerned with theory building and theory testing. Applied research uses theory to address social problems. The two kinds of research create a valuable synergy, as each informs and advances the others. Kurt Lewin, a founder of the field of social psychology, argued, "There is nothing so practical as a good theory" (Lewin, 1943b, p. 118). Few social psychologists would argue with Lewin's statement. Some of the best researchers in the field approach their work from both a theoretical and an applied perspective. Indeed, you can't properly apply a theory unless you know how it works, nor can you fully understand a theory until you see the many ways in which it plays out in the real world.

However, it is difficult to give equal weight to both kinds of research when resources such as funding, laboratory facilities, time, journal space, and human and animal experimental participants are limited. For example, many research supporters understandably want to know how their money is being used. It is much easier to see any direct benefits of funding when the research is applied than when it is theoretical.

This ongoing dilemma affects all aspects of the research process (see Anderson, Lindsay, & Bushman, 1999) and has caused tension between basic and applied researchers (e.g., Forsyth, 1989).

How can social psychology help solve the social problems facing the world today? Social psychology has a history of using research and theory to try to resolve pressing social problems (Jones, 1998; Aron & Aron, 1989). Today, the problems tearing at societies in the United States and around the world call for an even more focused application of social psychological research. In fact, after many years of theory building, social psychology is now more prepared than ever to tackle tough social issues. Researchers are working hard to reduce prejudice and stereotyping, mitigate the impact of television violence, foster helping behavior and cooperation, alleviate the problems caused by crowding and stress, promote healthy behaviors and better medical practices, improve the criminal justice system, encourage the prevention of and education about AIDS, reduce youth violence, prevent divorce or lessen its negative impact, help people cope with aging, and reduce conflict in the world.

❦ WHAT SOCIAL PSYCHOLOGISTS DO

"If the lives of individuals and social groups are full of mystery, then personality and social psychologists are the detectives investigating these mysteries. Systematically observing and describing people's actions, measuring or manipulating aspects of social situations, these sleuths use the methods of science to reveal the answers to the kinds of puzzling questions we each encounter every day" (Society for Personality and Social Psychology, SPSP, 1998).

Given this description of what social psychologists do, it is no surprise to find them working in numerous areas. Approximately 50 percent of them work in universities or colleges as researchers and teachers—in departments of psychology, business, education, political science, law, health sciences, and medicine (American Psychological Association, APA, 1996; SPSP, 1998). Others work in the private sector or in government. Some of these social psychologists work as consultants, researchers, marketing directors, managers, or political strategists. Others work as designers and evaluators of policy and programs in education, conflict resolution, and environmental protection (SPSP, 1998).

To become a social psychologist, you need more than an undergraduate degree with a major in psychology (though you may be able to land a job as a research assistant in a university or in a marketing research firm with such credentials). In some careers, a master's degree (M.A.) may be sufficient. However, most social psychologists have earned the doctoral degree (Ph.D.), which requires at least four or five years of study and qualifies people to be independent, professional researchers (SPSP, 1998).

Doctoral programs are highly selective and rigorous. Most of them teach the theoretical and conceptual foundations of social psychology and basic knowledge of the field; develop critical and theoretical thinking skills; and provide training in research methodology, data analysis, report writing, and research presentation (SPSP, 1998).

Graduate programs in social psychology differ in the areas of research they specialize in. As you discover areas of the field that interest you, you can learn more about the work of individual researchers by checking out the Web resources on that area. Many labs have their own Web sites, where they publish their latest findings, discuss key issues, and encourage visitors to participate in experiments being conducted by the lab group via the Internet.

You can also find out more about recent research in social psychology by reading the current issues of the major journals of the field. These include the *Journal of Personality and Social Psychology*, *Personality and Social Psychology Bulletin*, *Personality and Social Psychology Review*, and the yearly publication *Advances in Experimental Social Psychology*. In addition, the American Psychological Association (APA) encourages students to join as affiliate members to receive the APA's monthly magazine, *The Monitor*; to attend national and regional conferences; or to volunteer at a conference. Attending conferences is a great way to hear about the newest research in social and other areas of psychology.

Now you have an overview of the current themes and issues in the field of social psychology. The following articles, research reports, and newspaper- and magazine-article summaries will take you deeper into the field, including its history and methods. Perhaps the best way to find out what social psychology is all about is to turn the page and start reading!

REFERENCES

Alicke, M. D., Klotz, M. L., Breitenbecher, D. L., Yurak, T. J., & Vrendenburg, D. S. (1995). Personal contact, individuation and the better than average effect. *Journal of Personality and Social Psychology, 68*, 804–825.

Allport, G. (1954). The historical background of modern social psychology. In G. Lindzey (Ed.). *The handbook of social psychology* (1st ed., Vol. 1, pp.1–46). Reading, MA: Addison-Wesley.

American Psychological Association (1996). *Doctorate Employment Survey.* Washington, DC: author.

Anderson, C. A., Lindsay, J. J., & Bushman, B. J. (1999). Research in the psychology lab: Truth or triviality? *Current Directions in Psychological Science, 8*(1), 3–9.

Aron, A., & Aron, E. M. (1989). *The heart of social psychology.* Lexington, MA: Lexington Books.

Aronson, E., Wilson, T. D., & Akert, R. M. (1999). *Social psychology* (3rd ed.). New York: Addison-Wesley.

Asch, S. E. (1955, November). Opinions and social pressure. *Scientific American*, 31–35.

Batson, C. D. (1987). Prosocial motivation: Is it ever truly altruistic? In L. Berkowitz (Ed.). *Advances in experimental social psychology* (Vol. 20, pp. 65–122). New York: Academic Press.

Baumeister, R. F. (1998). The self. In D. Gilbert, S. T. Fiske, & G. Lindzey (Eds.). *The handbook of social psychology* (4th ed., Vol. 1, pp. 680–740). Reading, MA: Addision-Wesley.

Berkowitz, L., & LePage, A. (1967). Weapons as aggression-eliciting stimuli. *Journal of Personality and Social Psychology, 7*, 202–207.

Bowlby, J. (1969). *Attachment and loss: Attachment.* New York: Basic Books.

Cialdini, R. B., Borden, R. J., Thorne, A., Walker, M. R., Freeman, S., & Sloan, L. R. (1976). Basking in reflected glory: Three (football) field studies. *Journal of Personality and Social Psychology, 34*, 366–375.

Festinger, L. (1957). *A theory of cognitive dissonance.* Stanford: Stanford University Press.

Fiske, S. T., & Stevens, L. (1999). *Five themes for teaching social psychology.* Paper presented at the Teaching Institute at the Annual Meeting of the American Psychological Society, Denver.

Fiske, S. T., & Taylor, S. E. (1991). *Social cognition.* New York: McGraw-Hill.

Forsyth, D. R. (1989). Social psychology's three little pigs. In M. Leary (Ed.), *The state of social psychology.* Newbury Park, CA: Sage.

Funder, D. C. (1992). Psychology from the other side of the line: Editorial processes and publication trends at JPSP. *Personality and Social Psychology Bulletin, 18*, 493–497.

Higgins, E. T. (1992). Increasingly complex but less interesting articles: Scientific progress or regulatory problems? *Personality and Social Psychology Bulletin, 18*, 489–492.

Jones, E. E. (1998). Major developments in five decades of social psychology. In D. Gilbert, S. T. Fiske, & G. Lindzey (Eds.). *The handbook of social psychology* (4th ed., Vol. 1, pp. 3–57). Reading, MA: Addison-Wesley.

Jones, E. E., & Harris, V. A. (1967). The attribution of attitudes. *Journal of Experimental Social Psychology, 3*, 2–24.

Jones, E. E., & Pittman, T. S. (1982). Toward a general theory of strategic self-presentation. In J. Suls (Ed.), *Psychological perspectives on the self* (Vol. 1, pp. 231–262).

Kelley, H. H. (1967). Attribution theory in social psychology. In D. Levine (Ed.) *Nebraska symposium on motivation* (Vol. 15, pp. 192–240). Lincoln: University of Nebraska Press.

Kunda, Z. (1990). The case for motivated reasoning. *Psychological Bulletin, 108*, 480–498.

Langer, E. (1975). The illusion of control. *Journal of Personality and Social Psychology, 32*, 311–328.

Latané, B., & Darley, J. M. (1969). Bystander "apathy". *American Scientist, 57*, 228–238.

Lewin, K. (1943a). Defining the "field" at a given time. *Psychological Review, 50*, 292-310.

Lewin, K. (1943b). Psychology and the process of group living. *The Journal of Social Psychology. SPSSI Bulletin, 17*, 113-131.

Milgram, S. (1965). Some conditions of obedience and disobedience to authority, *Human Relations, 18(1)*, 57–75.

Miller, D. T., & Ross, M. (1975). Self-serving biases in the attribution of causality: Fact or fiction? *Psychological Bulletin, 82*, 213–225.

Newsday, (1995, December 27). *People.* p. A6.

Pettigrew, T. F. (1979). The ultimate attribution error: Extending Allport's cognitive analysis of prejudice. *Personality and Social Psychology Bulletin, 55*, 461–476.

Reis, H. T., & Stiller, J. (1992). Publication trends in JPSP: a three-decade review. *Personality and Social Psychology Bulletin, 18*, 465–472.

Ross, L. (1977). The intuitive psychologist and his shortcomings: Distortions in the attribution process. L. Berkowitz (Ed.). *Advances in experimental social psychology* (Vol. 10, pp. 174–221). New York: Academic Press.

Ross, L., & Nisbett, R. E. (1991). *The person and the situation: Perspectives of social psychology.* New York: McGraw-Hill.

Rubin, E. (1915). *Synoplevede Figurer.* Copenhagen: Gyldendalske.

Smith, E. R., & Mackie, D. M. (1995). *Social psychology.* New York: Worth.

Society for Personality and Social Psychology (1998). What is a personality/social psychologist? www.spsp.org/what.htm.

Swann, W. B., Jr. (1984). Quest for accuracy in person perception: A matter of pragmatics. *Psychological Review, 91*, 457–475.

Tajfel, H., Billig, M. G., & Bundy, R. P. (1971). Social categorization and intergroup behavior. *European Journal of Social Psychology, 2*, 149–178.

Taylor, S. E. (1981). The interface of cognitive and social psychology. J. Harvey (Ed.). *Cognition, social behavior, and the environment* (pp. 189–211). Hillsdale, NJ: Erlbaum.

Taylor, S. E. (1998). The social being in social psychology. In D. Gilbert, S. T. Fiske, & G. Lindzey (Eds.). *The handbook of social psychology* (4th ed., Vol. 1, pp. 680–740). Reading, MA: Addison-Wesley.

Tesser, A. (1988). Toward a self-evaluation maintenance model of social behavior. In L. Berkowitz, (Ed.). *Advances in experimental social psychology* (Vol. 21, pp. 181–227). San Diego, CA: Academic Press.

Wegner, D. M. (1992). The premature demise of the solo experiment. *Personality and Social Psychology Bulletin, 18*, 504–508.

Weinstein, N. D. (1980). Unrealistic optimism about future life events. *Journal of Personality and Social Psychology, 39*, 806–820.

West, S. G., Newsom, J. T., & Fenaughty, A. (1992). Publication trends in JPSP: Stability and change in topics, methods, and theories across two decades. *Personality and Social Psychology Bulletin, 18*, 473–484.

Zanna, M. P. (1992). My life as a dog (I mean editor). *Personality and Social Psychology Bulletin, 18*, 485–488.

Zimbardo, P. (1992). *Teaching social psychology.* Paper presented at the Teaching Institute of the Annual Meeting of the American Psychological Society, Washington, DC.

Zimbardo, P. (1975). Transforming experimental research into advocacy for social change. In M. Deutsch & H. A. Hornstein (Eds.). *Applying social psychology.* Hillsdale, NJ: Erlbaum.

Suggested Readings

American Psychological Association (1996). *Psychology/careers for the 21st century.* Washington, DC: author.

Argyle, M. (1992). *The social psychology of everyday life*. New York: Routledge.

Aron, A., & Aron, E. M. (1989). *The heart of social psychology*. Lexington, MA: Lexington Books.

Brannigan, G. C., & Merens, M. R. (1995). *The social psychologists: Research adventures*. New York: McGraw-Hill.

Carroll, J. L., Shmidt, J. L., Jr., & Sorensen, R. (1992). Careers in psychology: Or what can I do with a bachelor's degree. *Psychological Reports, 71*, 1151–1154.

Morgeson, F. P., Seligman, M. E. P., Sternberg, R. J., Taylor, S. E., & Manning, C. M. (1999). Lessons learned from life in psychological science: Implications for young scientists. *American Psychologist, 54*

RESEARCH METHODS

୬

"**S**cientists Discover Life on Mars." "New York City Is Sinking." "TV Violence Responsible for Copycat Killings." "Portable Phones Cause Brain Cancer." "Elvis spotted in Roswell, New Mexico." Take another look at each of these news headlines. Are they from supermarket tabloids or from *CNN*? As you've probably guessed from trying this little exercise, sometimes it's hard to tell fact from fiction. Fortunately, there is a powerful tool available that can help you scientifically evaluate any claims—whether you're a news "consumer" or a student of social psychology. This tool is called research methodology.

Social psychology is a *science*. That means that social psychologists have accumulated knowledge in the field by using the scientific method to devise and test theories through conducting research. Essentially *everything* you learn in your social psychology class is based on theory and research. This chapter gives you a closer look at the logic of theory building, the process of hypothesis testing, and the methods of social psychological research.

୬ THE RESEARCH PROCESS

The process of social psychological research involves a number of steps (see Table 1). Social psychologists, like all scientists, must go through a strict process: selecting a topic to study, reading past research to find out what's been discovered on that topic before, developing a theory, formulating a hypothesis, selecting a research method, collecting the data, analyzing the data, and reporting the results.

୬ EVALUATING A THEORY

Most social psychological knowledge is based on theory. Theories are abstract concepts or constructs that describe or explain the phenomenon under study. Theories advance the field by helping to identify or classify events, predict future events, explain past events, understand causes, and guide or inspire research (Pettigrew, 1996). From theories, researchers develop specific hypotheses, or predictions, which they then test in an experiment. The outcome of the experiment will either support or fail to support the researcher's hypothesis. With enough experimental evidence, theories are confirmed, modified, revised, or abandoned (see, for example, Levy, 1997).

In general, theories are considered "good" if they have an internal logic and coherence; predict events in a simple, parsimonious way; can be proven false; and are useful for understanding phenomena and for generating research. Theories that lack any of these qualities are either improved upon or abandoned for better theories.

Though it is tempting to believe that theories can be proved "true" or "false," in practice research is much more complicated than this. If the results of an experiment fail to support the hypothesis, there are always two potential explanations: (1) the theory on which the hypothesis is based is wrong, or (2) the experiment went wrong. Because human behavior is so complex, it is very difficult to design experiments with enough controls to account for all possible explanations. As a result, it is often much easier to see where an experiment went wrong than to see how a theory is wrong.

Table 1 *Steps in the Process of Social Psychological Research*

Step 1: *Select a topic and review past research.* Ideas come from a variety of sources, including existing theories, past research, current social events, and personal experiences. Social psychologists must also become knowledgeable about past research findings in their area of interest and keep abreast of recently published studies and those reported at scientific meetings.

Stop 2: *Develop a theory and hypotheses.* Once the research literature has been digested, a theory and/or hypotheses that can be empirically tested must then be developed.

Step 3: *Select a research method.* Research can be conducted in the laboratory or in the field, and the social psychologist can either employ correlational or experimental methodology.

Step 4: *Collect the data.* The three basic techniques of data collection are self-reports, direct observations, and archival information.

Step 5: *Analyze the data.* Data can be analyzed using either descriptive or inferential statistics, with the latter mathematical analysis being the more valuable because it allows researchers to generalize their findings to the population of interest.

Step 6: *Report the results.* Just because a social psychologist conducts a study doesn't mean it will be published and make its way into the social psychological literature. In most cases, a scientific journal will not publish a submitted article if there are problems with the hypotheses or methods, or flaws in the data analysis. In addition, articles are often rejected for publication because reviewers decide the research isn't very important. Due to these factors, the top journals in social psychology (*Journal of Personality* and *Social Psychology, Personality and Social Psychology Bulletin*) regularly publish less than 10 percent of the submitted research articles.

From Franzoi, 2000, p. 21.

Only after many failed experiments can a researcher say with any assurance that a theory is wrong. Therefore, science advances not so much by the "truth" of theories—because it is so difficult to evaluate the validity of a theory—but by the "usefulness" of theories to explain the outcomes of experiments.

❦ CHOOSING A RESEARCH METHOD

There are many methods that researchers can use to test their hypotheses (see Table 2). The method chosen depends on the hypothesis or question that the researcher wants to test. For example, a researcher might want to study the effect on children of watching violence on TV. Any of the five methods identified in Table 2 could be used; however, each method will yield a slightly different answer. But if a researcher wants to know exactly "what caused what," the only way is to conduct an experiment. The problem is that, for ethical or practical reasons, some of the most interesting and important

questions about human behavior can't be tested in a true controlled laboratory experiment. Thus, one of the other methods must be used. Each method has its strengths and weaknesses, so the best method to use depends on exactly what question the researcher wants to answer (see Maracek, Fine & Kidder, 1997, for a more in-depth discussion of these issues). In fact, good researchers often use many different methods to gain the most thorough understanding possible of their area of interest.

An example will help clarify this. Let's say a researcher wants to know the effects on adults and children of watching violence on TV. While she could use any of the methods, each method will answer a slightly different question and at the same time leave other questions unanswered (see Table 3). To put it differently, even if a researcher does everything right (which is no easy feat, as we will soon see), the method chosen will limit the kinds of conclusions he or she can draw from the results.

Table 2 *Major Research Methods and Level of Control*

<—Low Control				High Control —>
Observational Study	Survey, Interview, Archival Research	Natural Experiment	Field Experiment	Laboratory Experiment

From Moghaddam, 1998, p. 28.

Table 3 *The Impact of TV Violence: A Comparison of Research Methods*

Question	Study	Method	Unanswered Questions
Do children who watch violence on TV act aggressively?	Identify children who watch violence on TV and see if they act aggressively.	Observational Study	Aggressive compared to whom or what? Did watching the violence actually cause the aggression? Why do children watch violence on TV?
How much violent TV are children exposed to at home, on average?	Ask parents about the TV habits of their children. Look at school records of aggressive incidents from 1959 to 1999.	Survey	Are the parents telling the truth? What effect does watching TV have on children? Does watching violence on TV cause aggression?
Is there an increase in school violence over time? Is there an increase in TV viewing over time?	Look at TV-viewing habits of children from 1959 to 1999.	Archival Research	Does watching violence on TV cause aggression? Are there other reasons that childhood aggression might be increasing over time?
What effect does TV reporting of violence have on people?	Compare crime rates in areas where crimes are reported heavily on TV to areas where they are not.	Natural Experiment	Did watching the violence actually cause the aggression? Are there other reasons that the areas differ in crime rate?
What effect on children results from watching violent TV?	Control the TV content of children in an orphanage so that some watch violent TV while others don't. See how they act afterwards.	Field Experiment	How much violence are children exposed to on average? How long does the effect last?
What effect on children results from watching violent TV?	Have children come to the laboratory and some watch violent TV others watch non-violent TV for 1 hour. See how they act afterwards.	Laboratory Experiment	How much violence are children exposed to at home, on average? Does this effect occur outside the laboratory? How long does the effect last?

❧ DISTINGUISHING BETWEEN STUDIES AND EXPERIMENTS

Though the terms *study* and *experiment* seem interchangeable, their meanings aren't quite the same. *Study* is the more general term and refers to any kind of research, whether it's experimental or nonexperimental. The term *experiment* refers to a specific type of study that uses the experimental method. In an experiment, often called a true experiment, the researcher has controlled all aspects of the situation. He or she allows only one thing (a variable) to vary, so that any differences in participants' reactions must be due to the variable that was manipulated. In nonexperimental, or correlational research, we can't say for sure what caused the outcome because we haven't controlled all aspects of the situation. The variable the researcher manipulates is called the *independent variable*. The reaction of the participants that the researcher measures is called the *dependent variable*.

Look again at the examples of the observational, archival, and survey studies on TV aggression in Table 3. You can see that there are many other factors that the researcher did not control—such as violence in the home or what the child watches on TV—that may limit the results. This limited control affects what conclusion the researcher can be draw from the study. Specifically, the researcher cannot say with confidence that one variable has caused another. He or she can only say that there is a *relationship* between the two variables, watching violent TV and acting aggressively. This is why researchers refer to such study methods.

However, in the examples of natural, field, and laboratory experiments in the table, the researcher was able to control the variable of TV content. But for a study to be considered a true experiment, a researcher must also randomly assign participants to experimental conditions, in addition to controlling the independent variable. Participants shouldn't be left to choose which condition they would like to take part in, nor should the researcher leave this decision to extraneous factors such as who shows up for the experiment first. The random assignment of participants to conditions is the most important variable that a researcher can control. Without it, extraneous variables—like assertiveness on the part of the participants—may influence the result. This would invalidate the experiment, because the logic and power of a true experiment to determine causality relies on the experimenter's ability to successfully control all but the independent variable.

There are techniques by which a researcher can control for extraneous variables using statistics. However, a study in which such a technique is used is still not considered a true experiment. Nevertheless, it's an improvement on a study that hasn't controlled for extraneous variables either statistically or methodologically.

Suppose a researcher has designed an experiment such that participants have been randomly assigned to a condition and the difference between conditions is under the experimenter's total control. If there turns out to be a difference in participants' responses, then the difference must be due to the variable the researcher manipulated. In this case—and only in this case—can we say for certain what caused what. That's what makes experiments more powerful than studies.

❧ EVALUATING AN EXPERIMENT

Generally, an experiment is considered "good" if it is well designed and uses appropriate measures. A well-designed experiment has both validity and reliability. *Validity* refers to the meaning that we can draw from the experiment as a whole, depending on the soundness of its design. There are

two kinds of validity that apply to experiments: internal validity and external validity.

An experiment has *internal validity* if the researcher has successfully controlled all aspects of the situation so that it is clear that only the independent variable, and not some other factor, has caused a difference in the participants' responses. At the very least, this means that the researcher has effectively manipulated the independent variable and randomly assigned subjects to conditions. As we've seen, without internal validity, we cannot say for certain that the results were caused by the independent variable. Thus we cannot determine causality.

An experiment has *external validity* if the variables that were manipulated and the results that were obtained are generalizable to some situation outside the laboratory. Researchers who stress external validity are generally trying to understand some real-world phenomenon. Think of the earlier claims that TV violence causes human aggression or that cell phones cause cancer. In experiments designed to research such claims, external validity is important. Generally, applied researchers are highly interested in external validity.

Other researchers, called basic or theoretical researchers, are less concerned with external validity because they are testing theoretical links among variables. Sometimes this kind of research is called pure research. For example, if a theory suggests that people imitate behaviors they see, or that electromagnetic waves cause cancer, a theoretical researcher would want to design a highly controlled experiment to test the theory. For example, a cancer researcher might use mice to test the kind of substances that allegedly cause cancer—without thinking about how this knowledge might be used. Applied researchers would then step in to determine whether cell phones expose humans to these substances.

The difference between internal validity and external validity comes down to control. The more the experimenter controls all aspects of the experiment, the more internal validity the experiment has. However, such an experiment becomes less realistic and thus has less external validity. On the other hand, a highly realistic, natural, experiment would have low internal validity owing to the researcher's lack of control. So internal and external validity are often inversely related.

There is a place for both kinds of validity and for theoretical and applied research in the field of social psychology, but the difference between the two kinds of research has sparked a lively debate (see, for example, Anderson, Lindsay & Bushman, 1999, or Forsyth, 1989). Kurt Lewin, a founder of social psychology, emphasized the need for both kinds of research. He often reminded his colleagues that "a business man once stated, 'There is nothing so practical as a good theory' " (Lewin, 1943, p. 118). For example, our understanding of the effect of violence in the media or cancer-causing carcinogens in the environment advances because of both applied and theoretical research. To continue Lewin's quote,

"[We must] watch out that theory never breaks loose from its proper place as a servant, as a tool for human beings."

The validity of an experiment is only part of what makes an experiment good. Researchers must also use appropriate measures to asses changes in participants' behavior, for example, dependent variable. As with experiment design, measures must be both valid and reliable. The *validity* of a measure refers to its truth; that is, does a questionnaire, for example, measure what we want it to measure? For instance, if we want to see how extroverts act in an experiment, we need to be sure that we are truly measuring extroversion and not inadvertently measuring something else, like intelligence or emotionality. Or, if we're measuring the effect of TV on aggression, then we must be careful to measure aggression and not playfulness.

Reliability refers to the ability of a measure to produce consistent results. A measure, such as a questionnaire or a heart-rate monitor or the number of instances of aggressive behavior, is reliable if it gives a similar answer when used under similar conditions at another time or by another person. For example, you wouldn't want to measure your height one day and then find that the same yardstick you used gives you a totally different height the next week, or that your friend gets a different result for your height using the same yardstick. In measuring aggression with a reliable questionnaire, researchers should agree on the kinds of behaviors they think are aggressive (see for example, Schwartz, 1999, for a discussion of potential problems with questionnaire measures). Going back to the headlines at the opening of this introduction, if there were no other witnesses to an Elvis sighting except for the reporter, you would probably question the *reliability* of the report. And if you read the headline in a nonreputable newspaper, you would also suspect that the report was not *valid*.

❧ WHAT'S SO SPECIAL ABOUT SOCIAL PSYCHOLOGICAL RESEARCH?

We said earlier that social psychological research is conducted in the same way that any other scientific research is conducted. However, there are some unique things about research in this field. In 1982 the American Psychological Association (the professional organization of all psychologists) published guidelines for the conduct of research using human and animal participants (APA, 1982, 1992). For human participants, these guidelines require, among other things, that researchers protect participants from psychological or physical harm, that participants know all aspects of the experimental procedure ahead of time, that researchers be truthful whenever possible, that the information provided by

participants remains confidential, and that participants have the right to decline participation or to discontinue their participation at any time without penalty. These rights and the purpose of the experiment must be explained to potential participants ahead of time so that they can give their formal agreement, called informed consent, to take part in any study.

Social psychologists face a special challenge in designing their experiments that adhere to these guidelines. By definition, their research often requires participants to interact with others. This makes it hard for the experimenter to maintain experimental control. To resolve this dilemma, researchers often have participants interact with another person who is actually playing a role designed by the experimenter. This other person is called the experimental confederate, and participants are not informed ahead of time that this person is part of the experiment. This technique, which requires a level of deception, is unique to social psychological research.

Deception might be necessary in other kinds of psychological experiments as well. This is because people often act differently when they know they are being watched, or they might purposely try to "help" or "hurt" the experimenter by changing their responses. The ethical guidelines of the APA require that deception be used only when absolutely necessary and only when the nature of the deception can be fully explained to participants after the experiment.

Such an explanation takes place during the post-experimental interview (see Mills, 1976). During this interview, the researcher talks with participants to see whether they have any suspicions about the true purpose of the experiment or any discomfort about the experimental procedures. At this time, the experimenter must reveal the deception used and make sure that the participants understand why it was necessary.

To learn more about the ethics of research and to follow a debate among researchers about the ethical nature of the famous Milgram obedience to authority studies (Milgram, 1965), you may want to read Baumrind (1964), Milgram (1964), Orne and Holland (1968), and Milgram (1970).

So, do you believe that New York City is sinking or that Elvis is alive, or that violence in the media causes aggression? Your answer to all three questions should be that you'd like to hear more about the research that these headlines are based on. And soon you will, for the only true headline cited at the beginning of this introduction comes from research in an active and exciting area of social psychological research.

REFERENCES

American Psychological Association (1982). *Ethical principles in the conduct of research with humans*. Washington, DC: Author.

American Psychological Association (1992). Ethical principles of psychologists and code of conduct. *American Psychologist, 47,* 1597-1611.

Anderson, A. C., Lindsay, J. J., & Bushman, B. J. (1999). Research in the psychology lab: Truth or triviality? *Current Directions in Psychological Science, 8*(1), 3-9.

Baumrind, D. (1964). Some thoughts on ethics of research: After reading Milgram's "Behavioral Study of Obedience." *American Psychologist, 19,* 421-423.

Forsyth, D. R. (1989). Social psychology's three little pigs. In Mark Leary (Ed.). , *The state of social psychology*. Newbury Park, CA: Sage.

Franzoi, S. L. (2000). *Social psychology*. (2nd ed.). Madison, WI: Brown and Benchmark.

Levy, D. A. (1997). *Tools of critical thinking*. Boston: Allyn & Bacon.

Lewin, K. (1943). Psychology and the process of group living. *Journal of Social Psychology, SPSSI Bulletin, 17,* 113-131.

Maracek, J., Fine, M., & Kidder, L. (1997). Working between worlds: Qualitative methods and social psychology. *Journal of Social Issues, 53*(4), 631-644.

Milgram, S. (1964). Issues in the study of obedience: A reply to Baumrind. *American Psychologist, 19,* 848-852.

Milgram, S. (1965). Some conditions of obedience and disobedience to authority. *Human Relations, 18*(1), 57-75.

Milgram, S. (1970). Interpreting obedience: Error and evidence. A reply to Orne and Holland. In *The individual in a social world*. New York: McGraw-Hill.

Mills, J. (1976). A procedure for explaining experiments involving deception. *Personality and Social Psychology Bulletin, 2,* 3-13.

Moghaddam, F. M. (1998). *Social psychology*. New York: W. H. Freeman and Company.

Orne, M. T., & Holland, C. C. (1968). On the ecological validity of laboratory deceptions. *International Journal of Psychiatry, 6,* 282-293.

Pettigrew, T. F. (1996). *How to think like a social scientist*. New York: HarperCollins.

Schwartz, N. (1999). Self-reports: How questions shape the answers. *American Psychologist, 54,* 93-105.

Suggested Readings

Aronson, E., Ellsworth, P. C., Carlsmith, J. M., & Gonzales, M. H. (1997). *Methods of research in social psychology*. New York: McGraw-Hill.

Brannigan, G. G., & Merrens, M. R. (1995). *The social psychologists: Research adventures*. New York: McGraw-Hill.

Girden, E. R. (1996). *Evaluating research articles from start to finish*. Thousand Oaks, CA: Sage.

Levy, D. A. (1997). *Tools of critical thinking*. Boston: Allyn & Bacon.

McKenna, R. J. (1995). *The undergraduate researcher's handbook: Creative experimentation in social psychology*. Boston: Allyn & Bacon.

Pettigrew, T. F. (1996). *How to think like a social scientist*. New York: HarperCollins.

THE SELF

D o you have a self? Is self something you *have* or something you *become*? Point to yourself. Did you point to your head, your stomach, or your heart? Are you the same person now that you were back in kindergarten? Are you the same with your professors as you are with your friends? Are you one self or many selves? How do you know yourself?

These questions—and the varied answers they provoke—highlight a paradox of the self: We are one self, but with many different facets. Moreover, we come to know ourselves through a complex array of channels: through our own consciousness, through interactions with others, and through decision-making.

According to Baumeister (1998), there are three "patterns of experience" through which we can understand our "self" (p. 680). These patterns also reveal themes that have emerged in social psychologists' studies of the self. The three kinds of experiences are *reflexive consciousness*, *interpersonal being*, and *executive function*.

In brief, *reflexive consciousness* is awareness of oneself. Imagine taking all of the perceptive powers that you normally use to understand others and turning them inward to construct a concept of your self. As Baumeister wrote:

> . . . [Y]ou lie awake in bed at night, thinking about your failures and inadequacies, or glorying in your triumphs; when you look in the mirror or step on the scale or read your resume; ... when you contemplate your future or your spiritual center or your dwindling resources; or when you try to answer some

questions honestly about your opinions, traits, habits, qualifications, and past experiences.
> (Baumeister, 1998, p. 680).

Interpersonal being is the experience of understanding yourself through others. That is, we are who we are as a result of the myriad interactions that we have with others over the course of our lifetimes. However, we are not merely passive participants in these interactions. Instead, we may actively try to create an impression of who we are for others. Again, Baumeister offered some vivid examples of this kind of experience:

> When someone looks into your eyes and smiles a little and says your name, and you have a feeling of warm gladness; or the same happens and you feel anxious terror; when you join a group, or quit it; ... when you try to make a good impression on someone or live up to that person's expectations; when you discover that someone has been watching you and you blush; when you keep a promise to a friend.
> (Baumeister, 1998, p. 680).

Finally, *executive function* is that little voice inside your head that controls how you respond to life's demands. Just as the executive branch of government makes decisions and determines what actions to take or issues to think about, the executive function of the self controls your actions and thoughts and makes choices:

> When you make a resolution or vow; ... when you decide what it is that you really want to buy or work on or become; when you stop yourself from acting

on an impulse, such as to eat or drink or smoke, or to hit someone ...; when you vote, or when you take out a bank loan; when you resist fatigue and temptation and make yourself put forth the maximum effort, beyond the normal call of duty.

(Baumeister, 1998, p. 680).

In this chapter, we explore the major social psychological theories and findings on the self from these three perspectives—with a special emphasis on the interpersonal being, of course.

⅁ REFLEXIVE CONSCIOUSNESS

Reflexive consciousness consists of the ideas we hold about ourselves. We have self-concepts, self-schemas, self-awareness, and the evaluation of it all—our self-esteem.

Self-Concept. The reflexive consciousness experience of the self was identified formally over a hundred years ago by the first American psychologist, William James. He distinguished between the "I" and the "me" aspects of self (James, 1890). The "I" refers to the knower (or the subject of awareness), while the "me" is the known (or the object of awareness). This paradox—of the self simultaneously studying and being aware of being studied—has fascinated psychologists and philosophers for many years. Today, social psychologists call the act of thinking about ourselves *self-awareness*, and the specific knowledge we hold about who we are our *self-concept*. For example, one's self-concept might include things like "good at math, outgoing, good with elderly people, psychology major, and night owl."

Self-Schemas. To understand, explain, and predict the social world, we organize information into what are called schemas. In the same vein, we also organize information about our selves into *self-schemas* (Markus, 1977). We base these organized structures on our past behaviors and use them to understand ourselves, organize our memories, and make decisions. Self-schemas include the characteristics that we attribute to ourselves—especially those which we believe make us unique (McGuire & McGuire, 1981). For example, the self-concepts of "outgoing" and "good with elderly people" mentioned earlier might be organized into a schema of "sociable." People have well-developed self-schemas for characteristics that are important to them (like "sociability"), for qualities that they think are extreme (e.g., not everyone spends time with the elderly), and for traits that they are certain the opposite is not true of them (e.g., "I'm definitely not a 'wall flower'!") (Markus, 1977). Self-schemas can be negative as well as positive (Malle & Horowitz, 1995).

People also hold schemas about what they might be like in the future (Markus & Nurius, 1986). These *possible selves* embody goals, aspirations, and expectations—such as when you imagine yourself settled into a successful career. Possible selves may also include dreaded or feared future selves, such as being lonely in old age or contracting a serious illness. Like other self-schemas, possible selves help us to understand our behavior, remember events, and to make decisions about our future (Markus & Nurius, 1986).

We also may hold *self-guides* (Higgins, 1987). For example, we may have an idea in mind of our *ideal self,* or the kind of person we would *like* to be ("I want to be a psychologist"). We may also hold a mental picture of what we think we *should* be—our *ought self* ("I should be more organized"). When our actual self does not match our ideal self ("I was hoping for a high grade point average this semester"), the *self-discrepancy* may cause us to feel sadness, dissatisfaction, and disappointment (Higgins, 1987). A discrepancy between our actual self and our ought self may cause us to feel fear, worry, and tension ("I'm trying to be organized but I can't seem to get it together in time for that exam!") (Higgins, 1987). Interestingly, these ought and ideal selves are so powerful that we suffer from the same negative emotions if the discrepancy is between our actual self and a *parent's or friend's* notion of our ideal self (Higgins, 1987; 1989).

Self-Awareness. According to self-awareness theory, our attention can be directed either outward toward others and the world or inward toward ourselves (Duval & Wicklund, 1972). For example, standing in front of an audience, seeing oneself in a mirror or on a videotape, or hearing one's voice on a tape recorder or answering machine makes people highly self-aware. People who are self-conscious by nature may be especially prone to self-awareness even without being in these situations (Carver & Scheier, 1981).

When our attention is focused inward, we immediately become aware of some standard of character and of how we measure up to that standard—such as seeing ourselves in a mirror and becoming conscious of a few extra pounds. Becoming judgmental observers of ourselves in this way can feel uncomfortable, especially if we decide that we are deficient in some way. In response, we may either change ourselves so that we meet the standard (walk to class to use up calories instead of taking the bus), or try to escape these feelings of self-awareness (Duval & Wicklund, 1972). In this same example, we might escape by fleeing the situation (avoid mirrors) or taking refuge in distracting activities, such as watching TV, reading a book, or immersing ourselves in religion. Escape in its general sense can take more harmful forms as well, such as alcohol abuse, binge eating, sexual masochism, or even suicide (Baumeister, 1991). However, self-awareness is not always unpleasant. If we have met or exceed our standards (Greenberg & Musham, 1981), we might even enjoy taking stock of how we measure up (Carver & Scheier, 1981).

Self-Esteem. Perhaps the ultimate form of self-awareness is our overall evaluation of ourselves. Self-esteem is our general assessment of whether we are fundamentally good or bad (Rosenberg, 1965). We also hold more specific evaluations about our abilities in particular areas, such as academics or sports, which may in turn influence our overall self-esteem (Pelham, 1995). Much of social psychological research and theory is based on the premise that people are motivated to protect and enhance their self-esteem (Baumeister, 1998).

In his review of the extensive research on self-esteem, Baumeister (1998) came to some interesting conclusions. First, people with high self-esteem tend to have more elaborate and detailed—but not necessarily more accurate—self-knowledge than people with low self-esteem (Campbell, 1990). In contrast, people with low self-esteem have a more tentative or confused understanding of themselves (Campbell & Lavallee, 1993). This confusion may cause emotional turmoil and mood swings (Campbell, Chew, & Scratchley, 1991). Further, people with high self-esteem tend to protect their views of themselves, perhaps by attributing any good fortune they enjoy to their own skills, or blaming others for their failures, or selectively remembering only their successes (Blaine & Crocker, 1993). It may be this very ability that helps them stay emotionally stable during the ups and downs of daily life. People with low self-esteem don't tend to use these techniques and therefore may be more vulnerable to life's vicissitudes (Campbell, Chew, & Scratchley, 1991).

❧ INTERPERSONAL BEING

Our earliest way of coming to know ourselves, even before we can form thoughts into words, is probably through the reactions of others during our childhood. Yet, even after we reach adulthood, our interactions with others still shape how we see ourselves. Let's take a closer look at the various kinds of social interactions we experience, and what kinds of information we get from them.

Reflected Appraisals. When we are young children, we develop a "looking-glass self"; that is, an image of how we appear to others (Cooley, 1902; Mead, 1934). The smile of a parent, the scowl of an aunt, or the giggle of a sibling all tell us what the world thinks of us. Through these *reflected appraisals*, we see ourselves through the eyes of others. Eventually, we incorporate these appraisals into our self-concepts and use them to know ourselves.

Social Comparison. We can also come to know ourselves by directly comparing our emotions, reactions, talents, abilities, attitudes, and characteristics with those of others. Many social psychologists have studied this social comparison process, but Leon Festinger was the first to articulate a theory about it (Festinger, 1954). According to Festinger, we tend to compare ourselves to others when we feel uncertain about our attitudes or abilities, or when there is no objective standard to judge ourselves against (Suls & Miller, 1977). Though we may compare ourselves to whoever is around (Gilbert,

Giesler, & Morris, 1995), we gain more accurate self-knowledge by comparing ourselves with those who are similar to us on the relevant skill (Goethals & Darley, 1977; Miller, 1982). For example, if you are a beginner skater, it makes more sense to compare yourself to other beginners in your skating class than to compare yourself to the teacher or to tennis player André Agassi.

We can also compare ourselves with others in order to set high aspirations for ourselves, or to bolster a wilting self-image. Let's say you're considering setting a new record for the 50-yard dash at your school. It would make sense for you to compare your running ability with someone who is currently better than you are at this event (Thorton & Arrowood, 1966). This is called an *upward social comparison*. If, however, you want to make yourself feel better about your lukewarm record for the 50, you can engage in a *downward social comparison* and judge yourself against someone who is even worse at it than you (Pyszczynski, Greenberg, & LaPrelle, 1985).

Self-Evaluation Maintenance Theory. As we saw above, our choice of comparison strategy depends on our goals and emotional needs. Comparing ourselves with those who are worse—or better—off can even affect how well we cope with illness (e.g., Wood, Taylor, & Lichtman, 1985). However, if the person we are comparing ourselves to is a close friend, then the social comparison situation gets a little more tricky. Think about it: Suppose you consider yourself a skilled musician or a great golfer. You then discover that a new friend is better than you at your "great talent." How would this make you feel? According to the self-evaluation maintenance theory, another person's talents or abilities can severely threaten our self-concept (Tesser, 1988). The threat is especially great when the other person is a close friend or when the ability in question is important to our self-concept. In order to cope with this threat or maintain our self-concept, we could work to improve our ability, we could value the ability less or decide that it's not essential to our self-image, or we could distance ourselves from our friend (Tesser & Paulus, 1983). However, if a friend has special talents that are not parts of your self-concept, you can happily maintain the friendship—and even increase your self-esteem—by cheering your friend on and basking in his or her reflected glory (e.g., Cialdini et al., 1976).

Culture. Perhaps the most subtle way that our sense of self is affected by others is through culture. With reflected appraisals and social comparisons, the impact of others' views or abilities on our self-concepts are clear. By contrast, culture shapes our self-concepts in a more nuanced and perhaps more lasting way. There's an old bromide that says that a fish would be the last one to know that water is wet. Similarly, it is hard for us to see the influence of culture on our self-concepts. Yet culture may have a profound effect on our self-concepts (e.g., Rhee, Uleman, Lee, & Roman, 1995).

For example, in Western or other individualistic cultures—including the mainstream United States—people tend to have an independent view of the self (Markus & Kitayama, 1991). That is, they tend to define themselves as individuals with unique thoughts and feelings who are able to function independently from family, friends, and acquaintances. However, in Eastern or collectivistic cultures—such as Japan, China, India, and Amish and some African-American cultures in the United States—people tend to have an interdependent view of the self. In these cultures, the self is defined by relationships and connections to others. Just as you probably could not imagine living without a vital body organ, people with an interdependent view of the self could not imagine living away from family and friends. These differing cultural views affect self-definition, self-concept, life tasks, the role that others play in our lives, and the basis of self-esteem (see Table 1).

❧ CONSTRUCTING OURSELVES: IMPRESSION MANAGEMENT

Part of the experience of interpersonal being involves how we present ourselves to others; that is, the impressions we create and the selves we try to be in others' eyes. There are certain times—and certain people—who manage or create impressions by virtually remaking themselves for others, like social chameleons. This topic of impression management merits a closer look.

Self-Presentation. We engage in self-presentation when we try to convey information or images about ourselves to others through our clothing, mannerisms, or conversation (Baumeister, 1998). Sociologist Irving Goffman likened self-presentation strategies to theatrical performances and agreed with Shakespeare's statement that "all the world's a stage" (Goffman, 1959). According to Goffman, people play "roles" in their social lives by acting in a certain way and using various "props," such as the right clothes and car. Similarly, they act in a calculated way, following a set "script," in order to please or impress an "audience."

Why might we present ourselves in certain ways to others (Baumeister, 1982)? There are two reasons. First, we want to please our "audience," to gain some kind of benefit or rewards, or to manipulate others (e.g., Jones, 1964). Some of the most common forms of strategic self-presentation are *ingratiation*, *self-promotion*, *intimidation*, *exemplification*, and *supplication* (Jones, 1990; see Table 2). Second, we may be trying to please ourselves rather than an audience, or to corroborate our own view of ourselves. The assumption here is that we cannot truly be attractive, talented, trustworthy, or whatever unless others see us in these ways, too (Baumeister, 1998). Self-presentation, or more specifically, self-construction, is one way to achieve this social validation.

Self-Handicapping. Another way we may manage our presentation to others is by *self-handicapping*. This means setting things up ahead of time so that we have a handy excuse when things go wrong. For example, some people self-handicap before a test by drinking, taking drugs (Berglass & Jones, 1978), procrastinating (Tice & Baumeister, 1997), not sleeping or eating properly, or not studying beforehand. Then if

Table 1 *Summary of Key Differences Between Independent and Interdependant Perceptions of Self*

Feature Compared	Independent	Interdependent
Definition	Separate from social context	Connected with social content
Structure	Bounded, unitary, stable	Flexible, variable
Important features	Internal, private (abilities, thoughts, feelings)	External, public (statuses, roles, relationships)
Tasks	Be unique	Belong, fit in
	Express self	Occupy one's proper place
	Realize internal attributes	Engage in appropriate action
	Promote own goals	Promote others' goals
	Be direct: say what's on your mind	Be indirect: read other's mind
Role of others	*Self-evaluation:* others important for social comparison, reflected appraisal	*Self-definition:* relationships with others in specific contexts define the self
Basis of self-esteem[a]	Ability to express self; validate internal attributes	Ability to adjust, restrain self, maintain harmony with social context

[a]Esteeming the self may be primarily a Western phenomenon, and the concept of self-esteem should perhaps be replaced by self-satisfaction, or by a term that reflects the realization that one is fulfilling the culturally mandated task.
Source: Markus, H. R., & Kitayama, S. (1991). Culture and the Self: Implications for Cognition, Emotion, and Motivation. *Psychological Review*, 98, 224–253.

From Taylor, Peplau, & Sears, 2000, p. 109.

Table 2 *Self-Presentational Strategies*

	Attributions Sought	Negative Attributions Risked	Emotion to be Aroused	Prototypical Actions
1. *Ingratiation*	Likeable	Sycophant Conformist Obsequious	Affection	Positive self-characterization Opinion conformity Other enhancement Favors
2. *Self-promotion*	Competent (effective, "a winner")	Fraudulent Conceited Defensive	Respect (awe, deference)	Performance claims Performance accounts Performances
3. *Intimidation*	Dangerous (ruthless, volatile)	Blusterer Ineffectual	Fear Potential anger	Threats
4. *Exemplification*	Worth (suffers, dedicated) Exploitative	Hypocrite Sanctimonious	Guilt (shame, emulation) Militancy for a cause	Self-denial Helping
5. *Supplication*	Helpless (handicapped, unfortunate)	Stigmatized Lazy Demanding	Nurturance (obligation)	Self-deprecation Entreaties for help

Source: Adapted from Jones, 1990, p. 198.
From Feldman, 1998, p. 142.

they perform poorly on the test, they have a ready-made explanation ("I couldn't sleep" or "I was sick") that lets them preserve their self-esteem. If they perform well, then they look even better for succeeding despite the handicap! Of course, sabotaging one's own efforts like this may actually jeopardize one's performance. However, a person who self-handicaps is so anxious about performing well and looking good to him- or herself or to others that the risk is apparently worthwhile (Berglass & Jones, 1978).

Self-Monitoring. While everyone at times tries to create a favorable self-presentation for others, some people are con-stantly monitoring and adjusting their own behavior. Such people, called high self-monitors, are unusually sensitive to the social "climate." They vigilantly scope out the proper or most socially appropriate behavior for each situation (Snyder, 1974, 1980). They then change their own behavior in order to fit the requirements of the situation. In contrast, low self-monitors are less concerned with such things. They focus more on their own internal values and beliefs. High self-monitors might size up a social situation and say to themselves, "What does this situation want me to be?" Low self-monitors may think, "How can I be me in this situation?" (Snyder, 1987).

Table 3 *Sample Items From the Self-Monitoring Scale*

Items Relating to High Self-Monitoring
I would probably make a good actor.
I may deceive people by being friendly when I really dislike them.
I can make impromptu speeches on topics about which I have almost no information.
In different situations and with different people, I often act like very different persons.

Items Relating to Low Self-Monitoring
I find it hard to imitate the behavior of other people.
In a group of people, I am rarely the center of attention.
I can only argue for ideas which I already believe.
I feel a bit awkward in company and do not show up quite as well as I should.

Source: Snyder & Gangestad (1986).
From Feldman, 1998, p. 140.

Mead, G. H. (1934). *Mind, self, and society.* Chicago: University of Chicago Press.

Miller, C. T. (1982). The role of performance-related similarity in social comparison of abilities: A test of the related attributes hypothesis. *Journal of Experimental Social Psychology, 18,* 513–523.

Pelham, B. W. (1995). Self-investment and self-esteem: Evidence for a Jamesian model of self-worth. *Journal of Personality and Social Psychology, 69,* 1141–1150.

Pyszczynski, T. A., Greenberg, J., & LaPrelle, J. (1985). Social comparison after success and failure: Biased search for information consistent with a self-serving conclusion. *Journal of Experimental Social Psychology, 21,* 195–211.

Rhee, E., Uleman, J. S., Lee, H. K., & Roman, R. J. (1995). Spontaneous self-descriptions and ethnic identities in individualistic and collectivistic cultures. *Journal of Personality and Social Psychology, 69,* 142–152.

Rosenberg, M. (1965). Society and the adolescent self-image. Princeton, NJ: Princeton University Press.

Rotter, J. (1966). Generalized expectancies for internal versus external control of reinforcement. *Psychological Monographs, 80*(1, whole No. 609).

Seligman, M. E. P. (1990). *Learned optimism.* New York: Pocket Books.

Snyder, M. (1974). The self-monitoring of expressive behavior. *Journal of Personality and Social Psychology, 30,* 526–537.

Snyder, M. (1980, March). The many me's of the self-monitor. *Psychology Today,* 33–40.

Snyder, M. (1987). *Public appearances, private realities: The psychology of self-monitoring.* New York: Freeman.

Snyder, M., Berscheid, E., & Glick, R. P. (1985). Focusing on the exterior and the interior: Two investigations of the initiation of personal relationships. *Journal of Personality and Social Psychology, 48,* 1427–1439.

Snyder, M., & DeBono, K. J. (1989). Understanding the function of attitudes: Lessons for personality and social behavior. In A. R. Pratkanis, S. J. Breckler, & A. G. Greenwald (Eds.), *Attitude structure and function* (pp. 339–359). Hillsdale, NJ: Erlbaum.

Synder, M., & Gangestad, S. (1986). On the nature of self-monitoring: Matters of assessment, matters of validity. *Journal of Personality and Social Psychology, 51,* 125–139.

Suls, J. M., & Miller, R. L. (1977). (Eds.). *Social comparison processes: Theoretical and empirical perspectives* (pp. 259–278). Washington, DC: Hemisphere/Halstead.

Taylor, S, E., Peplau, L. A., & Sears, D. O. (2000). *Social psychology* (10th ed.). Upper Saddle River, NJ: Prentice Hall.

Tesser, A. (1988). Toward a self-evaluation maintenance model of social behavior. In L. Berkowitz (Ed.), *Advances in experimental social psychology* (Vol. 21, pp. 181–227). Orlando, FL: Academic Press.

Tesser, A., & Paulus, D. (1983). The definition of self: Private and public self-evaluation management strategies. *Journal of Personality and Social Psychology, 44,* 672–682.

Thorton, D., & Arrowood, A. J. (1966). Self-evaluation, self-enhancement, and the locus of social comparison. *Journal of Experimental Social Psychology* (Suppl. 1), 40-48.

Tice, D. M., & Baumeister, R. F. (1997). Self-esteem, self-handicapping, and self-presentation: The strategy of inadequate practice. *Journal of Personality, 58,* 443–464.

Wood, J. V., Taylor, S. E., & Lichtman, R. R. (1985). Social comparison in adjustment to breast cancer. *Journal of Personality and Social Psychology, 49,* 1169—1183

SUGGESTED READINGS

Baumeister, R. F. (1991). *Escaping the self: Alcoholism, spirituality, masochism, and other flights from the burden of selfhood.* New York: Basic Books.

Baumeister, R. F. (1998). The self. In D. Gilbert, S. T. Fiske, & G. Lindzey (Eds.), *The handbook of social psychology* (4th ed., Vol. 1, pp. 680–740). New York: McGraw-Hill.

Hattie, J. (1992). *Self-concept.* Hillsdale, NJ: Erlbaum.

Osborne, R. E. (1996). *Self: An eclectic approach.* Boston: Allyn & Bacon.

Snyder, M. (1987). *Public appearances, private realities: The psychology of self-monitoring.* New York: Freeman.

Stevens, R. (Ed.). (1996). *Understanding the self.* London: Sage.

Suls, J. (Ed.). (1993). *Psychological perspectives on the self* (Vol. 4: The self in social perspective). Hillsdale, NJ: Erlbaum.

Tyler, T. R., Kramer, R. M., & John, O. P. (1999). *The psychology of the self.*

THE MANY ME'S OF THE SELF-MONITOR

Mark Snyder

University of Minnesota

Do you have one self or many selves? Think about it: Are you the same person with your best friend as you are with your parents? Are you the same on a date as you are in your psychology class? Are you the same when playing sports as when visiting your grandparents?

According to Mark Snyder, there appear to be two kinds of people in the world: low self-monitors and high self-monitors. Low-self monitors tend to act similarly in different situations, while high self-monitors change their behavior from situation to situation. When faced with a new situation, low self-monitors may think something like "Who am I . . . and how can I be me in this situation," while high self-monitors might think "Who am I . . . and what does this situation want me to be?"

According to Snyder, high self-monitors constantly assess cues in a situation and adjust their behavior to fit the demands of the situation. They try to give off just the right impression and are able to pick up on the subtle responses and impressions of others. In contrast, low self-monitors are more attuned to their own feelings. They interact with others and the world in accord with Polonius' advice to Laertes in Hamlet: "to thine own self be true."

In this article, Snyder explains what causes people to act in these differing ways, and presents interesting research that he and his colleagues have done in this area. The idea of changing like a social chameleon, depending on the forces of the situation, raises intriguing philosophical questions about the nature of the self and of our social world.

"The image of myself which I try to create in my own mind in order that I may love myself is very different from the image which I try to create in the minds of others in order that they may love me."

W. H. Auden

The concept of the self is one of the oldest and most enduring in psychological considerations of human nature. We generally assume that people are fairly consistent and stable beings: that a person who is generous in one situation is also likely to be generous in other situations, the one who is honest is honest most of the time, that a person who takes a liberal stance today will favor the liberal viewpoint tomorrow.

It's not always so: each of us, it appears, may have not one but many selves. Moreover, much as we might like to believe that the self is an integral feature of personal identity, it appears that, to a greater extent, the self is a product of the individual's relationships with other people. Conventional wisdom to the contrary, there may be striking gaps and con-

tradictions—as Auden suggests—between the public appearances and private realities of the self.

Psychologists refer to the strategies and techniques that people use to control the impressions they convey to others as "impression management." One of my own research interests has been to understand why some individuals are better at impression management than others. For it is clear that some people are particularly sensitive to the ways they express and present themselves in social situations—at parties, job interviews, professional meetings, in confrontations of all kinds where one might choose to create and maintain an appearance, with or without a specific purpose in mind. Indeed, we have found that such people have developed the ability to carefully monitor their own performances and to skillfully adjust their performances when signals from others tell them that they are not having the desired effect. I call such persons "high self-monitoring individuals," and I have developed a 25-item measure—the Self-Monitoring Scale—that has proved its ability to distinguish high self-monitoring individuals from low self-monitoring individuals. (See box.) Unlike the high self-monitoring individuals, low self-monitoring individuals are not so concerned about taking in such information; instead, they tend to express what they feel, rather than mold and tailor their behavior to fit the situation.

"The Many Me's of the Self-Monitor," by Mark Snyder, reprinted from *Psychology Today*, March 1980. pp. 33–34, 36, 39–40, 92.

My work on self-monitoring and impression management grew out of a long-standing fascination with explorations of reality and illusion in literature and in the theater. I was struck by the contrast between the way things often appear to be and the reality that lurks beneath the surface—on the stage, in novels, and in people's actual lives. I wanted to know how this world of appearances in social relationships was built and maintained, as well as what its effects were on the individual personality. But I was also interested in exploring the older, more philosophical question of whether, beneath the various images of self that people project to others, there is a "real me." If we are all actors in many social situations, do we then retain in any sense an essential self, or are we really a variety of selves?

❧ SKILLED IMPRESSION MANAGERS

There are striking and important differences in the extent to which people can and do control their self-presentation and in social situations: some people engage in impression management more often—and with greater skill—than others. Professional actors, as well as many trial lawyers, are among the best at it. So are successful salespeople, confidence artists, and politicians. The onetime mayor of New York Fiorello LaGuardia, was particularly skilled at adopting the expressive mannerisms of a variety of ethnic groups. In fact, he was so good at it that in watching silent films of his campaign speeches, it is easy to guess whose vote he was soliciting.

Of course, such highly skilled performances are the exception rather than the rule. And people differ in the extent to which they can and do exercise control over their self-presentations. It is the high self-monitoring individuals among us who are particularly talented in this regard. When asked to describe high self-monitoring individuals, their friends say that they are good at learning which behavior is appropriate in social situations, have good self-control of their emotional expression, and can effectively use this ability to create the impression they want. They are particularly skilled at intentionally expressing and accurately communicating a wide variety of emotions both vocally and facially. As studies by Richard Lippa of California State University at Fullerton have shown, they are usually such polished actors that they can effectively adopt the mannerisms of a reserved, withdrawn, and introverted individual and then do an abrupt about-face and portray, just as convincingly, a friendly, outgoing, and extroverted personality.

High self-monitoring individuals are also quite likely to seek out information about appropriate patterns of self-presentation. They invest considerable effort in attempting to "read" and understand others. In an experiment I conducted with Tom Monson (then one of my graduate students), various cues were given to students involved in group discussions as to what was socially appropriate behavior in the situation.

For example, some of them thought that their taped discussions would be played back to fellow students; in those circumstances, I assumed they would want their opinions to appear as autonomous as possible. Others believed that their discussions were completely private; there, I assumed they would be most concerned with maintaining harmony and agreement in the group. High self-monitoring individuals were keenly attentive to these differences; they conformed with the group when conformity was the most appropriate behavior and did not conform when they knew that the norms of the larger student audience would favor autonomy in the face of social pressure. Low self-monitoring individuals were virtually unaffected by the differences in social setting: presumably, their self-presentations were more accurate reflections of their personal attitudes and dispositions. Thus, as we might have guessed, people who are most skilled in the arts of impression management are also most likely to practice it.

Although high self-monitoring individuals are well skilled in the arts of impression management, we should not automatically assume that they necessarily use these skills for deceptive or manipulative purposes. Indeed, in their relationships with friends and acquaintances, high self-monitoring individuals are eager to use their self-monitoring abilities to promote smooth social interactions.

We can find some clues to this motive in the way high self-monitoring individuals tend to react to, and cope with, unfamiliar and unstructured social settings. In a study done at the University of Wisconsin, psychologists William Ickes and Richard Barnes arranged for pairs of strangers to spend time together in a waiting room, ostensibly to wait for an experiment to begin. The researchers then recorded the verbal and nonverbal behavior of each pair over a five-minute period, using video and audio tapes. All possible pairings of same-sex undergraduates at high, moderate, and low levels of self-monitoring were represented. Researchers scrutinized the tapes for evidence of the impact of self-monitoring on spontaneous encounters between strangers.

In these meetings, as in so many other aspects of their lives, high self-monitoring individuals suffered little or no shyness. Soon after meeting the other person, they took an active and controlling role in the conversation. They were inclined to talk first and to initiate subsequent conversational sequences. They also felt, and were seen by their partners to have, a greater need to talk. Their partners also viewed them as having been the more directive member of the pair. It was as if high self-monitoring individuals were particularly concerned about managing their behavior in order to create, encourage, and maintain a smooth flow of conversation. Perhaps this quality may help self-monitoring people to emerge as leaders in groups, organizations, and institutions.

❦ DETECTING IMPRESSION MANAGEMENT IN OTHERS

High self-monitoring individuals are also adept at detecting impression management in others. To demonstrate this finely tuned ability, three communications researchers at the University of Minnesota made use of videotaped excerpts from the television program "To Tell the Truth." On this program, one of the three guest contestants (all male in the excerpts chosen for the study) is the "real Mr. X." The other two who claim to be the real Mr. X are, of course, lying. Participants in the study watched each excerpt and then tried to identify the real Mr. X. High self-monitoring individuals were much more accurate than their low self-monitoring counterparts in correctly identifying the real Mr. X. and in seeing through the deception of the other two contestants.

Not only are high self-monitoring individuals able to see beyond the masks of deception successfully but they are also keenly attentive to the actions of other people as clues to their underlying intentions. E. E. Jones and Roy Baumeister of Princeton University had college students watch a videotaped discussion between two men who either agreed or disagreed with each other. The observers were aware that one man (the target person) had been instructed either to gain the affection or to win the respect of the other. Low self-monitoring observers tended to accept behavior at face value. They found themselves attracted to the agreeable person, whether or not he was attempting to ingratiate himself with his discussion partner. In contrast, high self-monitoring observers were acutely sensitive to the motivational context within which the target person operated. They liked the target better if he was disagreeable when trying to ingratiate himself. But when he sought respect, they were more attracted to him if he chose to be agreeable. Jones and Baumeister suggest that high self-monitoring observers regarded agreeableness as too blatant a ploy in gaining affection and autonomy as an equally obvious route to respect. Perhaps the high self-monitoring individual felt that they themselves would have acted with greater subtlety and finesse.

Even more intriguing is Jones's and Baumeister's speculation—and I share their view—that high self-monitoring individuals prefer to live in a stable, predictable social environment populated by people whose actions consistently and accurately reflect their true attitudes and feelings. In such a world, the consistency and predictability of the actions of others would be of great benefit to those who tailor and manage their own self-presentation in social situations. From this perspective, it becomes quite understandable that high self-monitoring individuals may be especially fond of those who avoid strategic posturing. Furthermore, they actually may prefer as friends those comparatively low in self-monitoring.

How can we know when strangers and casual acquaintances are engaged in self-monitoring? Are there some channels of expression and communication that are more revealing than others about a person's true, inner "self," even when he or she is practicing impression management?

Both scientific and everyday observers of human behavior have suggested that nonverbal behavior—facial expressions, tone of voice, and body movements—reveals meaningful information about a person's attitudes, feelings, and motives. Often, people who engage in self-monitoring for deceptive purposes are less skilled at controlling their body's expressive movements. Accordingly, the body may be a more revealing source of information than the face for detecting those who engage in self-monitoring and impression management.

More than one experiment shows how nonverbal behavior can betray the true attitude of those attempting impression management. Shirley Weitz of the New School for Social Research reasoned that on college campuses where there are strong normative pressures supporting a tolerant and liberal value system, all student would avoid saying anything that would indicate racial prejudice—whether or not their private attitudes supported such behavior. In fact, she found that among "liberal" white males at Harvard University, the most prejudiced students (as determined by behavioral measures of actual attempts to avoid interaction with blacks) bent over backwards to *verbally* express liking and friendship for a black in a simulated interracial encounter. However, their *nonverbal* behaviors gave them away. Although the prejudiced students made every effort to say kind and favorable things, they continued to do so in a cool and distant tone of voice. It was as if they knew the words not the music: they knew *what* to say, but not *how* to say it.

Another way that prejudice can be revealed is in the physical distance people maintain between themselves and the target of their prejudice. To demonstrate this phenomenon, psychologist Stephen Morin arranged for college students to be interviewed about their attitudes toward homosexuality. Half the interviewers wore "Gay and Proud" buttons and mentioned their association with the Association of Gay Psychologists. The rest wore no buttons and simply mentioned that they were graduate students working on theses. Without the students' knowledge, the distance they placed their chairs from the interviewer was measured while the interviews were going on. The measure of social distance proved to be highly revealing. When the student and the interviewer were of the same sex, students tended to establish almost a foot more distance between themselves and the apparently gay interviewers. They placed their chairs an average of 32 inches away from apparently gay interviewers, but only 22 inches away from apparently nongay interviewers. Interestingly, most of the students expressed tolerant, and at time favorable, attitudes toward gay people in general. However, the distances they chose to put between themselves and the interviews they thought gay betrayed underlying negative attitudes.

❧ IMPRESSION MANAGERS' DILEMMAS

The well-developed skills of high self-monitoring individuals ought to give them the flexibility to cope quickly and effectively with a diversity of social roles. They can choose with skill and grace the self-presentation appropriate to each of a wide variety of social situations. But what happens when the impression manager must effectively present a true and honest image to other people?

Consider the case of a woman on trial for a crime that she did not commit. Her task on the witness stand is to carefully present herself so that everything she does and says communicates to the jurors clearly and unambiguously her true innocence, so that they will vote for her acquittal. Chances are good, however, that members of the jury are somewhat skeptical of the defendant's claims of innocence. After all, they might reason to themselves, the district attorney would not have brought this case to trial were the state's case against her not a convincing one.

The defendant must carefully manage her verbal and nonverbal behaviors so as to ensure that even a skeptical jury forms a true impression of her innocence. In particular, she must avoid the pitfalls of an image that suggests that "she doth protest her innocence too much and therefore must be guilty." To the extent that our defendant skillfully practices the art of impression management, she will succeed in presenting herself to the jurors as the honest person that she truly is.

It often can take as much work to present a truthful image as to present a deceptive one. In fact, in this case, just being honest may not be enough when facing skeptical jurors who may bend over backwards to interpret any and all of the defendant's behavior—nervousness, for example—as a sign of guilt.

The message from research on impression management is a clear one. Some people are quite flexible in their self-presentation. What effects do these shifts in public appearance have on the more private realities of self-concept? In some circumstances, we are persuaded by our own appearances: we become the persons we appear to be. This phenomenon is particularly likely to occur when the image we present wins the approval and favor of those around us.

In an experiment conducted at Duke University by psychologists E. E. Jones, Kenneth Gergen, and Keith Davis, participants who had been instructed to win the approval of an interviewer presented very flattering images of themselves. Half the participants (chosen at random) then received favorable reactions from their interviewers; the rest did not. All the participants later were asked to estimate how accurately and honestly their self-descriptions had mirrored their true personalities.

Those who had won the favor of their interviewers considered their self-presentations to have been the most honest of all. One interpretation of this finding is that those people were operating with rather pragmatic definitions of self-concept: that which produced the most positive results was considered to be an accurate reflection of the inner self.

The reactions of other people can make it all the more likely that we become what we claim to be. Other people may accept our self-presentations at face value; they may then treat us as if we really were the way we pretend to be. For example, if I act as if I like Chris, chances are Chris will like me. Chris will probably treat me in a variety of friendly ways. As a result of Chris's friendliness, I may come to like Chris, even though I did not in the first place. The result, in this case, may be beneficial to both parties. In other circumstances, however, the skilled impression manager may pay an emotional price.

High self-monitoring orientation may be purchased at the cost of having one's actions reflect and communicate very little about one's private attitudes, feelings, and dispositions. In fact, as I have seen time and again in my research with my former graduate students Beth Tanke and Bill Swann, correspondence between private attitudes and public behavior is often minimal for high self-monitoring individuals. Evidently, the words and deeds of high self-monitoring individuals may reveal precious little information about their true inner feelings and attitudes.

Yet, it is almost a canon of modern psychology that a person's ability to reveal a "true self" to intimates is essential to emotional health. Sidney Jourard, one of the first psychologists to hold that view, believed that only through self-disclosure could we achieve self-discovery and self-knowledge: "Through my self-disclosure, I let others know my soul. They can know it, really know it, only as I make it known. In fact, I am beginning to suspect that I can't even know *my own soul* except as I disclose it. I suspect that I will know myself "for real" at the exact moment that I have succeeded in making it known through my disclosure to another person."

Only low self-monitoring individuals may be willing or able to live their lives according to Jourard's prescriptions. By contrast, high self-monitoring individuals seem to embody Erving Goffman's view of human nature. For him, the world of appearances appears to be all, and the "soul" is illusory. Goffman defines social interactions as a theatrical performance in which each individual acts out a "line." A line is a set of carefully chosen verbal and nonverbal acts that express one's self. Each of us, in Goffman's view, seems to be merely the sum of our various performances.

What does this imply for the sense of self and identity associated with low and high self-monitoring individuals?

I believe that high self-monitoring individuals and low self-monitoring individuals have very different ideas about what constitutes a self and that their notions are quite well-suited to how they live. High self-monitoring individuals regard themselves as rather flexible and adaptive people who tailor their social behavior shrewdly and pragmatically to fit appropriate conditions. They believe that a person is whoever he appears to be in any particular situation: "I am me, the me

I am right now." This self-image fits well with the way high self-monitoring individuals present themselves to the world. It allows them to act in ways that are consistent with how they believe they should act.

By contrast, low self-monitoring individuals have a firmer, more single-minded idea of what a self should be. They value and strive for congruence between "who they are" and "what they do" and regard their actions as faithful reflections of how they feel and think. For them, a self is a single identity that must not be compromised for other people or in certain situations. Indeed, this view of the self parallels the low self-monitoring individual's consistent and stable self-presentation.

What is important in understanding oneself and others, then, is not the elusive question of whether there is a quintessential self, but rather, understanding how different people define those attributes of their behavior and experience that they regard as "me." Theory and research on self-monitoring have attempted to chart the processes by which beliefs about the self are actively translated into patterns of social behavior that reflect self-conceptions. From this perspective, the processes of self-monitoring are the processes of self—a system of operating rules that translate self-knowledge into social behavior.

❧ MONITOR YOUR SELF

On the scale I have developed to measure self-monitoring, actors are usually high scorers, as are many obese people, who tend to be very sensitive about the way they appear to others. For much the same reason, politicians and trial lawyers would almost certainly be high scorers. Recent immigrants eager to assimilate, black freshmen in a predominantly white college, and military personnel stationed abroad are also likely to score high on the scale.

The Self-Monitoring Scale measures how concerned people are with the impression they are making on others, as well as their ability to control and modify their behavior to fit the situation. I believe that it defines a distinct domain of personality that is quite different from the traits probed by other standard scales.

Several studies show that skill at self-monitoring is not associated with exceptional intelligence or with a particular social class. Nor is it related, among other things, to being highly anxious or extremely self-conscious, to being an extrovert, or to having a strong need for approval. They may be somewhat power-oriented or Machiavellian, but high self-monitoring individuals do not necessarily have high scores on the "Mach" scale, a measure of Machiavellianism developed by Richard Christie of Columbia University. (Two items from the scale: "The best way to handle people is to tell them what they want" and "Anyone who completely trusts anyone else is asking for trouble.") The steely-eyed Machiavellians are more manipulative, detached, and amoral than high self-monitoring individuals.

The Self-Monitoring Scale describes a unique trait and has proved to be both statistically valid and reliable, in tests on various samples. Below is a ten-item abbreviated version of the Self-Monitoring Scale that will give readers some idea of whether they are low or high self-monitoring individuals. If you would like to test your self-monitoring tendencies, follow the instructions and then consult the scoring key.

These statements concern personal reactions to a number of different situations. No two statements are exactly alike, so consider each statement carefully before answering. If a statement is true, or mostly true, as applied to you, circle the T. If a statement is false, or not usually true, as applied to you, circle the F.

1. I find it hard to imitate the behavior of other people. T F

2. I guess I put on a show to impress or entertain people. T F

3. I would probably make a good actor. T F

4. I sometimes appear to others to be experiencing deeper emotions than I actually am. T F

5. In a group of people I am rarely the center of attention. T F

6. In different situations and with different people, I often act like very different persons. T F

7. I can only argue for ideas I already believe. T F

8. In order to get along and be liked, I tend to be what people expect me to be rather than anything else. T F

9. I may deceive people by being friendly when I really dislike them. T F

10. I'm not always the person I appear to be. T F

SCORING: Give yourself one point for each of questions 1, 5 and 7 that you answered F. Give yourself one point for each of the remaining questions that you answered T. Add up your points. If you are a good judge of yourself and scored 7 or above, you are probably a highly self-monitoring individual; 3 or below, you are probably a low-self-monitoring individual.

❧ THE ROLES WE PLAY

"A man has as many social selves as there are individuals who recognize him and carry an image of him in their mind. . . . But as the individuals who carry the images form naturally into classes, we may practically say that he has as many different social selves as there are distinct *groups* of persons about whose opinions he cares. He generally shows a different side of himself to each of these different groups. Many a youth who is demure enough before his parents and teachers swears and swaggers like a pirate among his 'tough' young friends. We do not show ourselves to our children as to our club companions, to our masters and employers as to our intimate friends. From this there results what practically is a division of the man into several selves; and this may be a discordant splitting, as where one is afraid to let one set of his acquaintances know him as he is elsewhere; or it may be a perfectly harmonious division of labor, as where one tender to his children is stern to the soldiers or prisoners under his command."

—William James
The Principles of Psychology, 1890

REFERENCES

Gergen, K. (1971). *The concept of self.* Holt, Rinehart & Winston.

Goffman, E. (1959). *The presentation of self in everyday life.* Doubleday.

Snyder, M. (1979). Self-monitoring processes. In L. Berkowitz (Ed.), *Advances in experimental social psychology*, (Vol. 12). Academic Press.

Snyder, M. (1979). Cognitive behavioral, and interpersonal consequences of self-monitoring. In *Advances in the Study of Communication and Affect, (Vol. 5: Perception of emotion in self and others*). Plenum.

Snyder, M. (1974). Self-monitoring of expressive behavior. *Journal of Personality and Social Psychology, 30,* 526–537.

❧ Questions

1. Think about how you act in the following different situations: with your best friend, with your parents, on a date, in your psychology class, playing sports, and visiting your grandparents. Are you the same person in each situation? Or is it more like there are six different people inside of you? How can this be? How would Snyder explain this paradox?

2. Do you know people who are high self-monitors? What are these individuals like? Can you see them change their behavior from situation to situation? Do you know people who are low self-monitors? What are they like? Can you see them act the same despite what kind of behavior the situation calls for?

3. Why are high self-monitors so good at detecting lies, perceiving true intentions, and reading others' nonverbal behavior?

4. What would it be like to go on a first date with a high self-monitor? With a low self-monitor? Which date you would enjoy more? Why?

PERSON PERCEPTION

༄

Imagine driving in your car to school to attend your social psychology class. Suddenly, another driver cuts you off. Do you, like most people, mutter under your breath—or out loud even—and question the character or IQ of the offender? What makes you so quick to say, "What a jerk" rather than, "He must have done that to avoid hitting something"? In other words, how do we draw conclusions about the causes of other people's behavior?

Person perception, or social perception, is that branch of social psychology which studies how we form impressions of and make inferences about other people (Aronson, Wilson, & Akert, 1999) or how we seek to understand other persons and events (Taylor, Peplau, & Sears, 2000). In contrast to social cognition, which is a more general look at how people think about their social world, person perception is concerned with how we come to understand a specific person or event. In this chapter, we consider several aspects of this interesting field of study: nonverbal communication, impression formation, attribution of the causes of behavior, and the question of how accurate we are in our judgments of others.

༄ HOW DO WE COMMUNICATE WITH OTHERS?

The process of communication requires one person who *encodes* or expresses a message, and another person who *decodes* or interprets the message. It's easy to think that language is the most important means of receiving information about another person, but verbal communication is only one part of how we communicate. People communicate in nonverbal ways, too, through what are called a paralinguistic channel and a visible channel (Richmond, McCroskey, & Payne, 1991).

Paralanguage includes variations in speech—such as loudness, pitch, inflection, and hesitations—that are completely separate from the content of the speech. The same statement, "I just can't believe it," can signal different things—from anger to happiness—depending on the way the speaker modulates his or her voice while saying it. The *visible channel* includes eye contact and gaze, facial expressions, gestures, body posture, and distance between speakers. With facial expressions, for example, almost all cultures identify the same expressions as indicating certain emotions. There are six basic emotions: anger, happiness, sadness, disgust, surprise, and fear (Ekman et al., 1987). Individual cultures, however, have different cultural rules about the appropriateness of expressing certain emotions (Ekman, 1972). For example, in many cultures, including the United States, one should appear grateful when given a gift, even if one is disappointed with the present.

We understand another person most accurately when information from all three channels—verbal, paralinguistic, and visible—are combined (Chawla & Krauss, 1994). In fact, a mismatch between channels is often one sign of deception on the part of the speaker (Zuckerman, Larrance, Speigel, & Klorman, 1981). In order to deceive others, a person must control his or her emotional expressions in all of the channels at the same time, and this is very difficult to do skillfully.

☙ HOW DO WE FORM IMPRESSIONS OF OTHERS?

There are six general principles that summarize research in impression formation (see Table 1).

When we form an impression of another person, we focus our attention on what is most *salient* in the situation: that is, what seems unusual and stands out from the background. People who seem unusual in a social situation are more likely to be noticed, seen as more influential, and judged either more harshly or more leniently than those who do not seem unusual (Fiske & Taylor, 1991). Here are some examples of salience: A person looks different from others in a group (e.g., there is one man in a gathering of women). A person is in motion (e.g., someone is sitting in a rocking chair while others are in regular chairs). Someone is doing something unusual in the context of the situation, the group, or the person her- or himself (e.g., a person is talking loudly in a library; a man is knitting; or a normally conservative dresser is wearing a brightly colored print shirt). Any of these individuals would draw our attention. Further, we would judge these persons as more influential relative to their actual contributions to the group (e.g., the man in a gathering of women might be viewed as the leader). We would also judge these persons more extremely than we would other people in the same settings (e.g., the library-talker would be seen as particularly rude).

In addition to being influenced by salience effects, we may form certain impressions of others because we have been *primed* to think in a certain way—such as when our expectations are activated, or when certain information is particularly accessible in our minds (Higgins, Rholes, & Jones, 1977; Higgins, 1996). Similarly, we are highly likely to *categorize* a person as a member of a group as a shorthand way of figuring out what he or she might be like. Once we place some-

one in a category, such as "Asians" or "mothers," the person's individual characteristics also become assimilated into the category (Fiske & Neuberg, 1990). That is, we cease to make judgments about the person based solely on his or her own personality (Pendry & Macrae, 1994).

Once we form an initial impression, we quickly infer something about what the person is like. For example, we might decide that the person who is speaking loudly in a library is rude or ignorant, or that a driver who cuts us off is a jerk. We infer traits as a way of summarizing and understanding people instead of having to remember and evaluate each instance of their behavior (Fiske & Taylor, 1991). Moreover, we make such *trait inferences* spontaneously and automatically (Uleman, Hon, Roman, & Moskowitz, 1996).

We also tend to assume that certain traits go together. We derive an *implicit personality theory* from witnessing a single example of behavior by another person and, from there, imagining his or her entire personality (Fiske & Taylor, 1991). Once we construct an understanding of someone else's entire personality, we are more likely to remember a trait than to recall the actual behavior that led to our original inference (Fiske, Neuberg, Beattie, & Milberg, 1987). For example, if we see a young woman pet a dog, we might infer that she is kind. Based on what we know about kind people, we might infer that she is also friendly, warm, and helpful to her friends (Sedikides & Anderson, 1994).

Some traits have a particularly powerful effect on our perceptions because they are associated with many other characteristics. For example, Asch (1946) found that the addition of the word "warm" or "cold" to a description of a person led to different impressions of that person. He concluded that "warm" and "cold" are *central traits* because they cued many additional associations. Further, people often pay more attention to negative traits and weigh them more heavily than positive traits (Vonk, 1993). This tendency causes what's know as the *negativity effect*. As an example of this effect, we are more influenced by traits that imply a lack of moral character, such as dishonesty, than we are by positive traits like honesty (Fiske, 1980). When we see someone acting dishonestly—going against the norm that we should try to make positive impressions on others—we give this negative information more weight because we think it is more likely to indicate his or her genuine personality.

As we gather new pieces of information about another person, we also evaluate each piece in light of information that we already have (Asch, 1946). Thus the *context* of new information also influences how we will interpret the data. For example, we would tend to judge someone who is described as "a very warm person, industrious, critical, practical, and determined" much more positively than someone who is painted as "a very cold person, industrious, critical, practical, and determined" (Asch, 1946). Notice how the traits "industrious, critical, practical, and determined" take on different qualities in the context of "warm" than in the context of "cold."

Table 1 *Six Principles of Social Perception*

1. Perceivers form impressions of others quickly, on the basis of minimal information.
2. Perceivers pay special attention to the most obvious or unusual qualities of another person.
3. Perceivers infer the meaning of a person's actions from the social context.
4. Perceivers organize information by seeing other people as members of a particular group.
5. Perceivers judge a single member by using their knowledge of groups.
6. Perceivers' own needs and personal goals influence the perception process.

From Taylor, Peplau, & Sears, 2000, p. 63.

An example of this phenomenon is the *halo effect*. When we have an overall positive impression of a person, we evaluate new information about him or her in a positive way. In short, we give the person the benefit of the doubt (Cooper, 1981). For example, we tend to assume that honest and attractive people also possess other positive traits. Of course, if our evaluation of a person is negative, this too will color our evaluation of new information, albeit in a negative way. (Some have called this tendency the "horns effect.")

Finally, we combine our observations about another person's appearance and behavior into inferences about his or her personality. From there, we form an overall impression of the kind of person he or she is. Interestingly, we tend to evaluate people positively, despite mixed or negative information. This phenomenon is called the *person positivity bias* (Sears, 1983).

Researchers have theorized about other ways in which we combine pieces of information about others. One early model theorized that we use the *averaging principle* to blend the effects of positive and negative traits (Anderson, 1965). A later model suggested that people use the *additive principle* to combine traits into a total impression. According to the averaging model, a person who had a couple of positive traits would be viewed as moderately positive. According to the additive model, he or she would be viewed as much more positive than either trait alone would imply. However, a *weighted averaging model*—in which we weigh more heavily those traits that we think are more important, and then average them together—appears to capture the impression-formation process most accurately (Anderson, 1968).

As this summary suggests, we do not form impressions of others in a completely calculating, objective way. Rather, we do our best to make sense out of the raw materials of our incomplete observations and inferences.

❦ How Do We Understand the Causes of Behavior?

The study of how we understand the causes of behavior—others' as well as our own—is called *attribution theory*. According to Heider (1958), we have a need to form a coherent understanding of the world. We do this by making attributions, or inferences, about the causes of events. We tend to think that behavior is caused by either external (or situational) forces or by internal (or dispositional) forces. Think back to our earlier example of the driver who cut you off on the way to class. If your first thought was "What a jerk," then you are attributing the "jerk's" behavior to an internal or dispositional cause. If you said, "Wow—he must have been trying to avoid hitting something," you would be assuming an external or situational reason for the other driver's behavior.

Other theorists have built on Heider's basic principles. For example, according to correspondent inference theory, we infer that someone else's behavior is caused by their disposition under three conditions: (1) when the behavior is freely chosen, (2) when others probably would not behave similarly in that same situation, and (3) when the behavior causes an outcome not caused by other possible actions (Jones & Davis 1965). To see how this works, think again about the example of the driver who cut you off. If he chose to cut you off, if other drivers typically do not cut you off, and if this driver could have moved into a different lane instead of cutting you off, then you will probably infer that the driver's low character caused his behavior. However, if the driver was forced into your lane because a deer ran into the road, and if this sort of thing happens often during hunting season, then probably you would conclude that the situation caused the driver's behavior.

Still others have refined attribution theory further. For example, Kelly specified the conditions under which we make internal or external attributions with confidence (Kelly, 1967). When a behavior or outcome is *consistent* over time, is *distinctive* to the situation, and is what most others would do in the same situation (high *consensus*), we make a *situational* attribution. If a behavior or outcome is consistent over time, is *not* distinctive to the situation, and is probably *not* what others would do in the situation, then we make a *dispositional* attribution. But, if the behavior is not consistent over time, is not distinctive to this situation, and may or may not be what others would do, then we conclude that something unique about this particular event caused the behavior in question.

Let's use the driving example again to illustrate. If a driver often cuts you off, and you see him cut off other drivers, and most drivers are not cutting each other off, then you will likely conclude "He's a jerk" (a dispositional attribution). But, if this particular driver hardly ever cuts you off, but he does cut people off if there is a pothole or a deer in the road, *and* most other people would do the same, you would likely conclude that "he did that to avoid hitting something" (a situational attribution).

According to Kelly, we are like naive scientists conducting analyses of covariance to find out which causes and events covary over time, situation, and individuals. We evaluate these three pieces of information — *consistency*, *distinctiveness*, and *consensus* — to judge whether an outcome was caused by the person or by the situation.

❦ How Accurate Are We in Our Judgments?

At this point, you may be thinking that all this weighing of various pieces of information must be very cumbersome and time-consuming. Most of the time, we must make our attributions quickly, without carefully considering the various "if . . . then's." You would be right. You're also right if you think that our fondness for expediency sometimes leads us to make *incorrect* judgments. For example, we tend to significantly overemphasize the impact of someone's personality or disposition on his or her behavior. This bias is so pervasive—and yet so wrong—that it is called the *fundamental attribution error* (Ross, 1977) or the *correspondence bias* (Jones, 1990).

Why do we make this error? For one thing, we seem to be "personality psychologists" at heart. We simply believe that most behavior is caused by personality (Ross & Nisbett, 1991). United States Americans and other Westernized peoples may be more vulnerable to this error because their cultures emphasize individualism more than collectivistic cultures do (Morris & Peng, 1994).

Perceptual salience is another reason for the fundamental attribution error. As we saw, we tend to view salient individuals or events as causal (Fiske & Taylor, 1991). But what is salient to us depends on whether we are *observing* others' behavior or *behaving* ourselves. From the perspective of observers, we consider *other people* most salient. Therefore, we overestimate the impact of their disposition on their behavior (Jones & Nisbett, 1972; Taylor & Fiske, 1975). However, something interesting happens when we try to explain our own behavior: We tend *not* to make the fundamental attribution error. Instead, we make external, or situational, attributions. This is because, when we are in the role of actor (the person exhibiting the behavior), the *situation* is most salient. Therefore we notice it more and make external attributions for our behavior. The impact of these differing perspectives of the actor and the observer is called the *actor-observer effect* (Jones & Nisbett, 1972). Because actors are more able to see the situation's influence on their behavior, they are less likely to make the fundamental attribution error (see Schoeneman & Rubanowitz, 1985, for an illustration of the actor-observer effect from newspaper advice columns).

Although we may be less likely to make the fundamental attribution error when explaining our own behavior, we make another kind of attributional error called *the self-serving bias*. This bias causes us to take credit for our successes and to deny responsibility for our failures (Miller & Ross, 1975). One easy way of doing this is to make internal attributions for positive outcomes ("I got an A") and external attributions for negative outcomes ("The professor flunked me"). We do this in order to maintain our self-esteem and our positive view of ourselves—even if it means distorting reality. We also do this in order to present ourselves in the best possible light to others (Greenberg, Pyszczynski, & Solomon, 1982).

The self-serving bias leads to a number of interesting social phenomena. For example, sometimes people may *self-handicap* before taking a test by drinking, taking drugs (Berglass & Jones, 1978), procrastinating in studying (Tice & Baumeister, 1997), not sleeping or eating properly, or not studying at all. Then if they perform poorly on the test, they have a handy external attribution: "I couldn't sleep" or "I was sick." But if they perform well, then they look even better for succeeding despite the handicap! Of course, sabotaging one's

own efforts like this may actually jeopardize one's performance. However, a person who self-handicaps is so anxious about performing well and looking good to him- or herself or to others that the risk is apparently worthwhile (Berglass & Jones, 1978).

The self-serving bias also creates the *illusion of invulnerability* (Perloff, 1987), in which we believe that good things are *more* likely to happen to us than to others and that bad things are *less* likely to happen to us than to others. This illusion causes us to have *unrealistic optimism* about our futures. For example, we may believe that we will have better jobs, live in more beautiful homes, live longer and healthier lives, and be less vulnerable to cancer, alcoholism, and heart disease than our peers will (Weinstein, 1980).

Similarly, we tend to believe that we are more talented and able compared to others. This belief gives us a sense of *false uniqueness* (Snyder & Fromkin, 1980). Of course, statistically, we can't *all* be better than average! However, this tendency for groups of people to consistently rate themselves as better than average has been dubbed the *Lake Wobegon Effect* by some, after the mythical town of Lake Wobegon created by radio talent Garrison Keillor. As you may recall if you've ever listened to Keillor's show, in Lake Wobegon "the women are strong, the men are good-looking, and *all* of the children are above-average."

❦ "IF WE'RE SO DUMB, HOW COME WE MADE IT TO THE MOON?"

Given the inferences, shortcuts, leaps of intuition, and biases that characterize the attribution process, you might well be wondering how we make *any* correct judgments about others, let alone survive in a social world. Upon reading about the early work on biases in the attribution process, some psychologists wondered the same thing (Nisbett & Ross, 1980, p. 249).

We survive because, despite our flaws, we are surprisingly accurate perceivers of other people. When we do make mistakes about others, we often don't realize that we are wrong. Therefore, these biases and errors in the person-perception process do not affect us strongly (Aronson, Wilson, & Akert, 1999). This is especially likely if we make our false beliefs come true, as is the case with self-fulfilling prophecies (Snyder, Tanke, & Berscheid, 1977). (This occurs when the beliefs we hold about others are strong enough to lead those same others to act in ways that confirm our expectations [Merton, 1948]). Also, observers tend to make the same kinds of inferences, so that often we can find social support for our impressions (like gossiping about the new people you met at a party afterwards with friends) even when we are wrong (Kenny, 1991). Finally, we may not be as concerned with statistical accuracy as we are with pragmatic accuracy (Synder & Swann, 1978). That is, as long as we are able to function reasonably well in social interactions, the accuracy of our impressions may not matter much to us.

For example, people commonly think that they know a professor well, even though they have only interacted with him or her in one situation—the classroom. You may not know exactly how your professor is when she is not speaking in front of a large audience of social psychology students, or what she does to relax on the weekend. However, you probably know quite well what's the most important for getting a good grade—for example, how late you can come to class, how prepared you have to be, what kind of questions your professor is likely to ask on an exam, how tolerant she is of misbehavior, how smart she is, and what kind of sense of humor she has.

Despite various flaws in the person-perception process, the good news is that we are generally wrong in consistent ways. As a result, we can hone our awareness of these tendencies and try to overcome them. Even better, we become more accurate in our impressions and understandings of other people the more we get to know them. So, before you judge that driver too harshly, think about inviting him out for a pizza instead!

REFERENCES

Anderson, N. H. (1959). A test of a model for opinion change. *Journal of Abnormal and Social Psychology, 59,* 371-381.

Anderson, N. H. (1968). A simple model for information integration. In R. P. Abelson et al. (Eds.), *Theories of cognitive consistency: A sourcebook* (pp. 731-743). Chicago: Rand McNally.

Aronson, E., Wilson, T. D., & Akert, R. M. (1999). *Social psychology* (3rd ed.). New York: Longman.

Asch, S. E. (1946). Forming impressions of personality. *Journal of Abnormal and Social Psychology, 41,* 258-290.

Berglas, S., & Jones, E. E. (1978). Drug choice as a self-handicapping strategy in response to noncontingent success. *Journal of Personality and Social Psychology, 36,* 405-417.

Chawla, P., & Krauss, R. M. (1994). Gesture and speech in spontaneous and rehearsed narratives. *Journal of Experimental Social Psychology, 30,* 580-601.

Cooper, W. H. (1981). Ubiquitous halo. *Psychological Bulletin, 90,* 218-224.

Ekman, P. (1971). Universals and cultural differences in facial expressions of emotion. In J. K. Cole (Ed.). *Nebraska symposium on motivation* (pp. 207-283). Lincoln, NB: University of Nebraska Press.

Ekman, P., Friesen, W. V., O'Sullivan, M., Chan, A., Diacoyanni-Tarlatzis, I., Heider, K., Krause, R., LeComre, W. A., Pitcairn, T., Ricci-Bitti, P. E., Sherer, K., Tomita, M., & Tzavras, A. (1987). Universals and cultural differences in the judgments of facial expressions of emotions. *Journal of Personality and Social Psychology, 53,* 712-717.

Fiske, S. T. (1980). Attention and weight in person perception: The impact of negative and extreme behavior. *Journal of Personality and Social Psychology, 30,* 889-906.

Fiske, S. T., & Neuberg, S. L. (1990). A continuum of impression formation, from category-based to individuating processes: Influences of information and motivation of attention and interpretation. In M. P. Zanna (Ed.), *Advances in experimental social psychology* (Vol. 23, pp. 1-73). New York: Academic Press.

Fiske, S. T., Neuberg, S. L., Beattie, A. E., & Milberg, S. J. (1987). Category-based and attribute-based reactions to others: Some informational conditions of stereotyping and individuating processes. *Journal of Experimental Social Psychology, 23,* 399-427.

Fiske, S. T., & Taylor , S. E. (1991). *Social cognition.* New York: McGraw-Hill.

Greenberg, J., Pyszczynski, T., & Solomon, S. (1982). The self-serving attributional bias: Beyond self-presentation. *Journal of Experimental Social Psychology, 18,* 56-67.

Heider, F. (1958). *The psychology of interpersonal relations.* New York: Wiley.

Higgins, E. T. (1996). Knowledge application: Accessibility, applicability, and salience. In E. T. Higgins & A. R. Kruglanski, (Eds.), Social psychology: Handbook of basic principles (pp. 133-168). New York: Guilford.

Higgins, E. T., Rholes, W. S., & Jones, C. R. (1977). Category accessibility and impression formation. *Journal of Experimental Social Psychology, 13,* 141-154.

Jones, E. E. (1990). *Interpersonal perception.* New York: W. H. Freeman.

Jones, E. E., & Davis, K. E. (1965). From acts to dispositions: The attribution process in social psychology. In L. Berkowitz (Ed.), *Advances in experimental social psychology* (Vol. 2, pp. 219-266). New York: Academic Press.

Jones, E. E., & Nisbett, R. E. (1972). The actor and the observer: Divergent perceptions of the causes of behavior. In E. E. Jones, D. E. Kanouse, H. H. Kelley, R. E. Nisbett, S. Valins, & B. Weiner (Eds.), *Attribution perceiving the causes of behavior* (pp. 79-94). Morristown, NJ: General Learning Press.

Kelly, H. H. (1967). Attribution theory in social psychology. In D. Levine (Ed.), *Nebraska symposium on motivation* (pp. 192-238). Lincoln, NE: University of Nebraska Press.

Kenny, D. A. (1991). A general model of consensus and accuracy in interpersonal perception. *Psychological Review, 98,* 155-163.

Merton, R. (1948). The self-fulfilling prophecy. *Antioch Review, 8,* 193-210.

Miller, D. T., & Ross, M. (1975). Self-serving biases in the attribution of causality: Fact or fiction? *Psychological Bulletin, 82,* 213-225.

Morris, M. W., & Peng, K. (1994). Culture and cause: American and Chinese attributions for social and physical events. *Journal of Personality and Social Psychology, 67,* 949-971.

Nisbett, R. E. & Ross, L. (1980). *Human inference: Strategies and shortcomings of social judgment.* Englewood Cliffs, NJ: Prentice-Hall.

Pendry, L. F., & Macrae, C. N. (1994). Stereotypes and mental life: The case of the motivated but thwarted tactician. *Journal of Experimental Social Psychology, 30,* 303-325.

Richmond, V. P., McCroskey, J. C., & Payne, S. K. (1991). *Nonverbal behavior in interpersonal relations*. Englewood Cliffs, NJ: Prentice-Hall.

Ross, L. (1977). The intuitive psychologist and his shortcomings: Distortions in the attribution process. In L. Berkowitz (Ed.). *Advances in experimental social psychology* (Vol. 10, pp.171-221). New York: Academic Press.

Ross, L., & Nisbett, R. E. (1991). *The person and the situation*. New York: McGraw-Hill.

Schoeneman, T. J., & Rubanowitz, D. E. (1985). Attributions in the advice columns: Actors and observers, causes and reasons. *Personality and Social Psychology Bulletin, 11,* 315-325.

Sears, D. O. (1983). The person-positivity bias. *Journal of Personality and Social Psychology, 44,* 233-250.

Sedikides, C., & Anderson, C. A. (1994). Causal perceptions of intertrait relations: The glue that holds person types together. *Personality and Social Psychology Bulletin, 20,* 294-302.

Snyder, C. R., & Fromkin, H. L. (1980). *Uniqueness: The human pursuit of difference*. New York: Plenum Press.

Synder, M., & Swann, W. B. (1978). Hypothesis testing in social interaction. *Journal of Personality and Social Psychology, 36,* 1202-1212.

Snyder, M., Tanke, E. D., & Berscheid, E. (1977). Social perception and interpersonal behavior: On the self-fulfilling nature of social stereotypes. *Journal of Personality and Social Psychology, 35,* 656-666.

Taylor, S. E., & Fiske, S. T. (1975). Point of view and perceptions of causality. *Journal of Personality and Social Psychology, 32,* 439-445.

Taylor, S. E., Peplau, L. A., & Sears, D. O. (2000). *Social psychology* (10th ed.). Upper Saddle River, NJ: Prentice-Hall.

Tice, D. M., & Baumeister, R. F. (1997). Self-esteem, self-handicapping, and self-presentation: The strategy of inadequate practice. *Journal of Personality, 58,* 443-464.

Uleman, J. S., Hon, A., Roman, R. J., & Moskowitz, G. B. (1996). On-line evidence for spontaneous trait inferences at encoding. *Personality and Social Psychology Bulletin, 22,* 377-394.

Vonk, R. (1993). The negativity effect in trait ratings and in open-ended descriptions of persons. *Personality and Social Psychology Bulletin, 19,* 269-278.

Weinstein, N. D. (1980). Unrealistic optimism about future life events. *Journal of Personality and Social Psychology, 39,* 806-820.

Zuckerman, M., Larrance, D. T., Speigel, N. H., & Klorman, R. (1981). Controlling nonverbal displays: Facial expressions and control of voice. *Journal of Experimental Social Psychology, 17,* 506-524.

Taylor, S. E. (1998). The social being in social psychology. In D. T. Gilbert, S. T. Fiske, & G. Lindzey (Eds.). *The handbook of social psychology*, (4th ed., Vol. 1, pp. 58–95). New York: McGraw Hill.

SUGGESTED READINGS

Fiske, S. T., & Taylor , S. E. (1991). *Social cognition*. New York: McGraw-Hill.

Gilovich, T. D. (1991). *How we know what isn't so*. New York: Free Press.

Jones, E. E. (1990). *Interpersonal perception*. New York: W. H. Freeman.

Kunda, Z. (1999). *Social cognition*. Cambridge, MA: MIT Press.

Nisbett, R., & Ross, L. (1980). *Human inference: Strategies and shortcomings of social judgment*. Englewood Cliffs, NJ: Prentice-Hall.

SOCIAL COGNITION

A young singer waited for her cue backstage at a concert. The former astronaut Edwin "Buzz" Aldrin was scheduled to appear as narrator for a special performance of Gustav Holst's *The Planets* by the Philadelphia Orchestra. As a unique feature, the performance would be enhanced by footage from NASA space missions. The singer was casually reading some newspaper articles posted on a bulletin board in the hallway when a compact, older man in a suit and tie passed behind her in the hallway. As she turned to say "Excuse me" to make room for him in the narrow passageway, she noticed a NASA pin on his lapel. She glanced at his face—which was easy to do, since they were about the same height—smiled, and then turned back to her reading. Only much later did she realize that she had come in close contact with the great astronaut—and that she had virtually ignored him. She had always imagined Buzz Aldrin and the other participants in the early space program as "larger than life heroes," and was taken aback by the rather small physical stature of the man who walked by her in the hallway.

This anecdote powerfully illustrates a fundamental principle of social perception: Our perceptions, decisions, and actions are colored by our thoughts and motives. Such is the purview of social cognition—an area of study within social psychology that explores how we perceive, think about, understand, and remember events. Social psychologists have viewed human beings as thinking organisms (Fiske & Taylor, 1991), actively sensing, perceiving, inferring, judging, remembering, deciding, and acting in the world. Whether the social thinker is considered a naïve scientist (Kelly, 1967), weighing the co-variation of events, or an intuitive psychologist (Ross, 1977), trying to understand why others behave as they do, the common theme is that people actively and constantly make sense out of their world (Fiske, 1993).

Unfortunately, some psychologists have argued, we are neither very rigorous scientists nor very thoughtful psychologists. Instead, we are more like cognitive misers (Fiske & Taylor, 1984)—conserving our cognitive energies or indeed avoiding thinking entirely by acting mindlessly (Langer, 1989)! Even our memory is fallible (Schacter, 1999). As a result of these weaknesses, we take mental shortcuts as we respond to the world around us. We ignore useful information at times, overuse irrelevant information at other times, or fail to appreciate the unreliability of human memory.

On the one hand, these strategies do help us process complex information by breaking it into smaller, more manageable "pieces." After all, we are each called upon to make hundreds of decisions in the course of a day, and, with our limited cognitive capacities, it would be impossible to think through each one carefully. On the other hand, these shortcuts sometimes lead us to the wrong conclusions. True, we might imagine a science-fiction-like fantasy world in which humans figured each other out by using hand-held computers ("Hmm, he said hello to me; what are the statistical chances that he likes me? . . ."). However, most people would agree that this kind of cool, rational process is unrealistic and even inappropriate when it comes to making certain social decisions.

Recently, Fiske and Taylor (1991) suggested that in trying to understand the social world, people act like motivated tacticians. That is, we are flexible thinkers who choose from among many different cognitive strategies—including cold, calculating ones—based on our goals, motives, and needs.

Sometimes we choose a strategy based on accuracy; other times, our choice is based on needs such as speed or self-esteem. Part of what makes us most assuredly human—and puts the *social* in social cognition—are our foibles and follies. For social psychologists, how we choose from among our cognitive strategies can be the most interesting aspect of social cognition.

The study of social cognition encompasses the strategies people use to organize and interpret information; the ways in which our moods, motives, attitudes, and beliefs all influence how we perceive, understand, and recall information; and the shortcomings of the judgment process. Let us turn to the first of these aspects: how we organize our social world.

◁ SCHEMAS: HOW WE ORGANIZE OUR SOCIAL WORLD

The world around us generates a relentless stream of information. We would become quickly overwhelmed if every time we met a new person or encountered a new situation, we had no prior experience to help us interpret the new events. Instead, we rely on what are called schemas. A schema is an expectation we have regarding new experience. This expectation is based on our prior knowledge, impressions, and past experiences (Fiske & Taylor, 1991). For example, many people living in the American midwest have a schema of "life in California" that causes them to believe that they would be happier if they lived in California. This schema is derived from television shows, movies, and popular songs that portray California as a fun, beautiful, sunny place to live. (Interestingly, Californians—despite holding the same schema—are not in fact generally happier than midwesterners [Schkade & Kahneman, 1998]). (See Table 1 for a summary of the various kinds of schemas we use.)

Schemas help us to interpret, act on, and remember new information quickly and efficiently. Sometimes we also use schemas to fill in gaps in our knowledge. For example, if you are trying to use the public transit system in an unfamiliar city, you could call to mind how the buses work in your hometown and use this knowledge to figure out how to get

around. One important thing about schemas is that we are more likely to notice and to think about new information when it fits with our schemas. To illustrate, suppose you like to go out to clubs. If you scan the newspaper to find something to do over the weekend, you will be more likely to notice ads for clubs than for classical music concerts—and vice versa if you are a classical music fan. As a result of this tendency, our schemas become reinforced and ever more resistant to change. Additionally, our use of schemas is often unconscious and automatic. We often don't even realize that we are using them.

Of these six kinds of schemas, scripts and stereotypes are the ones of greatest interest to social psychologists. *Scripts* are schemas for events (Abelson, 1976). A script lets us know what sequence of occurrences to expect in a new situation, and thereby eases social interactions. For example, you probably have a well-defined script for going to a restaurant—a script that includes being seated, reading a menu, choosing what to order, eating, paying, and leaving a tip.

Stereotypes are schemas for people. Stereotypes are expectations about what people of a certain gender, age, race, ethnicity, or other social category may be like or how they will behave (Fiske & Taylor, 1991). For example, the singer described earlier had clear stereotypes for "astronaut" and "smaller older man" that were mutually exclusive. That is, she expected all astronauts to be young and tall. While stereotypes may be a useful way to organize new information about other people, they also can fuel prejudice and discrimination when we use negative or inaccurate stereotypes (Allport, 1954).

Schemas are organized in a hierarchical fashion, with the most specific concepts on the bottom and the most general concepts at the top (Fiske & Taylor, 1991). For example, the concept of "animal" might be at the top of a hierarchy containing "dog" at a lower level, "Dalmatian" at yet a lower level, and "Rover," the family pet, at the lowest level (Kunda, 1999). Higher-order schemas contain all members and attributes of the schemas below them. In our example, "animal" includes all dogs, and "dog" includes all Dalmatians. Schemas at different levels contain different attributes, so the same creature can be classified at different levels. We may refer to the family pet as an "animal," a "dog," or a "Dalmatian." "Animal" contains the schema "can breathe,"

Table 1 *Kinds of Social Schemas*

Social Schema	Contents
Person Schemas	An understanding of the traits and goals of a particular individual
Self-Schemas	An understanding of the traits and goals of oneself
Role Schemas	Assumptions about what behavior is appropriate for a specific social role
Stereotypes	Expectations of attributes of people from specific social categories
Scripts	Expectations of the sequence of events that unfold in well-known situations
Content-Free Schemas	Rules for processing, ordering, or organizing information

From Fiske & Taylor, 1991.

"dog" contains the schema "can bark," and "Dalmatian" contains the schema "has spots" (Kunda, 1999).

Further, schemas include *exemplars*, which are specific examples of the schema (e.g., "Rover," "Marmaduke," "Snoopy," "Wishbone") and *prototypes*, which are lists of features shared by all members of the category (Kunda, 1999). No doubt our singer was thinking of the prototypical astronaut—young, big, strong, brave—which the real Buzz Aldrin did not match. Researchers debate whether we use exemplars or prototypes most often when making judgments with our schemas (Kunda, 1999).

Schemas are also difficult to change. Once we use one to successfully organize or process information, it is reinforced and becomes especially difficult to discredit (Ross, Lepper, & Hubbard, 1975). This reinforcing process is called *belief perseverance* or the *perseverance effect*. In the case of a stereotype, if we meet a new person who does not conform to our schema, we may decide that the person is an exception that proves the rule, or we may develop subcategories—e.g. "*retired* astronauts"—that leave our original stereotype intact (Fiske & Taylor, 1991). This rigid quality of schemas is unfortunate because it means that we may dislike or discriminate against someone without getting to know him or her as an individual.

In sum, schemas help us process complex information about our social world quickly and efficiently. They make social events comprehensible and predictable. However, they may lead to wrong interpretations and inaccurate expectations if they are misapplied or overgeneralized (Taylor, Peplau, & Sears, 2000). After all, our singer was almost rude to a celebrated astronaut! Table 2 summarizes the advantages and disadvantages of using schemas.

❧ WHAT AFFECTS OUR PERCEPTIONS, INTERPRETATIONS, AND MEMORIES?

In perceiving, interpreting, and remembering events and people, we are not always purely rational. Rather, our moods, motives, preconceptions, attitudes, and social beliefs all influence our perceptions and memories.

Moods. Seeing the world through "rose-colored glasses" when you are happy or having "the blues" when you are sad are not just metaphors. People really do see things differently depending on their mood (e.g., Keltner, Ellsworth, & Edwards, 1993). For example, we tend to be more sociable, altruistic, and approving of things when we are in a good mood, as well as impulsive, cautious, and stereotypical in our decision-making. When we are in a negative mood, we may show less of these tendencies. However, we may also try to help ourselves out of a bad mood by being helpful to others or seeking the company of others (Fiske & Taylor, 1991).

Motives. Our motives and goals heavily influence our perceptions and judgments. As the model of the motivated tactician suggests, we are more accurate in our judgments of events or people when we are motivated to be accurate—perhaps because there are undesirable consequences for making an inaccurate judgment (Fiske & Taylor, 1991). However, our cognitive processes are not always under our conscious control. As a result, we may be only partially accurate in our judgments even when we are highly motivated to strive for accuracy (Nisbett & Wilson, 1977).

Preconceptions. Similarly, our preconceptions also influence what we see and how we interpret social events. For example, as the anecdote about Buzz Aldrin illustrated, studies have found that the more perceived status a speaker has, the taller his or her audience will perceive him or her to be (Wilson, 1968).

Attitudes. Many studies have shown that, because people interpret new information in such a way as to reinforce their attitudes, they are more likely to view neutral or information as biased against their side (Vallone, Ross, & Lepper, 1985). This *hostile media effect* has been shown to happen when students who were either pro-Arab or pro-Israel interpreted news broadcasts of political events in the Middle East (Giner-Sorolla & Chaiken, 1994; Vallone, Ross, & Lepper, 1985). It has even been detected in the way people from rival schools interpret what happened during a football game between their schools (Hastorf & Cantril, 1954). In addition, people tend to be more accepting of information when it supports their view (Ditto & Lopez, 1992).

Social Beliefs. Our social judgments are also shaped by assumptions or beliefs that we hold but that we might not be aware of. Because these beliefs are often nonconscious, we are not aware that we may be applying them inaccurately. Therefore, we risk making errors in our judgments. There are many such beliefs; Table 3 lists four common ones (Franzoi, 2000; see Table 3).

1. Others think and behave as we do (the false consensus effect). We often use ourselves as the standard for behavior. We assume that others think as we do or should behave as we do. As a result, we are likely to overestimate the extent to which others would agree with us (Ross, Greene, & House, 1977).

2. Our judgments are correct (confirmation bias). We tend to seek information that supports our beliefs and to ignore information that disconfirms or challenges our beliefs (Wason, 1960). In forming beliefs—whether about the rule that a sequence of three numbers follows or whether a dinner partner is shy—information that proves us wrong is just as useful as information that shows us to be correct. However, we don't like to be wrong, so we seek to confirm what we already know. This tendency may smooth social interactions, such as keeping the conversation going when

Table 2 *Advantages and Disadvantages of Schemas*

Schemas . . .	But they also . . .
Help us process information	May distort what we see and remember
Help us recall events	May fill in gaps in our knowledge with elements that don't belong
Speed up our processing time	May cause us to oversimplify
Help us draw automatic inferences	May not fit reality
Add information	May mislead us
Facilitate interpretation	May lead us to wrong interpretations
Provide expectations	May persist even after they are proved false
Contain emotional qualities	May lead us to be inflexible

From Fiske & Taylor, 1991.

we are talking to a stranger whom we know little about (e.g., Leyens, 1990, and Leyens & Dardenne, 1994, in Franzoi, 2000). However, it does not help us to see our social world for what it is.

3. Our dreams come true (self-fulfilling prophecies). Sometimes the beliefs that we hold about others are strong enough to lead those same others to act in ways that confirm our expectations (Merton, 1948). This process involves three steps: (1) the perceiver forms an impression of another person (a "target"), (2) the perceiver acts toward the target person in a manner consistent with that impression, and (3) the other person responds to the perceiver's actions in a way that confirms the perceiver's original impression (Snyder, Tanke, & Berscheid, 1977). In a classic study, men who thought they were having a telephone conversation with an attractive woman spoke to her in such a way that the woman behaved in a more warm and outgoing—i.e., attractive—manner, according to judges who heard only the woman's end of the conversation (Snyder et al., 1977).

4. The world is a fair place (belief in a just world). Another common social belief assumes that the world is a just place—that good things happen to good people, bad things happen to bad people, and "everyone gets what they deserve" (Lerner, 1980). Such beliefs make us feel good about ourselves and about life in general and give us the illusion of having more control over our lives than we really do. In fact, people who hold these beliefs may expe-

rience less stress and depression than those who believe otherwise (Lipkus, Dalbert, & Siegler, 1996). However, the just-world belief may also cause us to be less empathetic and forgiving of people who have been the victim of bad events. Instead, we may actually blame such victims for their misfortune in order to preserve our belief that "everyone gets what they deserve" (Burger, 1981).

❧ OTHER MENTAL SHORTCUTS

As we've seen, schemas help us to process complex social information. In this sense, they serve as a kind of mental shortcut. There's another category of mental shortcuts, called heuristics, that also help us to reduce complexity. Many different heuristics exist, (Kahneman, Slovic, & Tversky, 1982; McKean, 1985), but we will consider four of the most common ones (see Table 4).

Representativeness. Judging the probability or likelihood of an outcome, a cause, or of an object belonging to a category is particularly difficult and counterintuitive for us motivated tacticians. To simplify this task, we often assess how similar or "representative" the object, outcome, or cause is to some standard. We might use this *representativeness heuristic* in the following ways (Nisbett & Ross, 1980):

1. To judge the likelihood that something belongs to a certain category, we assess how well the object represents or

Table 3 *Social Beliefs*

Belief	Name
1. Others think and behave as we do	The False Consensus Effect
2. Our judgments are correct	Confirmation Bias
3. Our dreams come true	Self-Fulfilling Prophecies
4. The world is a fair and just place	Belief in a Just World

From Franzoi, 2000.

matches features that we believe characterize the category (Tversky & Kahneman, 1974). For example, as a kid, Tom W. liked math and science fiction. What are the chances that he is an engineer today? (Most people would say that it is highly likely that he is an engineer today, since Tom matches our stereotype of an engineer.)

2. To judge the likelihood of an outcome, we assess how it compares with its cause (Tversky & Kahneman, 1971). For instance, suppose you flipped a coin six times and got the sequence HTTHHT. What do you think the next coin flip will be? (Most people will say "heads," even though they know that the probability of getting either heads or tails is the same each time. However, "heads" makes the sequence look more random, and so it is judged as more likely.)

3. To judge the likelihood of a cause, we assess how similar that cause is to its effect (Tversky, 1977). For example, we believe that eating carrots is good for your eyesight, because rabbits have good eyesight and they eat a lot of carrots (Gilovich, 1990; Gilovich & Savitsky, 1996). (See Gilovich & Savitsky, 1996, for a discussion of other erroneous medical beliefs, including homeopathic medicine, that seem compelling because of representativeness.)

Availability. Similarly, people may judge the likelihood of an event by assessing how easily such an event is perceived or comes to mind, instead of by using the actual base rate probability (Tversky & Kahneman, 1973). For example, many people are afraid to travel on airplanes, even though air travel is far safer than automobile travel, because people have vivid images of plane crashes readily available to them from the media (Myers, 1999).

Simulation. A specific case of the availability heuristic occurs when people judge probability or likelihood by assessing how easily they can construct counterexamples from their imagination. In other words, people simplify a judgment process by imagining various possible outcomes—i.e., by running mental simulations—of events that they wished had happened instead of the actual event. Then they judge the likelihood of an alternative outcome by seeing how easily they could think of it as a possible outcome (Kahneman & Tversky, 1982). "If only" thinking, as in "if only Mr. Tees didn't get that red light" (Kahneman & Tversky, 1982) or "if only I had jumped higher, I could have gotten the gold medal" (Medvec, Madey, & Gilovich, 1995), is a common technique for simplifying a difficult prediction problem. Such counterfactual thinking strongly shapes a person's expectations, causal attributions, impressions, and emotions—and may cause regret (Medvec & Savitsky, 1997).

Anchoring and Adjustment. Sometimes we have to make a decision without having the proper information at hand. In such cases, we might start with our best guess—an

Table 4 *Four Heuristic Strategies for Making Judgments Under Uncertainty*

Heuristic	Definition	Example
Representativeness	Representativeness is a judgment of how relevant A is to B; high relevance yields high estimates that A originates from B	Deciding that George (A) must be an engineer because he looks and acts like your stereotype of engineers (B)
Availability	Availability is the estimate of how frequently or likely a given instance or occurrence is, based on how easily or quickly an association or examples come to mind	Estimating the divorce rate on the basis of how quickly you can think of examples of divorced friends
Simulation	Simulation is the ease with which a hypothetical scenario can be constructed	Getting angry because of a frustrating event on the basis of how easily you can imagine the situation occurring otherwise.
Anchoring and Adjustment	Anchoring and adjustment is the process of estimating some value by starting with some initial value and then adjusting it to the new instance	Judging how hard a friend studies based on how hard you study

From Taylor, Peplau, & Sears, 2000, p. 50.

"anchor"—and then make adjustments from there. But if the anchor is completely arbitrary, and if we don't adjust enough later to account for this, we may be end up making a grossly inaccurate judgment (Tversky & Kahneman, 1974). For example, some unscrupulous realtors have been known to show clients houses that they know are out of the clients' price range. This is a device for getting potential buyers to raise their expectations of what is a reasonable selling price (Cialdini, 1993). Similarly, when making judgments about other people, we may use ourselves as the anchor and then judge others by how they compare to us, instead of using an objective standard such as actions or achievements (Markus, Smith, & Moreland, 1985).

Armed with this overview of how we perceive, interpret, and remember people and events, you probably have a lot more empathy for the young singer who failed to recognize Buzz Aldrin. By misapplying her schema about astronauts, she also missed getting an autograph from one of her favorite heroes. Her story contains an important lesson about the power of schemas and the advantages of knowing more about how we process reality—something that the following readings will help you begin to do.

REFERENCES

Abelson, R. P. (1976). Script processing in attitude formation and decision making. In J. S. Carroll & J. W. Payne (Eds.), *Cognition and social behavior* (pp. 13–32). Hillsdale, NJ: Erlbaum.

Allport, G. W. (1954). *The nature of prejudice*. Garden City, NY: Doubleday.

Burger, J. M. (1981). Motivational biases in the attribution of responsibility for an accident: A meta-analysis of the defensive-attribution hypothesis. *Psychological Bulletin, 90*, 496–512.

Cialdini, R. B. (1993). *Influence: Science and practice* (3rd ed.). New York: HarperCollins.

Ditto, P. H., & Lopez, D. E. (1992). Motivated skepticism: Use of differential decision criteria for preferred and non-preferred conclusions. *Journal of Personality and Social Psychology, 63*, 568–584.

Fiske, S. T. (1993). Social cognition and perception. In M. R. Rosenzweig & L. W. Porter (Eds.), *Annual Review of Psychology, 44*, 2–23.

Fiske, S. T., & Taylor, S. E. (1984). *Social cognition*. Reading, MA: Addison-Wesley.

Fiske, S. T., & Taylor, S. E. (1991). *Social cognition*. New York: McGraw-Hill.

Franzoi, S. L. (2000). *Social psychology* (2nd ed.). New York: McGraw-Hill.

Gilovich, T. (1990). The anatomy of questionable and erroneous beliefs. *Cornell University Arts and Sciences Newsletter, 11*(2), 2, 5.

Gilovich, T., & Savitsky, K. (1996, March/April). Like goes with like: The role of representativeness in erroneous and psuedo-scientific beliefs. *The Skeptical Inquirer*, 34–40.

Giner-Sorolla, R., & Chaiken, S. (1994). The causes of hostile media judgments. *Journal of Experimental Social Psychology, 30*, 165–180.

Hastorf, A. H., & Cantril, H. (1954). They saw a game: A case study. *Journal of Abnormal and Social Psychology, 49*, 129–134.

Kahneman, D., Slovic, P., & Tversky, A. (1982). *Judgment under uncertainty: Heuristics and biases*. New York: Cambridge University Press.

Kahneman, D., & Tversky, A. (1982). The psychology of preferences. *Scientific American, 246*, 160–173.

Kelly, H. H. (1967). Attribution theory in social psychology. In D. Levine (Ed.), *Nebraska symposium on motivation* (Vol. 15, pp. 192–240). Lincoln: University of Nebraska Press.

Keltner, D., Ellsworth, P. C., & Edwards, K. (1993). Beyond simple pessimism: Effects of sadness and anger on social perception. *Journal of Personality and Social Psychology, 64*, 740–752.

Langer, E. J. (1989). Minding matters: The consequences of mind-lessness-mindfulness. In L. Berkowitz (Ed.), *Advances in experimental social psychology* (Vol. 22, pp. 137–173). New York: Academic Press.

Lerner, M. J. (1980). *The belief in a just world: A fundamental delusion*. New York: Plenum.

Lipkus, I. M., Dalbert, C., & Siegler, I. C. (1996). The importance of distinguishing the belief in a just world for self vs. for others: Implications for psychological well-being. *Personality and Social Psychology Bulletin, 22*, 666–677.

Markus, H., Smith, J., & Moreland, R. L. (1985). Role of the self-concept in the perception of others. *Journal of Personality and Social Psychology, 49*, 1494–1512.

McKean, K. (1985, June). Decisions, decisions. *Discover*, 22–30.

Medvec, V. H., Madey, S. F., & Gilovich, T. (1995). When less is more: Counterfactual thinking and satisfaction among Olympic medalists. *Journal of Personality and Social Psychology, 69*, 603–610.

Medvec, V. H., & Savitsky, K. (1997). When doing better means feeling worse: The effects of categorical cutoff points on counterfactual thinking and satisfaction. *Journal of Personality and Social Psychology, 72*, 1284–1296.

Merton, R. (1948). The self-fulfilling prophesy. *Antioch Review, 8*, 193–210.

Myers, D. G. (1999). *Social psychology* (6th ed.). Boston, MA: McGraw-Hill.

Nisbett, R. E., & Ross, L. (1980). *Human inference: Strategies and shortcomings of social judgment*. Englewood Cliffs, NJ: Prentice-Hall.

Nisbett, R. E., & Wilson, T. D. (1977). Telling more than we can know: Verbal reports on mental processes. *Psychological Review, 84*(3), 231–259.

Ross, L. (1977). The intuitive psychologist and his shortcomings. In L. Berkowitz (Ed.), *Advances in experimental social psychology* (Vol. 10, pp. 173–220). New York: Academic Press.

Ross, L., Greene, D., & House, P. (1977). The "false consensus effect": An egocentric bias in social perception and attribution processes. *Journal of Experimental Social Psychology, 13*, 279–301.

Ross, L., Lepper, M. R., & Hubbard, M. (1975). Perseverance in self-perception and social perception: Biased attributional processes in the debriefing paradigm. *Journal of Personality and Social Psychology, 32,* 880–892.

Schacter, D. J. (1999). The seven sins of memory. *American Psychologist, 54,* 182–203.

Schkade, D. A., & Kahneman, D. (1998). Attributions in the advice columns: Actors and observers, causes and reasons. *Personality and Social Psychology Bulletin, 11,* 315–325.

Snyder, M., Tanke, E. D., & Berscheid, E. (1977). Social perception and interpersonal behavior: On the self-fulfilling nature of social stereotypes. *Journal of Personality and Social Psychology, 35,* 656–666.

Taylor, S. E., Peplau, L. A., & Sears, D. O. (2000). *Social psychology.* Upper Saddle River, NJ: Prentice-Hall.

Tversky, A. (1977). Features of similarity. *Psychological Review, 84,* 327–352.

Tversky, A., & Kahneman, D. (1971). Belief in the law of small numbers. *Psychological Bulletin, 76,* 104–110.

Tversky, A., & Kahneman, D. (1973). Availability: A heuristic for judging frequency and probability. *Cognitive Psychology, 5,* 207–232.

Tversky, A., & Kahneman, D. (1974). Judgment under uncertainty: Heuristics and biases. *Science, 185,* 1124–1131.

Vallone, R. P., Ross, L., & Lepper, M. R. (1985). The hostile media phenomenon: Biased perception and perceptions of media bias in coverage of the Beirut massacre. *Journal of Personality and Social Psychology, 49,* 577–585.

Wason, P. C. (1960). On the failure to eliminate hypotheses in a conceptual task. *Quarterly Journal of Experimental Psychology, 12,* 129-140.

Wilson, P. R. (1968). Perceptual distortion of height as a function of ascribed academic status. *The Journal of Social Psychology, 74,* 97–102.

Kunda, Z. (1999). *Social cognition.* Cambridge, MA: MIT Press.

SUGGESTED READINGS

Fiske, S. T., & Taylor , S. E. (1991). *Social cognition.* New York: McGraw-Hill.

Gilovich, T. D. (1991). *How we know what isn't so.* New York: Free Press.

Kunda, Z. (1999). *Social cognition.* Cambridge, MA: MIT Press.

Nisbett, R., & Ross, L. (1980). *Human inference: Strategies and shortcomings of social judgment.* Englewood Cliffs, NJ: Prentice-Hall.

Taylor, S. E. (1989). *Positive illusions: Creative self-deception and the healthy mind.* New York: Basic Books.

Taylor, S. E. (1998). The social being in social psychology. In D. T. Gilbert, S. T. Fiske, & G. Lindzey (Eds.), *The handbook of social psychology* (4th ed., Vol. 1, pp. 58–95). New York: McGraw Hill.

GENDER

∂

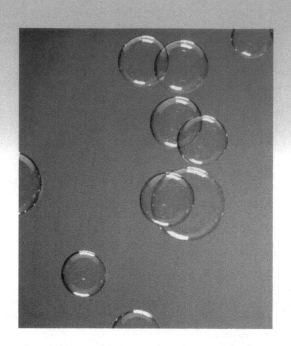

"**S**o, what is it, a boy or a girl?"

Before we know a baby's name or its health or even the health of the new mother, we know the baby's sex. From the very first moments of life, gender becomes a fundamental part of who we are and determines our place in the social world. No other aspect of who we are is so constant and yet so controversial.

∂ WHAT IS THE DIFFERENCE BETWEEN GENDER AND SEX?

You may think that the terms gender and sex are interchangeable, but many psychologists would disagree. The biological category of maleness or femaleness is called *sex*. The social role associated with each of these biological categories is called *gender*. Sometimes the difference between sex and gender is clear. For example, the reproductive differences between males and females are considered sex differences. The fact that women are the primary caretakers of children or that men more often take the leadership role on a date are considered gender differences. This is because these behaviors stem from social expectations that have little to do with biological differences.

However, sometimes the difference between sex and gender is not so clear. For example, consider the finding that males are more physically aggressive than females. Is this a sex difference caused by hormones? Or is it a gender difference caused by socialization and expectations of what is considered acceptable behavior for males and females? In fact, both sex and gender may cause certain behaviors—and for this reason, many psychologists use the terms interchangeably. Despite the differing views on this issue, honing our awareness of the differences between sex and gender offers an important benefit: It opens the possibility that some differences between men and women are not biologically determined and therefore can be changed.

∂ HOW DO WE UNDERSTAND GENDER DIFFERENCES?

Many psychologists have attempted to answer this question (e.g., Eagly & Wood, 1999). As a result, there are at least four different theoretical perspectives that researchers have used to define and explain gender differences. These include biology, socialization, social roles, and social situation (Taylor, Peplau, & Sears, 2000; see Table 1).

As we saw earlier, we might attribute differences in behavior to biological factors such as reproductive function or hormonal differences, or to socialization. As Table 1 shows, men and women might also act differently depending on the social role they occupy. For example, in many societies the role of boss requires that one act dominant, while the role of worker requires one to behave more passively. If men are more likely than women to hold positions of power in

Table 1 *Four Perspectives on Gender*

Perspective	Causes of Differences Between Men's and Women's Behavior
Biology	Biological factors, including physical differences, reproductive differences, and hormonal differences
Socialization	Societal expectations and standards of behavior for males and females as communicated by parents, peers, teachers, and the media
Social roles	The different roles that men and women occupy in their daily lives, such as teacher, boss, worker, mother, father, wife, and husband
Social situation	The specific situation in which behavior occurs, such as with peers vs. with family, with a job interview vs. a potential date, etc.

From Taylor, Peplau, & Sears, 2000.

society, then any differences in their behavior may be more due to the "boss" role they are occupying than to physical differences (biology) or expectations about gender (socialization). Indeed, when men and women occupy the same social roles, they tend to act in similar ways. This suggests that differences in social roles strongly foster differences in behavior between the two genders (Eagly, 1987).

Finally, certain social situations may cause men and women to behave differently (Deaux & Major, 1987). In two separate studies, both men and women changed their behavior to conform to what they thought was expected of them by someone they wanted to impress—either a job interviewer, in the case of the women (von Baeyer, Sherk, & Zanna, 1981) or an attractive woman, in the case of the men (Morier & Seroy, 1994).

❧ How Do Psychologists Conceptualize Gender?

Early psychological conceptualizations of gender treated gender as a typology. That is, researchers believed that people could be classified as one type or the other, as if put in boxes labeled "feminine" or "masculine" (Hyde, 1996). This rather conservative view oversimplified the complexities of gender. Later, psychologists viewed masculinity and femininity as two extremes on a single continuum of gender (Hyde, 1996). But on such a bipolar scale, in which the two dimensions are mutually exclusive, people who rank high in one quality must necessarily rank low in the other. This view conceptualizes femininity and masculinity as opposites.

Recently, some researchers have begun asking whether a person can be *both* feminine and masculine. In 1974, Sandra Bem developed the concept of psychological androgyny, which states that a person can be both feminine and masculine by having feminine and masculine psychological characteristics (Bem, 1974). According to this theory, there are feminine people, masculine people, and androgynous people (Hyde, 1996).

Bem herself admits that the concept of androgyny may be limiting, because it is based on traditional conceptualiza-tions of femininity and masculinity (Bem, 1981). In fact, Bem has come to question the importance that our society places on gender. She would like to see individuals transcend gender rather than accept society's limited construction of how they should behave (Bem, 1993). In her latest book, she candidly and poignantly tells her own story of raising androgynous children and striving for an egalitarian marriage (Bem, 1998).

❧ How Do We Develop Gender Identity?

How is it that we come to see ourselves as male or female? A sense of *gender constancy*—i.e., the idea that a person's sex is a stable property that is linked to physical and biological attributes rather than to superficial characteristics (Kohlberg, 1966, 1969)—unfolds in a series of developmental stages that roughly parallel cognitive development (Intons-Peterson, 1988). By the time children are two-and-a-half years old, they show the earliest form of gender self-awareness, called *gender identity* (Shaffer, 2000). They know that there are two categories of gender and are able to label themselves as a boy or as a girl. Further, they use this social category to decide how to behave: They act in ways dictated by their category, and avoid acting in ways dictated by the other category. Children also have very stereotypical ideas of gender at this age. They understand the categories but have only a rudimentary grasp of where the categories come from, what they mean, and what they imply for development and reproduction. For example, children tend to believe that wearing a dress or playing with dolls makes a person a girl, whereas a short hair cut or a shaved head makes one a boy.

Next, children develop *gender stability:* They recognize that gender remains constant over time (Shaffer, 2000). When children who have not yet reached this stage are asked "When you grow up, will you be a mommy or a daddy?" they may believe that they could become either. Some children may believe that one could be a mommy or a daddy "if you really wanted to be."

By age six or seven, children attain *gender consistency:* They understand that a person's gender does not change with his or her appearance or activities (Shaffer, 2000). Early in this stage, children may also still have only a rudimentary knowledge of genital and reproductive differences between males and females (McConaghy, 1979).

After children have learned what gender is, they begin learning the larger cultural meaning of *gender roles.* This is a socialization process. Through observation, imitation, and experience, the children learn expected ways that people of both genders behave, as defined by their society (Franzoi, 1996). By puberty, adolescents strive to develop their own unique identities by incorporating their concepts of gender. Interestingly, this entire process of forming a gender identity starts by being biologically determined, moves rather quickly to being socially defined, and finally becomes individually defined and internalized.

◑ IS GENDER IN THE EYE OF THE BEHOLDER?

Although we are born male or female, our gender is defined and taught to us by society. But how much of this gender-role differentiation is due to biology, and how much is socially determined?

Consider the following experiment, in which participants are shown a video of an infant watching a Jack-in-the-Box. The infant stares intently at the colorful box as the music plays, but when the puppet jumps out, the infant starts to cry. When asked what emotion the baby showed, participants who were told that the infant was a boy thought that he was angry. Participants who were told that the infant was a girl thought that she was fearful (Condry & Condry, 1976).

What caused these different responses? In reality, the same infant—and, in fact, the same video clip—was shown to all the subjects. The gender of the infant was only *in the mind of the participant.* Yet this assumption of the infant's gender had a huge effect on participants' interpretation of the infant's emotion. Other studies have shown similar effects, even when the stimulus is only an infant cooing in "his" or "her" cradle (Vogel, Lake, Evans, & Karraker, 1991).

Equally interesting, gender stereotypes, once primed, lead to self-fulfilling prophecies. In one study, participants played with a baby who wore neutral clothing (an undershirt and diaper) while sitting on a blanket with a doll, a football, and a teething ring (Sidorowicz & Lunney, 1980). Most male and female participants, after being told that the baby's name was Jenny, gave the baby the doll. When told that the baby's name was Johnny, participants gave the baby the football. Even more telling, when the experimenter admitted, "I don't know which infant we are using today," participants grew visibly awkward. They then asked the baby's gender or tried to guess it from the baby's behavior. Some relied on the teething ring to entertain the baby.

Stereotypes are especially likely to become activated when we have little information about a person, when gender is especially salient (or noticeable), or when we hold greater social power over the person about whose personality we're making assumptions (Sears, Taylor, & Peplau, 2000). In experiments, the most important variable was not the actual sex of the baby or of the participant but the *assigned* gender of the baby. Although gender starts out as a biological construct, in our society it quickly becomes a social one because of its salience.

There are many stereotypes of how males and females should be treated and how they should act in our society. When asked to list various gender stereotypes, college students readily generated differences in abilities, personalities, traits, and behaviors (Myer & Gonda, 1982). The majority of their responses reflected personality traits (30 percent) or social roles (19 percent), while a lesser percentage encompassed biological differences (22 percent) or physical differences (16%).

Notions of how males and females differ appear to be universal. In a study of male and female college students in 25 countries, Williams and Best (1982) found close agreement on which personality characteristics are most strongly associated with men versus with women. The researcher's sample included three African countries, 10 European countries, seven Asian countries, and six South American countries. Perhaps not surprisingly, males were considered more masculine, dominant, and strong, while females were considered more feminine, submissive, and sensitive (see Table 2).

Table 2 *Characteristics Associated with Males and Females in Twenty-Five Countries*

Males	Females
Adventurous	Affectionate
Aggressive	Dreamy
Autocratic	Feminine
Daring	Sensitive
Dominant	Sentimental
Enterprising	Submissive
Forceful	Superstitious
Independent	
Masculine	
Robust	
Stern	
Strong	

From Williams and Best (1982). To be considered a gender difference, two-thirds of the respondents within a country indicated that the adjective was more descriptive of one gender or the other. The items listed here achieved such consensus in at least 24 of the 25 countries sampled.

Despite the strong agreement that certain traits characterize each gender, applying gender stereotypes to a specific person can create many problems (Sears, Taylor, & Peplau, 2000). First, the stereotype may be wrong or overgeneralized. For example, not all women are sentimental or dreamy. Second, stereotypes often exaggerate the differences between males and females and minimize differences among individual men or individual women. For instance, to say that males are independent is not the same as saying that *all* males are more independent that *all* females. Yet this is how we interpret gender differences when we hear about them. Finally, stereotypes have a tendency to become self-fulfilling. For example, care-givers who expect boys to be more aggressive may ignore rowdy behavior in boys but reprimand it in girls. Similarly, if a man assumes that women are not smart, he would probably never think to ask a woman her opinion of current events or books. Instead, he might limit the conversation to the weather or the woman's clothing. In both cases, the stereotype holders might come away with their stereotypes intact—without being aware of their own role in further cementing those stereotypes. Given these problems, we might well ask whether there is any truth to gender stereotypes.

❧ ARE GENDER DIFFERENCES REAL OR IMAGINED?

In thinking about gender differences and trying to separate fact from stereotype, it is important that we keep three questions in mind. First, is there a difference? Second, if there is a difference, is it important? And third, what causes this difference?

As it turns out, there are few actual psychological differences between males and females (Hyde, 1996). That is, in terms of our personalities, men and women are more similar than different. Where differences do exist, researchers using the technique of meta-analysis (in which the size of the gender effect is calculated over many studies) found that the actual differences are statistically small or moderate (Hyde & Frost, 1993). In fact, there are more close-to-zero differences in the area of gender than in other aspects of psychological make-up (Hyde & Plant, 1995). Further, any differences are due to socialization or social-role expectations rather than biological predisposition.

For example, variations in physical strength and muscle distribution between males and females are probably the biggest differences but perhaps the least relevant from a psychological perspective (Hyde, 1986). All other psychological differences pale in comparison to these, however. Consider the area of cognition. Functions such as verbal ability, math, spatial visualization, and moral reasoning show insignificantly small differences between men and women (Hyde, 1996). However, there are moderate differences in spatial perception and large differences in mental rotation (imagin-

ing what a cube or other figure would look like from a different side), such that males outperform females in these functions (Hyde, 1996).

In terms of social behaviors, there are no gender differences in sociability, but there are moderate differences in aggression (Hyde, 1986). Males are more aggressive and dominant than females (Perry, Perry, & Weiss, 1989; Sidanius, Pratto, & Bobo, 1994). Males also tend to have a greater sense of personal entitlement than females, in that they expect more from their jobs or personal relationships (Major, 1989, 1993). Females are better at understanding nonverbal communication than males are, especially when reading facial expressions (Hall, 1998).

The evidence for gender differences in influence ability, helping behavior, anxiety, empathy, and leadership tends to be more equivocal. Women sometimes appear to be somewhat more influenceable or more conforming than men. However, this depends on the kind of task or the nature of the social influence involved; for example, the familiarity of the task, or the gender of the experimenter (Eagly, 1978, 1983, 1987). With helping behavior, men are more likely than women to act the "hero," gaining awards and public recognition for offering aid to strangers. Women are more likely to be cast in the role of "mother" or "friend," engaging in quiet acts of heroism and self-sacrifice or offering aid to friends and family (Eagly & Crowley, 1986). Females also score higher than males on self-report measures of anxiety and empathy; however, behavioral and observational studies find very little gender differences in these traits (Hyde, 1986). Finally, while no difference in leadership *ability* exists, it appears that women are more likely to use a democratic *style* of leadership than men are (Hyde, 1996).

What can we conclude about gender differences? Taking all of these results together, we can say three things. First, we must keep in mind that for all of these variables, we are concerned with differences between males and females *on average*. When a difference is found, it does not mean that *all* males differ from *all* females. It means that there is some overlap in the kinds of behaviors that males and females show, but that on average there tends to be a difference. So, we need to take care not to overemphasize the differences (Hyde & Frost, 1993).

Second, the existence of differences does not mean that these behaviors are un-changeable. Anyone can readily learn how to read nonverbal cues, ask for more on the job, or become less conforming (Taylor, Peplau, & Sears, 2000).

Finally, it appears that these differences in social behavior strongly depend on the situation in which the behavior is measured or observed. Unfortunately, current models of gender-related behavior do not take social context into account when theorizing about gender differences (Deaux & LaFrance, 1998).

❧ TOWARD A SOCIAL PSYCHOLOGICAL MODEL OF GENDER

In the latest *Handbook of Social Psychology*, Deaux and LaFrance (1998) propose a new model for understanding the social psychology of gender. They claim that for the past 100 years or so, psychologists have used an overly simple, incomplete gender-difference model (Shields, 1975). Deaux and LaFrance cite Sandra Bem in their reasoning. Bem argues that social psychologists (like most individuals) have approached the study of gender with three hidden assumptions (1994): first, that male and female are mutually exclusive categories (gender polarization); second, that the male experience is seen as the standard or norm for behavior (*androcentrism*; e.g. Tavris, 1992); and third, that differences in behavior naturally and inevitably follow from differences in biology (biological essentialism). As a result, psychologists have inadvertently stressed opposites rather than overlap in gendered behavior and functioning, ignored the situational determinants of behavior, and focused on biology rather than on the social structures that place women and men in different and unequal positions in society (Deaux & LaFrance, 1998).

Deaux and LaFrance propose a gender-in-context model that rejects these assumptions. Instead, the model states that first we must "recognize and incorporate the context in which women and men act and react . . . looking to broader societal structures and cultural norms as well as to the immediate and micro features of experimental settings" (Deaux & LaFrance, 1998, p. 789).

Deaux and LaFrance's model starts with the idea that a perceiver and a target (the individual being perceived) interact with each other (see Figure 1). To this interaction, the perceiver brings his or her beliefs about gender, expectations of the behavior of men and women, gender stereotypes, gender-role attitudes, and his or her own gender identity. These all act as filters or lenses that color how the perceiver will behave toward the target. The resulting behaviors may have self-fulfilling consequences that perpetuate the perceiver's gender-belief system.

The exact same process is occurring within the target. That is, a target also comes to the interaction with his or her own gender-belief system. This system may become activated, or called to mind, by the specific interaction, by the purpose or outcome of the interaction, or by the context or situation in which the interaction occurs.

Deaux and LaFrance emphasize that certain contexts may make gender more salient and thereby cue gender-belief systems in both the perceiver and the target. For example, gender may be especially salient at a professional football

Figure 1 *A Simplified View of the Deaux and LaFrance Gender-in-Context Model*

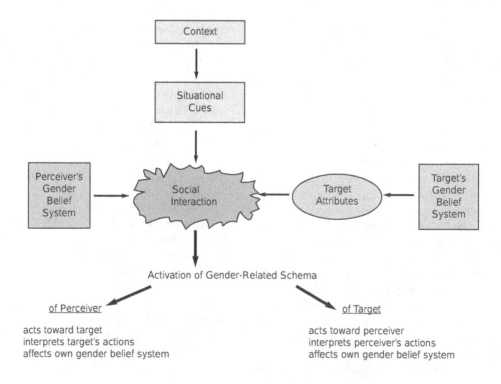

Based on Deaux & LaFrance 1998 p. 790

game, a Miss America pageant, or a singles bar (Deaux & LaFrance, 1998). These researchers believe that social psychologists need to pay more attention to the situation in which behavior occurs, and to the interaction between the person and the situation, than to the individual behavior.

For example, imagine that a man is meeting a woman. From the way she is dressed and his own stereotypes of women, he decides that she is a feminine sort of person. The woman senses his decision and, wanting to please him, may act in a more feminine manner than she might otherwise. According to Deaux and LaFrance's model, if this interaction took place on a date, it would mean something very different than if it took place during a job interview. Indeed, Deaux and LaFrance argue that we could not draw any conclusions about why the man is thinking as he is or why the woman is acting as she is unless we know the context of their interaction.

This new gender-in-context model not only integrates past research into a unified theoretical model, but it also provides an effective way to understand and study gender-related behavior. The model acknowledges that the behavior of males and females must be considered from many different levels of perspectives: from the individual, to the dyad (or pair of individuals), to the situation, and to the larger social system. The model also accepts the influences of both biology and socialization on gender-related behavior. Finally, and perhaps most importantly, by taking into account the social situation, the model emphasizes the variation, flexibility, and contingency of gender-related behavior (Deaux & LaFrance, 1998).

A model like this cannot help but be healthier for individuals than a model that emphasizes differences and limits behaviors. With such a model guiding psychological research, theory, and practice, every new baby—male or female—would grow up in a society that welcomes the best that each individual has to offer, regardless of gender.

REFERENCES

Bem, S. L. (1974). The measurement of psychological androgyny. *Journal of Consulting and Clinical Psychology, 42*, 155–162.

Bem, S. L. (1981). Gender schema theory: A cognitive account of sex-typing. *Psychological Review, 88*, 354–364.

Bem, S. L. (1993). *The lenses of gender.* New Haven, CT: Yale University Press.

Bem, S. L. (1998). *An unconventional family.* New Haven, CT: Yale University Press.

Condry, J., & Condry, S. (1976). Sex differences: A study in the eye of the beholder. *Child Development, 47*, 812–819.

Deaux, K., & LaFrance, M. (1998). Gender. In D. Gilbert, S. T. Fiske, & G. Lindzey (Eds.), *The handbook of social psychology* (4th ed., Vol. 1, pp. 788–827). Reading, MA: Addison-Wesley.

Deaux, K., & Major, B. (1987). Putting gender into context: An integrative model of gender-related behavior. *Psychological Review, 94*, 369–389.

Eagly, A. H. (1978). Sex differences in influenceability. *Psychological Bulletin, 85*, 86 116.

Eagly, A. H. (1983). Gender and social influence: A social psychological analysis. *American Psychologist, 38*, 971–981.

Eagly, A. H. (1987). *Sex differences in social behavior: A social role interpretation.* Hillsdale, NJ: Erlbaum.

Eagly, A. H., & Crowley, M. (1986). Gender and helping behavior: A meta-analytic review of the social psychological literature. *Psychological Bulletin, 100*, 283–308.

Eagly, A. H., & Wood, W. (1999). The origins of sex differences in human behavior. *American Psychologist, 54*, 408–423.

Franzoi, S. L. (1996). *Social psychology.* Madison, WI: Brown & Benchmark.

Hall, J. A. (1998). How big are nonverbal sex differences? The case of smiling and sensitivity to nonverbal cues. In D. J. Canary & K. Dindia (Eds.), *Sex differences and similarities in communication* (pp. 155–178). Mahwah, NJ: Erlbaum.

Hyde, J. S. (1996). *Half the human experience: The psychology of women* (5th ed.). Lexington, MA: D. C. Heath.

Hyde, J. S., & Frost, L. A. (1993). Meta-analysis in the psychology of women. In F. L. Denmark & M. A. Paludi (Eds.), *Psychology of women: A handbook of issues and theories* (pp. 67–104). Westport, CT: Greenwood Press.

Hyde, J. S., & Plant, E. A. (1995). Magnitude of psychological gender differences. *American Psychologist, 50*, 159–161.

Intons-Peterson, M. J. (1988). *Children's concepts of gender.* Norwood, NJ: Ablex.

Kohlberg, L. (1966). A cognitive-developmental analysis of children's sex role concepts and attitudes. In E. Maccoby (Ed.), *The development of sex difference.* Stanford, CA: Stanford University Press.

Kohlberg, L. (1969). Stage and sequence: The cognitive-developmental approach to socialization. In D. A. Goslin (Ed.), *Handbook of socialization theory and research.* Chicago: Rand McNally.

Major, B. (1989). Gender differences in comparisons and entitlement: Implications for comparable worth. *Journal of Social Issues, 45*, 99–115.

Major, B. (1993). Gender, entitlement, and the distribution of family labor. *Journal of Social Issues, 49*, 141–160.

McConaghy, M. J. (1979). Gender permanence and the genital basis of gender: Stages in the development of constancy of gender identity. *Child Development, 50*, 1223–1226.

Morier, D., & Seroy, C. (1994). The effect of interpersonal expectancies on men's self-presentation of gender role attitudes to women. *Sex Roles, 31*, 493–504.

Myers, A. M., & Gonda, G. (1982). Utility of the masculinity-femininity construct: Comparison of traditional and androgyny approaches. *Journal of Personality and Social Psychology, 43*, 514–523.

Perry, D. G., Perry, L. C., & Weiss, R. J. (1989). Sex differences in the consequences that children anticipate for aggression. *Developmental Psychology, 25*, 312–319.

Shaffer, D. R. (2000). *Social and personality development.* Belmont, CA: Wadsworth.

Shields, S. (1975). Functionalism, Darwinism, and the psychology of women: A study in social myth. *American Psychologist, 30,* 739–754.

Sidanius, J., Pratto, F., & Bobo, L. (1994). Social dominance orientation and the political psychology of gender: A case of invariance? *Journal of Personality and Social Psychology, 67,* 998–1011.

Sidorowicz, L. S., & Lunney, G. S. (1980). Baby X revisited. *Sex Roles, 6*(1), 67–73.

Tavris, C. (1992). *The mismeasure of woman.* New York: Simon & Schuster.

Taylor, S, E., Peplau, L. A., & Sears, D. O. (2000). *Social psychology* (10th ed.). Upper Saddle River, NJ: Prentice Hall.

Vogel, D. A., Lake, M. A., Evans, S., & Karraker, K. H. (1991). Children's and adults' sex-stereotyped perceptions of infants. *Sex Roles, 24,* 605–616.

von Baeyer, C. L, Sherk, D. L., & Zanna, M. P. (1981). Impression management in the job interview: When the female applicant meets the male (chauvinist) interviewer. *Personality and Social Psychology Bulletin, 7,* 45–52.

Williams, J. E., & Best, D. L. (1982). *Measuring sex stereotypes: A thirty-nation study.* Newbury Park, CA: Sage.

SUGGESTED READINGS

Bem, S. L. (1993). *The lenses of gender.* New Haven, CT: Yale University Press.

Bem, S. L. (1998). *An unconventional family.* New Haven, CT: Yale University Press.

Caplan, P. J., & Caplan, J. B. (1994). *Thinking critically about research on sex and gender.* New York: HarperCollins.

Deaux, K., & LaFrance, M. (1998). Gender. In D. Gilbert, S. T. Fiske, & G. Lindzey (Eds.), *The handbook of social psychology* (4th ed., Vol. 1, pp. 788–827).

Denmark, F. L., & Paludi, M. A. (Eds.). (1993). *Psychology of women: A handbook of issues and theories.* Westport, CT: Greenwood Press.

Diamant, L., & McAnulty, R. D. (Eds.). (1995). *The psychology of sexual orientation, behavior, and identity.* Westport, CT: Greenwood Press.

Keller, E. F. (1985). *Reflections on gender and science.* New Haven, CT: Yale University Press.

Maccoby, E. E. (1997). *The two sexes: Growing up apart, coming together.* Cambridge, MA: Harvard University Press.

Swann Jr., W. B., Langlois, J. H., & Gilbert, L. A. (1999). *Sexism and stereotypes in modern society: The gender science of Janet Taylor Spence.* Washington, DC: American Psychological Association.

Tavris, C. (1992). *The mismeasure of woman*

THE ABC'S OF ATTITUDES AND PERSUASION

W hat do you think about social psychology? Should the drinking age be reduced to 18? How about them Yankees/Cubbies/Bulls/whatever? Are you a Democrat or a Republican? What's the best toothpaste? What's your favorite flavor of ice cream? What do you want to do today?

These questions all have something in common: They are all asking about your attitudes. An attitude is an "overall evaluation of persons (including oneself), objects and issues" (Petty & Wegener, 1998, p. 323). Our attitudes are unobservable to others. Therefore they must be inferred from our responses—approval or disapproval, approach or avoidance, and like or dislike—to an entity (Eagly & Chaiken, 1998). Some researchers have defined attitude as a learned tendency to think about some issue, person, or object in a particular way (Zimbardo & Leippe, 1991).

The objects of our attitudes, which psychologists call, simply, the *attitude objects*, can be abstract or concrete. They can include social policies (e.g., the death penalty), social groups (e.g., lawyers or Asian Americans), individual persons (e.g., your roommate), specific behaviors (e.g., cigarette smoking), and general classes of behaviors (e.g., maintaining a healthy lifestyle) (Eagly & Chaiken, 1998). Psychologists often use specialized terms to refer to specific kinds of attitudes (see Table 1).

We human beings are very quick to form attitudes or judgments, no matter how trivial the entity or brief our exposure to it (Zajonc, 1980). Once we form an attitude, it easily influences our subsequent perceptions and thoughts (Zimbardo & Leippe, 1991). Attitudes thus become the "lenses" or "eyeglasses" (think of "rose-colored glasses") through which we view the world (see Table 2).

Yet attitudes do not stand alone. The attitude "I like chocolate chip ice cream," for example, is tied into an attitude *system* that includes affect (or emotion), behavior, and cognitions (or thoughts and beliefs). Hence we can think of the ABC's of attitudes (see Table 3 and Figures 1 and 2).

Table 1 *Specialized Terms for Attitudes*

Attitudes Toward. . .	Are Called. . .
Minority groups	Prejudices
Individuals	Liking or interpersonal attraction
Oneself	Self-esteem
Abstract goals (e.g., equality, freedom)	Values
Governmental policy or relations between social groups	Social or political attitudes

From Eagly & Chaiken, 1998.

Table 2 *Attitudes. . .*

. . . are organized such that changes in one component of
    an attitude often cause changes in other components
    of the attitude.

. . . guide our perceptual and cognitive processes.

. . . are easily accessible evaluative summaries.

. . . may serve and sustain our self-definition, self-percep-
    tion, and self-esteem.

From Zimbardo & Leippe, 1991, pp. 36-37.

Let's look at another example, the attitude "I like social psychology." This attitude might include affective elements such as "I enjoy learning about social psychology" or "Social psychology piques my curiosity." It might also include cognitions or beliefs about social psychology: "The course is required for the major" or "Social psychology will help me to understand human behavior better." Finally, behaviors associated with this attitude might include daily class attendance, note-taking, and intentions to study very hard for the test and get an A in the class.

Because attitudes are part of a system, any change in one part of the system will cause a change in other parts of the system. For example, suppose you found the material in your social psychology class boring (affect). Maybe you would stop liking social psychology (attitude). If you stopped liking social psychology (attitude), you might stop going to class (behavior). If you stopped going to class (behavior), you might like social psychology even less (attitude) because it is too frustrating (affect) to catch up on all the information you

Table 3 *Terms That Illustrate the A-B-C Components of Attitude*

Component	Terms	
A: affect	liking	loathing
	disliking	angriness
	loving	happiness
	hating	sadness
	fearing	pride
	wanting	boredom
B: behavior	buy	destroy
	hit	endorse
	kiss	hire
	rent to	fire
	vote for	choose
	donate to	reject
C: cognition	will lead to	causes
	goes with	yields
	has/have	produces
	are	costs
	comes from	prevents
	results in	mediates

From Rajecki, 1990, p. 39.

missed. By now, you might be thinking that social psychology is all a waste of time anyway (cognition).

Saying that attitudes are part of a system sounds simple enough. But this notion has led to a number of fascinating and controversial ideas. It seems not only that affect, behavior, and cognitions follow from attitudes, but also that attitudes can follow *from* these three. The six major areas of research in the study of attitudes and attitude change shown in Table 4 reflect these complex ideas. Let's explore each of these research areas in more detail.

Figure 1 *The Tripartite Model of Attitude Structure*

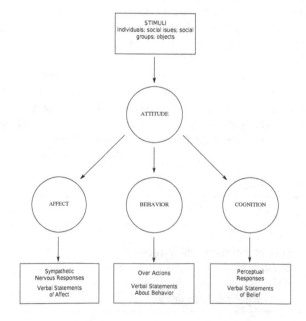

From Breckler, 1984, p. 1192.

Figure 2 *An Attitude System*

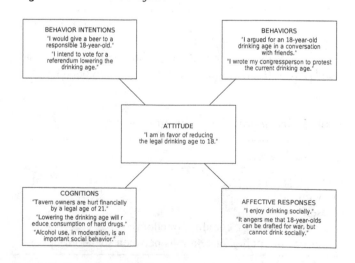

From Zimbardo & Leippe, 1991, p. 33.

Table 4 *Six Research Questions*

1. How does affect influence attitudes?
2. Do we always act in accord with our attitudes?
3. What if there is an inconsistency between or within our attitude systems?
4. Can people act their way into believing something new?
5. What is the relationship between our self-concept and the attitudes we hold?
6. How can attitudes be changed?

1. How does affect influence attitudes? At first, it may strike you as unusual to include emotions in a discussion of attitudes. Yet there are some interesting and important links between affect and attitudes and between affect and cognitions.

For example, basic research on emotions suggests that there is a great deal of similarity in the physiological processes our bodies experience in response to very different emotions (Zajonc & McIntosh, 1992). For instance, with both sexual attraction and fear, our pupils dilate, our hearts beat rapidly, and our breathing quickens. Yet despite these similarities, we make sharp distinctions among different emotions (Ekman et al., 1987). It seems that what distinguishes emotions is not the physiological phenomena but the thoughts or beliefs that individuals have about the source of the emotion and the context in which it occurs (Schachter & Singer, 1962). In fact, when people are feeling an intense emotion, they may label it with different names depending on their understanding of the source. For example, young men who are anxious about crossing a dangerous footbridge may misattribute their emotion as sexual arousal if they meet an attractive research assistant while crossing the bridge (Dutton & Aron, 1974).

Other research on affect suggests that behaving in a certain way—e.g., holding a pen with the teeth or with the lips—influences affect. In one experiment, subjects who held a pen between their teeth, thereby activating a smiling muscle, rated neutral cartoons as funnier than subjects who held a pen between their lips (Strack, Martin, & Stepper, 1988). Similarly, people who were instructed to move their facial muscles into a frown, without knowing that they were actually frowning, reported feeling angry (Laird, 1974). Clearly, the relationship between affect and attitude is more complicated than we might think.

2. Do we always act in accord with our attitudes? The relationship between attitude and behaviors is also complex. Although we might assume that behaviors are follow from attitudes ("I am a Democrat, so I will vote for a Democrat as mayor") some early studies found that this was not the case (e.g., LaPierre, 1934). In a classic literature review, Wicker (1969) found an average correlation of only .3 between expressed attitude and actual behavior. Wicker concluded that it was "considerably more likely" that attitudes are unrelated or only slightly related to behavior (1971, p. 65). This conclusion led to his famous suggestion that social psychology abandon the concept of attitude (Wicker, 1971). The German poet Goethe may well have had it right when he said, "Thinking is easy, acting difficult, and to put one's thoughts into action, the most difficult thing in the world."

Still, some studies *have* found impressive correlations between attitude and behavior (Fazio & Zanna, 1981). For example, voting behavior showed a nearly perfect relationship to attitudes (Kelley & Mirer, 1974). Such correlations inspired social psychologists to shift their attention to the kinds of conditions under which attitudes do consistently predict behavior (Fazio & Zanna, 1981).

As it turns out, there are certain identifiable conditions that fall into this category (Myers, 1999; see Table 5). First, when people feel safe enough to give their honest opinion, a correspondence between attitude and behavior will occur. An apt example of this is when you wait until the host is out of earshot before asking your friend what he or she *really* thinks about the party.

Second, the relationship between attitude and behavior becomes stronger the more samples of behavior we look at. That is, it is much more difficult to predict isolated behaviors than to predict average behavior.

Third, the more specific an attitude is, the better it will predict behavior. For example, your attitude toward *studying* will be a better predictor of how much you actually study than will your more general attitude toward *school* will.

Fourth, the more *potent* an attitude is, the more our behavior will align with the attitude. By potency, social psychologists mean strength, saliency, or relevancy. For example, doubtless there are some political issues that you care more about than others. For those that you care most strongly about, there is likely a closer match between your attitude and your behavior. Similarly, salient attitudes (i.e., those that especially attract our attention) will correspond strongly with behavior. For example, keeping a mirror on the refrigerator—which makes your attitude about your weight or appearance quite salient—will help to curb the midnight munchies if you are trying to diet. Last, attitudes that have been formed through experience are quite potent, resistant to change, and more likely to correlate closely with behavior. For instance, many people who have been involved in car accidents faithfully use their seatbelts afterward.

Table 5 *Attitudes Will Predict Behavior When . . .*

. . . situational demands are minimized.
. . . behavior is averaged over many instances.
. . . specific attitudes are studied.
. . . attitudes are potent; that is, strong, salient, and/or formed through experience.

From Myers, 1999.

3. What if there is an inconsistency between or within our attitude systems? In his theory of cognitive dissonance, Leon Festinger proposed that people like to maintain consistency within an attitude system or between two attitude systems (Festinger, 1957). If an inconsistency arises, people experience an uncomfortable sensation of arousal that Festinger called dissonance. This sensation is so uncomfortable that it motivates people to take action to restore the consonance, or consistency, within their attitude systems (Festinger, 1957). For example, suppose you believe that homelessness is a problem, but you realize that you don't do anything to solve it. Knowing that your beliefs don't match your actions would probably cause you to feel dissonance. But there are many ways of regaining consistency between your attitude and your behavior. For example, you could change the dissonant cognition and decide that homelessness is not a problem after all. You could add consonant cognitions by thinking about the times that you volunteered at a soup kitchen or helped out at a nursing home. You could lessen the importance of the dissonant cognitions by saying that you are busy with school right now, so it's not a big deal that you're neglecting the problem of homelessness. You could also increase the importance of the consonant cognitions by saying that hunger is a more pressing problem than homelessness. Or you could change your dissonant behavior by immediately writing a letter to Congress demanding that they implement policies to solve the homelessness problem.

Again, because cognitive dissonance involves attitude systems, a change in one part of the system will force a change in another part. This implies that you can change people's attitudes by getting them to act in a way that is *inconsistent* with their attitude. There is a fascinating series of experiments that illustrate this phenomenon. In the experiments, people are manipulated into performing behaviors or expressing opinions that go against their beliefs (dissonant actions). Surprisingly, their attitudes change to align with their dissonant actions. For example, participants rated a boring experiment as more interesting if they told the next participant that the experiment was actually interesting for $1 than if they lied to the next participant for $20. Lying for a small amount of money caused dissonance in these participants (presumably $20 is a good reason for lying), so only participants in the $1 condition needed to justify their behavior by changing their attitude toward the task (Festinger & Carlsmith, 1959).

4. Can people act their way into believing? Though it's easy to assume that behavior is caused directly by attitudes, the cause-effect relationship sometimes works in reverse. This is yet another implication of cognitive dissonance theory. Even people who have no particular attitudes toward an object can be made to form attitudes if they are manipulated into certain behaviors.

This phenomenon is a prediction of Daryl Bem's self-perception theory (Bem, 1972). Self-perception theory states that when we are unaware of our own attitudes, we must infer them from our behavior (Bem, 1972). This may sound counterintuitive. But think about how children often can't tell when they are overtired—even when they are practically falling asleep standing up. Perhaps you also know people who get grouchy when they are hungry or tired, without being aware of it. Bem claims that this is not so unusual. In fact, it may explain how we come to form numerous different attitudes (Bem, 1972). Take Bem's example of seeing a friend eating brown bread (Bem, 1970):

"Do you like brown bread?" you ask.

"Mmm, I don't know," she answers. "I never thought about it. I'm eating some now. Yeah, I guess I must like brown bread."

Or, imagine a young man who doesn't know how he feels about his girlfriend:

"Do you like her?"

"Oh, I dunno."

"Well, this is the third time you've seen her this week."

"Uh, yeah, I guess I like her."

The most provocative aspect of Bem's theory is his claim that, when we are inferring our own attitudes from our behavior, we adopt the perspective of an observer. That is, we have no more privileged information than a stranger has in trying to understand our own internal states. Like a stranger, we must guess our attitude from our own behavior.

Our ability to act our way into believing something new explains a number of phenomena—among them brain-washing, believing one's own false confessions, and self-persuasion. It may even explain the results of many cognitive dissonance studies (Bem, 1970). For example, in the Festinger and Carlsmith study (1959), participants judged the experiment more interesting in the $1 condition because they had no particular opinion about it until they told the next participant that it was interesting. Because $1 is hardly enough to justify a lie, they decide that they must really believe that the experiment was interesting. Despite theoretical and empirical battles over which theory is "right," both cognitive dissonance and self-perception theory have important and counterintuitive lessons to teach about the relationship between attitude and behavior.

5. What is the relationship between our self-concept and our attitudes? As we've seen, attitudes powerfully influence our perceptions and are firmly linked to our emotions, behaviors, and thoughts. It should come as no surprise to find out that some attitudes actually help define who we are as individuals (Pratkanis & Greenwald, 1989). It is difficult to change such self-defining attitudes. However, if we are persuaded to change how we perceive ourselves, then these attitudes may shift as well (Zimbardo & Leippe, 1991).

This idea is Elliot Aronson's modification to cognitive dissonance theory (Aronson, 1968; 1969). Aronson claims that dissonance is strongest when our self-concept is threatened; that is, when our actions or beliefs are not consonant with what we believe or want to believe about ourselves. For example, knowing that you have lied is dissonant with the idea that you are a person of integrity (Aronson, 1995). Again, we saw this theory at work in the study where subjects were paid $1 to tell the next subject that an experiment was interesting (Festinger & Carlsmith, 1959).

Aronson and his colleagues have been able to get college students to agree to practice safer sex (Stone, Aronson, Crain, Winslow, & Fried, 1994) and water conservation (Dickerson, Thibodeau, Aronson, & Miller, 1992) by targeting not the students' attitudes but their self-concepts. In each experiment, participants are reminded of their past failures to live up to their ideals. In essence, this makes them feel like hypocrites. Later, when given a chance to align their behavior with their self-concepts, the participants apparently seized the opportunity by buying condoms or taking shorter showers.

6. How can attitudes be changed? Attitudes can be changed in a more straight-forward way by targeting the attitude itself, by changing people's beliefs, or by changing people's emotional reactions. This is where theories of persuasion and advertising come in (e.g., Azar, 1999; Han & Shavitt, 1994; Petty & Cacioppo, 1986).

What is the difference between persuasion and propaganda, or between education and persuasion? While the differences between these terms are not always apparent (Pratkanis & Aronson, 1992), we can find some interesting distinctions (Petty & Wegener, 1998). When information is presented in a relatively objective way, it is considered *education*. When it is presented in a biased way, it is considered *propaganda* (Zimbardo, Ebbesen, & Maslach, 1977). Today, the less pejorative term *persuasion* is used to connote the process of trying to change attitudes by the strategic presentation of information (Petty & Wegener, 1998).

But what is meant by the strategic presentation of information? Social psychologists have identified numerous variables that increase or decrease the persuasiveness of a communication. These variables include qualities of the communicator ("who"), the message itself ("what"), the way in which the message is delivered ("by what means"), and the nature of the audience ("whom"). The classic question "Who says what to whom with what effect?" has driven much of the research in this area (Lasswell, 1948). Slightly modified, this question provides a handy way to remember the key variables (Myers, 1999; see Table 6).

The *Elaboration Likelihood Model* (ELM) explains how some of the elements in Table 6 produce attitude change (Petty & Cacioppo, 1981). According to this theory, there are two ways or routes through which a listener processes a message. The *central route* is taken when a person thinks carefully about the merits of the information presented. The *peripheral route* is taken when a person instead makes a hasty decision based on simple cues, such as the attractiveness of the source.

Moreover, the amount of elaboration, or processing, that a person engages in in response to a message depends on both individual and situational factors (Petty & Cacioppo, 1986). For example, people who are highly motivated to understand the message, who have the cognitive ability to carefully evaluate the message, or who like to think about issues are more likely than others to use central-route processing. People who might not care about the issue, who aren't willing to think about it, or who don't have the time are likely to use peripheral-route processing (Petty & Cacioppo, 1986).

By knowing his or her audience, a communicator can thus emphasize either the contents of the message (for central-route processing) or simpler cues (for peripheral processing) in order to make the message as persuasive as possible. For example, some magazine ads present a lot of information in the text about the specific features of the product advertised. Such ads require central-route processing (at least for those who stop and read the ad). Other ads present the product in a flashy manner, without any detailed text. These ads require peripheral-route processing from the audience.

Generally, central-route processing leads to more permanent attitude change than peripheral-route processing does. So, one way to make a communication more persuasive is to use rhetorical questions or multiple speakers to get your audience to think about the message (Myers, 1999). This means that central-route processing, or thinking carefully about a message, makes strong arguments seem *more* persuasive and weak arguments *less* persuasive. However, communicators can also use the peripheral route to block deeper processing by their audience if their arguments are weak or if they know that the audience is likely to be distracted when receiving the message (Petty & Cacioppo, 1986). Similarly, communicators can get an audience to process a message more carefully—and therefore effect more attitude change—by having an *un*expected or *un*trustworthy source present the message (Petty, Cacioppo, & Goldman, 1981).

The ELM is not only useful for understanding how listeners react to messages, it also shows how the elements of persuasion interact to affect persuasiveness. In addition, the ELM has been applied to counseling (Petty, Cacioppo, & Heesacker, 1984) and mass-media advertising (Petty & Cacioppo, 1983).

How can you use all this information about attitudes and persuasion? Try this: The next time you are asked your opinion about an issue, notice your emotions, behavior, and thoughts or beliefs about the issue. Think about why you hold your attitude and where you got your information. In other words, take the central route. This exercise will help you to see how your own attitudes were formed and thus deepen your under-

Table 6 *The Elements of Persuasion: Who Says What by What Means to Whom?*

WHO . . .

* Credible, believable sources who are (or who at least are perceived as) expert and trustworthy (or thoughtful and considerate, in collectivist cultures) are more persuasive than noncredible sources. Credibility can be achieved by:
    saying things the audience agrees with,
    being introduced as knowledgeable,
    speaking confidently,
    speaking quickly,
    seeming not to try to persuade,
    arguing against one's own self-interest, and
    arguing an unexpected position.

* Attractive sources are more persuasive than nonattractive sources. Attractiveness is achieved through:
    physical appearance,
    likability, and
    similarity to the audience.

. . . SAYS WHAT . . .

* The following message qualities make the communication more persuasive:
    Vividness (as long as it doesn't interfere with the audience's comprehension)
    Evoking of good feelings (which enhances positive thinking)
    Fear-inducing messages (which are successful only if the audience believes that they are serious and probable, and if there are specific protective actions that the audience can take)
    Humorous messages (as long as the humor doesn't interfere with comprehension)
    Repeated exposure (if it is varied)

* Presentation of one or both sides of an issue:
    If the audience is initially in agreement with your position, use a one-sided argument.
    If the audience is initially opposed to your position, or well-informed, or likely to hear the opposing side in the future, use a two-sided argument.

* Order of presentation:
    Primacy effect: If two different messages are presented back to back, and especially if the audience must respond to them at a later time, then the first message will be more persuasive.
    Recency effect: If two different messages are presented separately in time, and the audience must respond to them soon after the second message, then the second message will be more persuasive.

* Discrepancy of the message from the audience's attitude:
    If the audience cares about the issue, use of slight discrepancy will make the message more persuasive.
    If the audience does not care about the issue, use of greater discrepancy will make the message more persuasive.
    Credible sources can more persuasively advocate extreme positions than noncredible sources can.

. . . BY WHAT MEANS . . .

* Medium:
    Direct, face-to-face appeals work best for persuasion.
    Print media (newspapers, magazines) make complex messages more persuasive.
    Other media (TV, radio) are better for simple, understandable messages.

* Fast-talking pulls for peripheral route processing, which:
    helps persuade an opposed audience, and prevents a sympathetic audience from adequately processing the message.

* Powerful speech is generally more persuasive than powerless speech (hesitation, disclaimers, qualifiers, tag questions).

. . . TO WHOM

* People in a positive mood (via food, music) are generally more easily persuaded.
    Strong arguments are more persuasive to a neutral or mildly depressed audience, but may be difficult for a positive-mood audience to process.

* A forewarned audience is less easily persuaded than an audience taken by surprise.

* An audience who has practice defending mild attacks on their beliefs are inoculated against stronger attacks.

* Distracted audiences can't counterargue, so messages get processed via the peripheral route.

* Uninvolved audiences use the peripheral route; involved audiences use the central route.

* People who have a high need for cognition generally use the central route; people who have a low need for cognition use the peripheral route.
    High self-monitors are more persuaded by "soft sell" (ads that promote image); low self-monitors are more persuaded by "hard sell": ads that promote quality, value, and utility of a product.

standing of the theories about attitudes and persuasion discussed in this chapter.

REFERENCES

Aronson, E. (1968). Dissonance theory: Progress and problems. In R. P. Abelson, E. Aronson, W. J. McGuire, T. M. Newcomb, M. J. Rosenberg, & P. H. Tannenbaum (Eds.), *Theories of cognitive consistency: A sourcebook* (pp. 5–27). Chicago: Rand McNally.

Aronson, E. (1969). The theory of cognitive dissonance: A current perspective. In L. Berkowitz (Ed.), *Advances in experimental social psychology* (Vol. 4, pp. 1–34). New York: Academic Press.

Aronson, E. (1995). *The social animal* (7th ed.). New York: W. H. Freeman.

Azar, B. (1999, January). Antismoking ads that curb teen smoking. *APA Monitor*, 14.

Bem, D. J. (1970). *Beliefs, attitudes, and human affairs*. Monterey, CA: Brooks/Cole.

Bem, D. J. (1972). Self-perception theory. In L. Berkowitz (Ed.), *Advances in experimental social psychology* (Vol. 6, pp. 1–62). New York: Academic Press.

Breckler, S. J. (1984). Empirical validation of affect, behavior, and cognition as distinct components of attitude. *Journal of Personality and Social Psychology, 47*, 1191–1205.

Dickerson, C. A., Thibodeau, R., Aronson, E., & Miller, D. (1992). Using cognitive dissonance to encourage water conservation. *Journal of Applied Social Psychology, 22*, 841–854.

Dutton, D. B., & Aron, A. P. (1974). Some evidence for heightened sexual attraction under conditions of high anxiety. *Journal of Personality and Social Psychology, 30*, 510 517.

Eagly, A. H., & Chaiken, S. (1998). Attitude structure and function. In D. Gilbert, S. T. Fiske, & G. Lindzey (Eds.), *The handbook of social psychology* (4th ed., Vol. 1, pp. 269–322). Cambridge, MA: Addison-Wesley.

Ekman, P., Friesen, W. V., O'Sullivan, M., Chan, A., Diacoyanni-Tarlatzis, I., Heider, K., Krause, R., LeCompre, W. A., Pitcairn, T., Ricci-Bitti, P. E., Scherer, K., Tomita, M., & Tzavras, A. (1987). Universals and cultural differences in the judgments of facial expressions of emotions. *Journal of Personality and Social Psychology, 53*, 712–717.

Fazio, R. H., & Zanna, M. P. (1981). Direct experience and attitude-behavior consistency. In L. Berkowitz (Ed.), *Advances in experimental social psychology* (Vol. 14, pp. 161–202). New York: Academic Press.

Festinger, L. (1957). *A theory of cognitive dissonance*. Stanford, CA: Stanford University Press.

Festinger, L., & Carlsmith, J. M. (1959). Cognitive consequences of forced compliance. *Journal of Abnormal and Social Psychology, 58*, 201–210.

Han, S., & Shavitt, S. (1994). Persuasion and culture: Advertising appeals in individualistic and collectivistic societies. *Journal of Experimental Social Psychology, 30*, 326–350.

Kelley, S., & Mirer, T. W. (1974). The simple act of voting. *American Political Science Review, 68*, 572–591.

Laird, J. D. (1974). Self-attribution of emotion: The effects of expressive behavior on the quality of emotional experience. *Journal of Personality and Social Psychology, 29*, 475–486.

LaPiere, R. T. (1934). Attitudes versus actions. *Social Forces, 13*, 230–237.

Lasswell, H. D. (1948). The structure and function of communication in society. In L. Bryson (Ed.), *The communication of ideas: Religion and civilization series* (pp. 37–51). New York: Harper & Row.

Myers, G. (1999). *Social psychology* (6th ed.). Boston: McGraw-Hill.

Petty, R. E., & Cacioppo, J. T. (1981). *Attitudes and persuasion: Classic and contemporary approaches*. Dubuque, IA: William C. Brown.

Petty, R. E., & Cacioppo, J. T. (1983). Central and peripheral routes to persuasion: Application to advertising. In L. Percy & A. Woodside (Eds.), *Advertising and consumer psychology* (pp. 3 23). Lexington, MA: Heath.

Petty, R. E., & Cacioppo, J. T. (1986). The elaboration likelihood model of persuasion. In L. Berkowitz (Ed.), *Advances in experimental social psychology* (Vol. 19, pp. 123–205). New York: Academic Press.

Petty, R. E., Cacioppo, J. T., & Goldman, R. (1981). Personal involvement as a determinant of argument-based persuasion. *Journal of Personality and Social Psychology, 41*, 847-855.

Petty, R. E., Cacioppo, J. T., & Heesacker, M. (1984). Central and peripheral routes to persuasion: Application to counseling. In R. McGlynn, J. Maddux, C. Stoltenberg, & J. Harvey (Eds.), *Social perception in clinical and counseling psychology* (pp. 59–89). Lubbock, Texas, Texas Tech University Press.

Petty, R. E., & Wegener, D. T. (1998). Attitude change: Multiple roles for persuasion variables. In D. Gilbert, S. T. Fiske, & G. Lindzey (Eds.), *The handbook of social psychology* (4th ed., Vol. 1, pp. 323–390).

Pratkanis, A. R., & Aronson, E. (1992). *Age of propaganda: The everyday use and abuse of persuasion*. New York: Freeman.

Pratkanis, A. R., & Greenwald, A. G. (1989). A sociocognitive model of attitude structure and function. In L. Berkowitz (Ed.), *Advances in experimental social psychology* (Vol. 2, pp. 245–285). New York: Academic Press.

Rajecki, D. W. (1990). *Attitudes*. Sunderland, MA: Sinauer Associates.

Schachter, S., & Singer, J. (1962). Cognitive, social and physiological determinants of emotional state. *Psychological Review, 69*, 379–399.

Stone, J., Aronson, E., Crain, A. L., Winslow, M. P., & Fried, C. B. (1994). Inducing hypocrisy as a means of encouraging young adults to use condoms. *Personality and Social Psychology Bulletin, 20*, 116–128.

Strack, F., Martin, L. L., & Stepper, S. (1988). Inhibiting and facilitating conditions of the human smile: A nonobtrusive test of the facial feedback hypothesis. *Journal of Personality and Social Psychology, 54*, 768–777.

Wicker, A. W. (1969). Attitudes versus actions: The relationship of verbal and overt behavioral responses to attitude objects. *Journal of Social Issues, 25*, 41–78.

Wicker, A. W. (1971). An examination of the "other variables" explanation of attitude-behavior inconsistency. *Journal of Personality and Social Psychology, 19*, 18–30.

Zajonc, R. B. (1980). Feeling and thinking: Preferences need no inferences. *American Psychologist, 35*, 151–175.

Zajonc, R. B., & McIntosh, D. N. (1992). Emotions research: Some promising questions and some questionable promises. *Psychological Science, 3*, 70–74.

Zimbardo, P. G., Ebbesen, E., & Maslach, C. (1977). *Influencing attitudes and changing behavior.* Reading, MA: Addison-Wesley.

Zimbardo, P. G., & Leippe, M. R. (1991). *The psychology of attitude change and social influence.* New York: McGraw-Hill.

Suggested Readings

Clark, E. M., Brock, T. C., & Stewart, D. W. (1994). *Attention, attitude, and affect in response to advertising.* Hillsdale, NJ: Erlbaum.

Eagly, A., & Chaiken, S. (1993). *The psychology of attitudes.* Fort Worth, TX: Harcourt Brace Jovanovich.

Petty, R. E., & Cacioppo, J. T. (1986). *Communication and persuasion: Central and peripheral routes to attitude change.* New York: Springer-Verlag.

Pratkanis, A. R., & Aronson, E. (1992). *Age of propaganda: The everyday use and abuse of persuasion.* New York: Freeman.

Zimbardo, P. G., & Leippe, M. R. (1991). *The psychology of attitude change and social influence.* New York: McGraw-Hill.

"From the Very First, the Things That Were Me, That Comprised My Very Soul, Began to Die."

Andrew Cohen
Bucknell University

While it is one thing to learn about theories of social influence, it is quite another to actually experience it strongly enough to feel yourself and your soul dissolve. This is how Andrew Cohen felt when he joined a fraternity as a freshman and experienced the pledging process. Later, as a senior, he reflected back on his experiences and described what it felt like to lose his identity for the group. He also detailed the negative things that occurred as a result: irresponsibility, sexism, racism, and alcoholism. This excerpt, published in the Chronicle of Higher Education, *was taken from the longer article that Cohen wrote for the* The Bucknellian, *the campus newspaper at Bucknell University, where these events took place. The tremendous power of the social situation comes to light in Cohen's moving story.*

I swallowed the Greek bait, hook, line, and sinker. People said, "Going Greek is a good experience. You get to meet people, you have a body of brothers/sisters so close they'll do anything for you, you have leadership opportunities, and besides, the social scene here is so Greek-based, you've got to do it."

Nothing could be further from the truth.

I joined a fraternity and served as its vice-president and public-relations chair. I was elected by the presidents of the fraternities to the Interfraternity Council Executive Board, where I served until my deactivation in the spring of 1992. I do not speak from a disenfranchised perspective, but rather as someone who experienced the "essence" of the system.

It is also important that I am honest about my reasons for leaving. I left not because of any moral awakening, but because I could barely stay sober long enough to write my name. This was my problem, not the system's. Yet my time away from Greek life has led me to realize that while in the system, there is a tendency to forget the "kind of person" you think you are, in favor of the inclinations of the herd.

As a first-year student, I came to Bucknell University berating my parents for their interference in my life. I was my own person, not their juvenile, dependent son. I came to school eager to experience my individuality for the first time. Yet, within a few months, the burden was too great, and I sought refuge in the acceptance of a group.

I said that I was only going to rush. But it was so enticing. People seemed to like me. With no more than a beer in hand and an hour or so of small talk in common, I decided that they were going to be my best friends.

From the very first, the things that were me, that were pointedly Andrew Cohen, that comprised my very soul, began to die. The physical pain of being paddled bare-assed was, at that point in my life, indescribable. Some "pops" (older fraternity members picked as big brothers for pledges) and their "sons" never talked after that night. But I learned that *silence* was precious. I did not let out a peep, and the brothers "respected that," many shook my hand. That made it all *worth* it. I was proud of my welts, they were a badge of *courage.*

However, it was the psychological torture during pledging that really broke me. I was expected to sit in silence when I saw things that made me sick to my stomach. When brothers senselessly decried my very being, made me feel inhuman, I had to suck it up, to let go of my thoughts, to ignore them, to become numb. This was a hard lesson for me to swallow, and I voiced objections. I even mentioned the word "hazing," as I was told to do at an anti-hazing program we had been required to attend. I found out from an officer of the house that I was not being hazed because I could dissociate myself at any time.

It was too late. My identity was bound into the group. So I learned to ignore myself. One of the brothers told me that it was a simple psychological process whereby the individual is broken down only to be built up as a member of the group. It worked.

From the Very First, the Things That Were Me, That Comprised My Very soul, Began to Die," by Andrew Cohen, reprinted from *Chronicle of Higher Education*, March 3, 1993. p. B2.

By the end of "Hell Week," I had discarded any remnants of myself as an individual and rather began to enjoy my debasement. I was so excited that I would soon become a member and there would be others for me to terrorize. By the next year, I had become what I had held in contempt.

I miss my friends from my first year at Bucknell. After pledging, it was never the same. Paradoxically, my social opportunities were enlarged and shrunken all at once. I had an instant group of friends called brothers. But everyone outside of the group was somehow not as good as those in it. Social options immediately became limited by a set of letters.

As a brother, little changed. I ceased to be a thinker, if I ever was one. I was always busy jumping on the bandwagon or trying to lead one. But as for doing anything for myself, that was impossible; my self had long since left. The silence I had learned as a pledge took a turn for the worse; I put on my mask and joined the masses.

It was really no one's fault. An opening for a sexist remark or act would occur, someone would take it, everyone would take it. Never in my year and a half as an active member did I hear anyone really stand up against sexism during the hundreds of times that it occurred. I did not pride myself as a sexist, but it was just so damn funny, everyone roared with *approving* laughter.

I always thought I was the "kind of person" who deplored racism. Yet, when a small group got together and began making racist remarks, my courage had disappeared like the welts. Dumb silence pervaded my psyche. I did not know what to say, how to say it. Everyone was having such a good time, how could I spoil it?

Frequently, Jews were the target of disparaging remarks. While the anger rose within me, I shut up and smiled. Now it was my so-called "people." How could there be "my people" when there was no *me*?

So it was that I forgot myself. My insecurity had been filled by the ethos of the herd. I was now a leader of the system. I wrote scathing newspaper stories against those who opposed it. And I made the thing look so beautiful on paper that no one would dare write the libel you are reading. I wrote letters praising "our diverse brotherhood which maintains a close-knit sense of unity." All the while, my *experience* told a very different story.

I do not believe that Greeks are bad people. The majority of my close friends are Greek. But I do think that the system encourages people to value their membership in the group above their individuality and sense of self, which makes it easy for people to become foreign to themselves.

Students need not be slaves to the system. *Students can change the way things are.* They do not *validate* the system, it will cease to rule a university's social climate. People will be able to transcend the herd mentality to embark upon genuine relationships that are supportive of their individuality. Such a decision takes a lot of courage, though, a lot more than I had during my time in a fraternity.

Questions

1. What principles of social influence do you see at work in Cohen's story? For example, can you find evidence for conformity, obedience, compliance, groupthink, and deindividuation?

2. Cohen says that the Greek system "encourages people to value their membership in the group above their individuality and sense of self." What were some results of this? Why is this a bad thing, according to Cohen?

3. What does Cohen mean when he says that his social opportunities were both enlarged and shrunken at the same time? What enlarged? Why? What shrank? Why? Why does he miss his old friends? Why does he not enjoy his new friends?

4. If you were in Cohen's place, what would you have done? Why? What could Cohen have done to change things?

THE PSYCHOLOGY OF SOCIAL IMPACT

Bibb Latané, *Ohio State University*

What do conformity, imitation, bystander intervention, bystander non-intervention, and social loafing all have in common? At first glance, these five behaviors may seem very different. Nevertheless, we can view them all as instances of what Bibb Latané calls social impact: changes in thoughts, emotions, or behaviors resulting from the real, implied, or imagined presence or actions of other people.

This admittedly broad definition encompasses many core principles and fundamental findings of social psychology. Indeed, a common criticism of social psychology has been that it lacks unifying principles and integration across research areas. Social-impact theory is an important answer to that criticism.

In this classic article, Latané defines three fundamental principles of social behavior. He describes each principle in an abstract, mathematical, and graphic form and explores several real-world applications of each. The excerpt below includes only a few of the many applications Latané discusses in the full article. However, the three principles of social impact that he presents can explain a broad array of thoughts, emotions, and behaviors.

People affect each other in many different ways. As social animals, we are drawn by the attractiveness of others and aroused by their mere presence, stimulated by their activity and embarrassed by their attention. We are influenced by the actions of others, entertained by their performances, and sometimes persuaded by their arguments. We are inhibited by the surveillance of others and made less guilty by their complicity. We are threatened by the power of others and angered by their attack. Fortunately, we are also comforted by the support of others and sustained by their love.

I call all these effects, and others like them, "social impact." By social impact, I mean any of the great variety of changes in psychological states and subjective feelings, motives and emotions, cognitions and beliefs, values and behavior, that occur in an individual, human or animal, as a result of the real, implied, or imagined presence or actions of other individuals.

Clearly, this is a rather broad definition.

In the present article I offer a general theory of social impact. Depending on one's philosophy of science, one may wish rather to regard the theory as a quantitative description, an empirical generalization, a discovery, a set of fundamental laws, a model, an organizing theme, a framework, or a perspective. In any event, the theory is not itself very specific. It

does not say when social impact will occur or detail the exact mechanisms whereby social impact is transmitted. It does not purport to "explain" the operation of any of the number of particular social processes that are necessary to account for all the effects I have labeled "social impact" or to substitute for theories that do. It does, however, provide general overall rules that seem to govern each and all of these individual processes. The theory consists of three principles that represent an attempt to adapt, integrate, and formalize ideas initially developed by sociologist Stewart Dodd, astronomer J. Q. Stewart, anthropologist-geographer-linguist George Kingsley Zipf, and psychologists Kurt Lewin and S. S. Stevens, among others. Although the principles comprise a general theory, they lead to specific quantifiable and verifiable predictions. In the remainder of this article, I develop the theory and briefly review evidence from ten areas of application.

☙ THREE PRINCIPLES OF SOCIAL IMPACT

To start I suggest that one can usefully think of social impact as being the result of social forces (like the physical forces of light, sound, gravity, and magnetism) operating in a social force field or social structure. As an example of what I mean by a social force field, Figure 1 depicts the plight of a hapless striped target beset by a variety of spotted sources, all having some impact.

"The Psychology of Social Impact," by Bibb Latané, reprinted from *American Psychologist*, vol. 36, 1981. pp. 343–356.

❧ PRINCIPLE 1: SOCIAL FORCES, I = f(SIN)

As a first principle, I suggest that when some number of social sources are acting on a target individual, the amount of impact experienced by the target should be a multiplicative function of the strength, S, the immediacy, I, and the number, N, of sources present. By strength, I mean the salience, power, importance, or intensity of a given source to the target—usually this would be determined by such things as the source's status, age, socio-economic status, and prior relationship with, or future power over, the target. By immediacy, I mean closeness in space or time and absence of intervening barriers or filters. By number, I mean how many people there are.

This can be called a light bulb theory of social relations: As the amount of light falling on a surface is a multiplicative function of the wattage or intensity of the light bulbs shining on the surface, their closeness to the surface, and the number of bulbs, so the impact experienced by an individual is a multiplicative function of the strength, immediacy, and number of people affecting him or her. It seems reasonable to expect that an individual will experience more impact the higher the status, the more immediate the influence, and the greater the number of other people affecting him or her, and data typically bear this out. In general, I am suggesting that the laws governing the intensity of a social flux are comparable to the laws governing the intensity of a luminous flux.

I concentrate on the number dimension here because this is the dimension for which there are the most data. The line of thought I shall pursue, however, is also translatable into the other dimensions, and I do not mean to imply that number is more important than strength or immediacy in moderating impact.

Figure 1 *Multiplication of impact: I = f (SIN)*

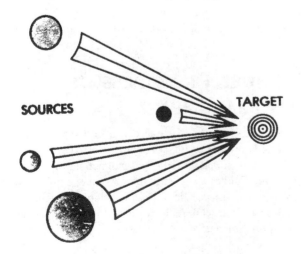

SOURCES   TARGET

❧ PRINCIPLE 2: THE PSYCHOSOCIAL LAW, $I = sN^T, t < 1$

Any economist will tell you that the first dollar you have, devalued as it might be, is worth more than the hundredth. Likewise, I think, the first other person in a social force field should have greater impact than the hundredth. This is not to say that one wouldn't rather have $100 than $1 or that 100 people won't have more impact than a single person but that the difference between 99 and 100 is less than the difference between 0 and 1. Thus, I suggest, there is a marginally decreasing effect of increased supplies of people as well as of money.

From Fechner's day, psychologists have studied similar relationships between objective and subjective reality, between external value and internal valuation, under the rubric of "psychophysics." In 1957, S. S. Stevens distilled all this activity into an elegant but simple law: $\psi = \kappa\phi^\beta$. For prothetic stimulus dimensions (in which qualities vary in intensity), the subjective psychological intensity, ψ, equals some power, β, of the objective physical intensity of the stimulus, ϕ, times a scaling constant, κ.

I would like to suggest my own *psychosocial* law to parallel Stevens's psychosphysical law: $I = sN^t$. When people are in a multiplicative force field, the amount of social impact, I, they experience will equal some power, t, of the number of sources, N, times a scaling constant, s. Further, the value of the exponent t should be less than one: Impact will increase in proportion to some root of the number of people present.

My task in this article is to convince you that SIN has a special role in psychology and that $I = sN^t$ is.

Application 1: Conformity and Imitation

Eighty years of experimental evidence strongly shows that individuals are influenced by the actions and expectations of others. These effects have long been studied under such rubrics as allelomimetic behavior, behavioral contagion, conformity, compliance, group pressure, imitation, normative influence, observational learning, social faciliation, suggestion, and vicarious conditioning. In general, the theory of social impact suggests that each of these kinds of influence can be understood as resulting from the operation of social forces in a multiplicative force field: Increases in the strength, immediacy, and number of people who are the source of influence should lead to increases in their effect on an individual. In this section, I discuss research on conformity, which presents only mixed support for the principles of social impact.

Asch and the magic number three

Ironically, some of the first and most famous research involving parametric variations in the number of people serving as the source of social impact appears to suggest a relationship quite different from that proposed here. In his classic studies on independence and conformity, Asch (1951, 1952, 1956) asked Swarthmore College students to choose which of a set of three disparate lines matched a standard, either alone or after 1, 2, 3, 4, 8, or 16 confederates had first given a unanimously incorrect answer. Figure 2a shows the percentage of trials on which participants overruled their own senses and conformed to majority judgment. In discussing the implications of these data, Asch focused on the concept of group "consensus," concluding that increasing group size leads to increased conformity only to the point, 3, where there is a perception of consensus among group members.

Although the most striking feature of Asch's data is that conformity does not seem to increase with increases in group size beyond three members, the most troubling aspect for social impact theory is that people faced with but one or two incorrect conformers conformed so little—in the present theory, the first person added to a social setting is expected to have the most impact. However, for such counterfactual judgments, Swarthmore students may be sufficiently independent as to require a substantial amount of social pressure just to bring them up to a yielding threshold; the first one or two incorrect models may in fact reduce restraints, making it possible for the addition of further confederates to have a more visible effect.

In a replication by Gerard, Wilhelmy, and Conolley (1968) 154 high school students (who might not have had so much initial resistance to making counterfactual judgments) were exposed to one to seven confederates giving incorrect answers. Gerard et al. expected and found conformity to increase with group size. Furthermore, the first few confederates had the most impact. Figure 2b presents their data (circles) and the best fitting power function (dashed line) calculated from the formula $I = sN^t$, which does a good job in fitting these data, accounting for 80% of the variance in means (better than the 61% best linear fit). In this case, the exponent is .46: Conformity seems to grow in proportion to the square root of majority size.

Craning and gawking

Milgram, Bickman, and Berkowitz (1969) conducted an interesting experiment at the Graduate Center of the City University of New York, where the laboratory facilities include 42nd Street. Confederates in groups ranging in size from 1 to 15 would stop, congregate, and crane their necks, gawking up at a window on the sixth floor, behind which, dimly visible, stood Stanley Milgram taking movies. These movies were later analyzed to see how many passersby were stimulated themselves to crane and gawk. Increasing the number of confederates craning and gawking led to an increase in the number of passersby craning and gawking, but additional craning and gawking caused by each additional craner and gawker grew smaller with increasing numbers of confederates The fit between the data (circles in Figure 2c) and the best fitting power function (dotted line in Figure 2c) is again impressive, with the squared correlation coefficient indicating that the power law accounts for 90% of the variance in the percentage of passersby imitating. The exponent of .24 is less than one, as predicted, and craning and gawking is proportional to the fourth root of the number of craners and gawkers. On balance, research on conformity and imitation appears to support the general principles of social impact.

. . .

Figure 2 *Conformity and imitation as a function of a group size: a. Data from Asch (1951); b. Data from Gerard, Wilhelmy, and Conolley (1968); c. Data from Milgram, Bickman, and Berkowitz (1969).*

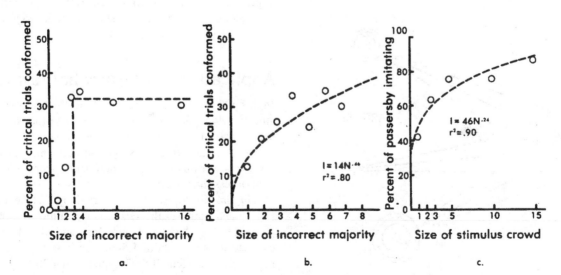

❧ PRINCIPLE 3: MULTIPLICATION VERSUS DIVISION OF IMPACT

In addition to force fields in which a given individual is the target of social forces and experiences impact as a multiplicative function of the strength, immediacy, and number of sources, I now suggest that there exists a different type of force field or social structure in which other people stand with the individual as the target of forces coming from outside the group. In such situations, schematized in Figure 3, I suggest that increasing the strength, immediacy, or number of other targets should lead to a division or diminution of impact, with each person feeling less than he or she would if alone. For example, consider a person giving a speech. As the target of social forces emanating from each member of the audience and the impact of their attention, he or she is in a multiplicative force field and should feel greater tension the larger the audience. Members of the audience, on the other hand, stand, or rather sit, together as the target of forces coming from the speaker. Unfortunately, the impact of the speaker's arguments is probably divided, and the larger the audience, the less each member will be persuaded.

Consistent with my earlier arguments about marginal impact, I suggest that the psychosocial law still applies in divisive force fields and that the effect of a social force from outside the group is divided and not by the actual number of people present, but by some root of that number, with $I = s/N^t$. This is mathematically equivalent to $I = sN^{-t}$ making the formula the same as in the case of mulitplicative social structures but with the sign of the exponent changed. Thus, according to social impact theory, the exponent of t in divisive social structures should be negative with an absolute value of less than one.

Figure 3 *Division of impact: I = f (1/SIN).*

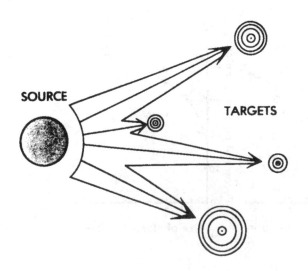

Application 2: Social Inhibition of Emergency Response

The present theory grew out of a program of research with John Darley on bystander intervention in emergencies (Latané & Darley, 1970). One might recall that one of several processes we postulated to explain our finding that people are less likely to intervene if they believe other people are also available to respond was diffusion of responsibility—if others are present, the responsibility for intervention is psychologically diffused or divided among them, leaving each person less motivated to act. I suggest now that this process is more general and can lead to the diffusion or division of other social forces.

The discovery of the social inhibition of bystander intervention has been widely replicated: Latané and Nida (1981) cite 56 published and unpublished comparisons of helping by people who were alone with helping by those who were tested in the presence of confederates or believed other people to be present. In 48 of these 56 comparisons, involving a total of more than 2,000 people, there was less helping in the group condition. Overall, three quarters of individuals tested alone helped; only half of those tested with others did so. Further, in 31 of an additional 37 comparisons between persons tested alone and actual groups of 2–8 people, the effective individual probability of helping was less than the alone response rate, while in 4 others, the comparison was indeterminate. About half of the 2,028 individuals tested alone in these studies helped, whereas the effective individual response rate for the more than 1,600 people tested in groups was only 22%. Clearly, social inhibition occurs in both laboratory and field settings employing a wide variety of emergencies designed by a multitude of independent investigators.

According to the psychosocial law, the biggest increment in social inhibition should occur with the addition of the first other bystander; subsequently ones should have decreasing marginal impact. In fact, the results of the original Darley and Latané (1968) experiment bear out this expectation. In that experiment, speed of helping decreased in proportion to the cube root of the number of bystanders believed to be present.

. . .

Application 3: Chivalry in Elevators

In this and the next two sections I briefly describe three field studies which are consistent with the proposition that in social structures in which many people stand together as the target of forces from a single source, impact will be an inverse power function of the number of people with an exponent of less than one.

Figure 4b shows data reported by Latané and Dabbs (1975) and includes the responses of almost 5,000 elevator passengers in Atlanta, Columbus, and Seattle who were exposed to one of about 1,500 occasions on which a fellow passenger "accidentally" dropped a handful of pencils or

Figure 4 *Division of impact: a. Effective individual probability of response as a function of number in room, based on data from Freeman (1974); b. Picking up objects as a function of the sex and number of elevator passengers, based on data from Latané and Dabbs (1975); c. Size of tip as a function of number of people eating together, based on data from Freeman, Walker, Borden, and Latané (1975).*

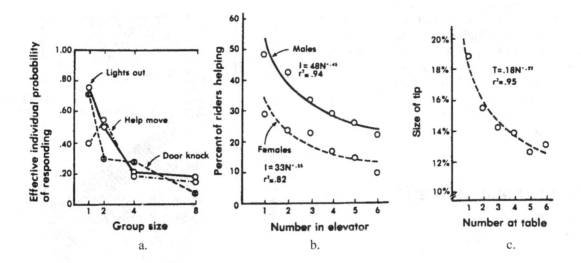

a.   b.   c.

coins. In addition to our primary interest in regional differences in sex role differentiation, we found highly significant group size effects: As the number of people available to respond increased from one to six, the individual probability of response decreased from 40% to 15%. This systematic decrease can best be described by an inverse power function with an exponent of about .5. Although there were big differences between the sexes in the overall likelihood of helping, the effect of other people was similar for both sexes—helping to pick up objects decreased in proportion to the square root of the number of people available to pick up objects. The impact of the need for help shown by the clumsy coin dropper was seemingly divided among those who were the target of this need.

I might put in a parenthetical plug for the utility of elevators as portable psychological laboratories (see also Petty, Williams, Harkins, & Latané, 1977). Never cluttered up with surplus equipment or old data sheets, always available for scheduling, they generate a steady stream of subjects who come inside of their own volition and, once there, act with no more than their normal paranoia. Far more representative of the general population than the typical college sophomore, elevator passengers are far less suspicious or anxious to do the right thing for science. And unlike other public places, elevators are self-contained with clearly defined boundaries, so one knows exactly who is present and who is not.

Application 4: Tipping in Restaurants

The custom of tipping—leaving some money for the waiter after one has finished a meal—is interesting for several reasons. Unlike most other economic transactions, it is at least partly voluntary. Although most waiters have the reasonable expectation that one will leave a tip, whether one does and how much one leaves are personal choices. Unlike one's obligation to the restaurant owner for the price of the meal, one cannot go to jail or be forced to wash dishes if one chooses not to tip.

Reasoning that a primary motive for leaving a tip is a feeling of responsibility or obligation to the waiter, and that this feeling of obligation should be diffused or divided to the extent that several people eat together on the same bill, Freeman, Walker, Borden, and Latané (1975) enlisted the cooperation of 11 waiters, unfamiliar with the theory, who unobtrusively recorded size of party, amount of bill, and size of tip for 408 groups of 1,159 evening diners at the Steak and Ale Restaurant in Columbus, Ohio. Twelve parties had more than 6 members and were excluded from analysis, since they required special services; the remaining 396 parties consisted of an average of 2.67 people, who were billed an average of $6.95 per person and tipped an average of $1.00 per person.

Although the best linear prediction of tip from bill was 15.02% minus .09 cents, indicating rather close adherence to a 15% norm, group size also made a major contribution to tipping. As seen in Figure 4c, individuals dining alone tipped almost 19%, while groups of five to six people tipped less than 13%. This systematic decrease can best be described by an inverse power function with an exponent of about .2:

Tipping seems to decrease in proportion to the fifth root of the number of people eating together. The impact of the responsibility for giving money to the waiter was seemingly divided among those who were the target of this responsibility.

This result has considerable practical significance. Americans spend about $30 billion a year in eating out and probably leave about $2 or 3$ billion a year in tips, accounting for two thirds of the total income of more than one million waiters in the United States. This result suggests, although it does not prove, that waiters might be far better off if they were a little more willing to write separate checks for large parties—this might short-circuit diffusion of responsibility and result in larger tips.

. . .

Application 5: Many Hands Make Light the Work

An unpublished experiment that has not perished in the classic study by Ringelmann, reported only in summary form by Moede (1927) in German but cited and analyzed by many later scientists. In that experiment, the collective group performance of co-workers pulling on a rope was less than the sum of their individual performances, with dyads pulling at 93% of their individual capability, trios at 85%, and groups of eight at only 49%. As the old saw has it, "Many hands make light the work."

In a recently published replication (Latané, Williams, Harkins, 1979), groups of six undergraduate males gathered in Ohio Stadium and were asked to make as much noise as possible by shouting or clapping hands alone, in pairs, or in groups of six. As in pulling ropes, it appears that when it comes to clapping or even shouting out loud, many hands do in fact make light the work: Even though total output increased with group size, the output of each member decreased, with six-person groups performing at only 36% of capacity (see Figure 5, "actual groups"). Part of this deficit can be attributed to the fact that sound waves tend to cancel each other out, reflecting one form of faulty coordination of social effort (Steiner, 1972). Another part, however, may be due to the fact that participants did not shout as loud or clap as hard in groups as they did when alone (a process I call "social loafing").

Individuals in another set of conditions shouted in "pseudogroups" in which they believed that others were yelling with them, although they actually yelled alone. This change eliminates coordination loss as a factor, allowing social loafing to be measured directly. Consistent with the view that pressures to work hard in groups are diffused, individual effort decreased as pseudogroup size increased, and the addition of the second through fifth other pseudoshouters had much less negative effect than the addition of the first (see Figure 5, "pseudogroups"). The data are well fit by an

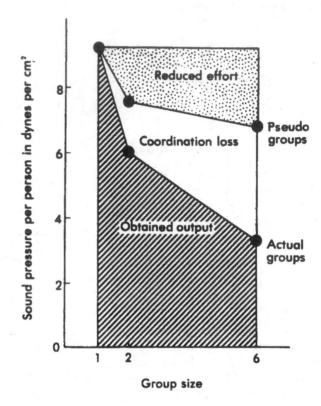

Figure 5 *Sound pressure per person as a function of group or pseudogroup size, based on data from Latané, Williams, and Harkins (1979).*

inverse power function which an exponent of less than one: Effort seems to decrease in proportion to the sixth root of the number of people working together. Similar effects have been obtained in the case of cognitive effort (Petty, Harkins, Williams, & Latané, 1977).

. . .

❧ CONCLUSION

In the preceding sections of this article, I have discussed three principles of social impact and have presented data consistent with the principles from ten areas of empirical research. In conclusion, I briefly list six unresolved questions relating to the theory and two problems with it in its present form. Finally, I mention four characteristics of the theory that commend it, I believe, to our further attention.

Six Unresolved Questions

1. Can we achieve better measurement of social outcomes? This kind of theory, with its greater precision and specificity, requires ratio scaling. If it is to be useful in other domains of social psychology, we will have to improve our standards of measurement.

2. If indeed the psychosocial law involves a power function, what is the meaning of the exponent? Stevens (1975) believes there to be a characteristic psychophysical exponent for each sensory modality. Is there one for social impact?

3. How does one deal with individual differences in susceptibility to social impact? Perhaps individuals can be seen as differing in their mass, inertia, or resistance to change.

4. How do the acute effects of short-term exposure to impact transmute over time into chronic effects?

5. What happens when two or more groups act as simultaneous sources of impact, groups serve both as source and target of impact, social groups are heterogeneous with respect to the strength or immediacy of their members, and/or different psychological processes are triggered off at the same time? The general answer to these questions would seem to relate to how one combines and decomposes power functions.

6. Is the model descriptive or explanatory, a generalization or a theory?

Two Problems with the Theory

1. The model views people as passive recipients of social impact and not as active seekers. A more perfected theory would incorporate mechanisms for people to control and direct their exposure to social impact.

2. The model is static and at present does not have a needed dynamic aspect. A more perfected theory would specify the means whereby the consequences of social impact cumulate as the people in a social setting react to and interact with each other.

Four Characteristics of the Theory

1. It is a *general* theory, drawing on basic laws, predicting to many domains, and encompassing a variety of processes.

2. But it is also *specific* in the sense that it is quantifiable, deals with parametric variations, and makes precise predictions about observable variations, and makes precise predictions about observable aspects of the real world.

3. Thus, it is *falsifiable*—if relationships turn out to be nonmonotonic, or if exponents are greater than one or have the wrong sign, the theory will be disconfirmed.

4. The theory is *useful*. It not only can provide a baseline for assessing interesting exceptions to these general laws, but it can provide a foundation for the development of many areas of social engineering (Latané & Nida, 1980). Every day people need to decide on which people to appoint to a committee, on whether to make a telephone call or write a letter, on how many students should be in a classroom, or on any of a number of other choices concerning the strength, immediacy, and number of people to involve in a social setting. We live in a period of great societal growth—populations are getting larger and people are becoming more interdependent. It is becoming more and more important to understand both the positive and the negative ways in which people have impact on each other and to design our physical and social environments so as to maximize the quality of life for all. I would like to think this theory will help.

REFERENCES

Asch, S. E. (1951). Effects of group pressure upon the modification and distortion of judgments. In H. Guetzkow (Ed.), *Groups, leadership, and men*. Pittsburgh, PA: Carnegie Press.

Asch, S. E. (1952). *Social psychology*. Englewood Cliffs, NJ: Prentice-Hall.

Asch, S. E. (1956). Studies of independence and conformity: I. A minority of one against a unanimous majority. *Psychological Monographs, 70*(9, Whole No. 416).

Darley, J. M., & Latané, B. (1968). Bystander intervention in emergencies: Diffusion of responsibility. *Journal of Personality and Social Psychology, 8*, 337–383.

Freeman, S., Walker, M. R., Borden, R., & Latané, B. (1975). Diffusion of responsibility and restaurant tipping: Cheaper by the bunch. *Personality and Social Psychology Bulletin, 1*, 584–587.

Gerard, H. B., Wilhelmy, R. A., & Conolley, E. S. (1968). Conformity and group size. *Journal of Personality and Social Psychology, 8*, 79–82.

Latané, B., & Dabbs, J. (1975). Sex, group size and helping in three cities. *Sociometry, 38*, 180–194.

Latané, B., & Darley, J. M. (1968). Group inhibition of bystander intervention in emergencies. *Journal of Personality and Social Psychology, 10*, 215–221.

Latané, B., & Nida, S. (1980). Social impact theory and group influence: A social engineering perspective. In P. B. Paulus (Ed.), *Psychology of group influence*. Hillsdale, NJ: Erlbaum.

Latané, B., & Nida, S. (1981). Ten years of research on group size and helping. *Psychological Bulletin, 89*, 307–324.

Latané, B., Williams, K., & Harkins, S. (1979). Many hands make light of the work: The causes and consequences of social loafing. *Journal of Personality and Social Psychology, 37*, 822–832.

Milgram, S., Bickman, L., & Berkowitz, L. (1969). Note on the drawing power of crowds of different size. *Journal of Personality and Social Psychology, 13*, 79–82.

Moede, W. Die Richtlinien der Leistungs-Psychologie. (1927). *Industrielle Psychotechnik, 4*, 193–207.

Petty, R. E., Harkins, S. G., Williams, K. D., & Latané, B. (1977). The effects of group size on cognitive effort and evaluation. *Personality and Social Psychology Bulletin, 3*, 575–578.

Petty, R. E., Williams, K. D., Harkins, S. G., & Latané, B. (1977). Social inhibition of helping yourself: Bystander response to a cheeseburger. *Personality and Social Psychology Bulletin, 3*, 579–582.

Steiner, I. D. (1972). *Group process and productivity*. New York: Academic Press.

Stevens, S. S. (1957). On the psychophysical law. *Psychological Review, 64,* 153–181.

Stevens, S. S. (1975). *Psychophysics.* New York: Wiley.

❧ Questions

1. What other social psychological phenomena not discussed in this article might we better understand through social-impact theory? For example, how would this theory account for the various results that Stanley Milgram obtained in his obedience-to-authority studies?

2. Suppose a candidate is running for public office and must deliver a number of speeches to her constituents. According to social-impact theory, would she have a greater impact on her listeners if she spoke at large rallies, or at small dinner parties? What might she do to increase her impact at large rallies?

3. Would you rather give a speech in front of your social psychology class, or defend a thesis in front of a panel of five faculty members? Why? What does social-impact theory have to say about your predicament?

4. Consider Figures 1 and 2. What would happen to the social pressures felt by the "target" in each of these scenarios if the targets could talk to the "sources"? In Figure 1, what would happen to the social pressures felt by the target if the sources talked to each other but not to the target? In Figure 2, what would happen to the social pressures felt by the targets if the targets talked to each other but not to the source?

SOCIAL INFLUENCE

&

What do the following situations all have in common?

- At a party, you drink whatever everyone else is drinking.

- Your favorite supermarket is one that gives out free food samples.

- You are working with two laboratory partners, and one of them is not doing her fair share of the work.

- Your club made a disastrous decision about what to sell to raise money, and now you are stuck with 100 unsold cases of pencils with the name of your club imprinted on them.

- You and a friend like running with each other because you both run faster when you do it together.

- You screamed, you yelled, and you danced with strangers at a rock concert, even though you are usually a quiet person.

- You lied to a customer because your supervisor told you to do so.

All of these situations involve the presence, persuasion, or power of others; in a word, influence. We are affected by others in numerous ways, and social psychology seeks to understand the exact nature of such influence. The major forms of social influence are conformity, compliance techniques, group influences, social facilitation, deindividuation, and obedience (see Table 1). While these might seem similar, there are some interesting and important differences among them.

& SOCIAL FACILITATION AND INHIBITION

Social facilitation is the most basic form of influence. When you work alongside another person without interacting with him or her, you perform differently than when you work alone. If the task is easy for you or well learned, you are likely to perform better in the presence of others, as in the above example of running with a friend. This influence is called *social facilitation*. If the task is difficult or if you have not yet learned well, then you are likely to perform worse when in the presence of others. This is called *social inhibition*. Both facilitation and inhibition represent a magnification of the dominant or most likely response that occurs when an individual acts in the presence of others (Zajonc, 1965).

Social psychology's very first experiment explored the topic of social facilitation (Triplett, 1898). In the hundred-plus years of research on this same topic since then, researchers have documented the effect in many situations, including simple motor tasks (Travis, 1925), learning (Dashiell, 1930), eating (deCastro & Brewer, 1991), and even shopping (Sommer, Wynes, & Brinkley, 1992).

Table 1 Forms of Social Influence

Perceived Choice of Going Along	Social Influence	Power Differential Among Participants	Overt Compliance Pressure
Very high	Conformity	Equals	Very low
	Compliance Techniques:		
	Reciprocity		
	Door-in-the-Face		
	Foot-in-the-Door		
	The Low-Ball Technique		
	That's Not All		
	Even a Penny	Equals	
	Group Influences:		
	Social Loafing		
	Groupthink	Equals	
	Social Facilitation	Equals	
	Deindividuation	Equals	
Very low	Obedience	Authority	Very high

❧ GROUP INFLUENCES: SOCIAL LOAFING AND GROUPTHINK

Now suppose you are actually interacting with others. In this case, you are subject to *group influences*, perhaps without even knowing it. Group influences or group dynamics can take many forms, but two of the more interesting ones are social loafing and groupthink (see Dennis & Valacich, 1993; and Hall, 1971).

Social loafing occurs when there are many people who are working on the same task. Specifically, people have a tendency to work *less* when sharing a task with others than when working alone. Under certain conditions, we might even say that the whole becomes *less* than the sum of its parts—as in the earlier example of the group laboratory project. People are especially likely to exert less effort when individual contributions are not identified, when the task is boring, when the group members are all friends, and when rewards are divided equally regardless of individual inputs (Karau & Williams, 1993).

Groupthink, in the words of Irving Janis, is "the mode of thinking that persons engage in when concurrence-seeking becomes so dominant in a cohesive in-group that it tends to override realistic appraisal of alternative courses of action" (Janis, 1971, p. 43). This phenomenon occurs when a highly cohesive group becomes so intent on preserving the group and the good feelings that everybody has about the group that they fall victim to bad decision-making. In failing to consider alternative courses of action or the possibility that they might be wrong, such groups will make unwise decisions (for example, ending up with 100 unsold boxes of pencils). Janis developed his theory about the conditions, symptoms, and defective decision-making that typify groupthink, along with ideas for preventing groupthink, by analyzing historical decisions. He and others believe that the United States' Bay of Pigs invasion of Cuba and lack of preparedness for World War II, as well as the escalation of the Vietnam War and the *Challenger* space-shuttle disaster, all stemmed from groupthink (see Janis, 1971; and Moorehead, Ference, & Neck, 1991).

❧ DEINDIVIDUATION

The forms of social influence we have considered so far have involved individuals acting with one other person (social facilitation) or interacting with a few others (group influences). But what happens when you are part of a crowd or a mob, such as at a rock concert? Evidence suggests that when people are in a large group, are anonymous, and are involved in arousing and distracting activities, they lose their individual identities and take on the identity of the group. Often, social controls weaken in these situations, and unrestrained behaviors result. This state is called *deindividuation* (Festinger, Pepitone, & Newcomb, 1952). What we might call "mob behavior" is more likely to occur under deindividuating conditions. Such behavior may include antisocial or non-normative behaviors like yelling or screaming, dancing crazily, and throwing things, and may even escalate to violent rioting.

❧ CONFORMITY, OBEDIENCE, AND COMPLIANCE

Conformity occurs when we go along with perceived group pressure. The scenario of drinking what everyone else is drinking would be an example of conformity. Groups often develop social norms, which are behaviors that members are expected to go along with. Often a group will enforce these norms by shunning a group member who does not adhere to the norm (see Mitchell, 1995, for a child's perspective on this). Norms can powerfully shape people's behavior, for better or for worse (see Prentice & Miller, 1993, or DeAngelis, 1994, for an example of conformity to group norms of alcohol use).

Classic studies of conformity pressures include the Muzifer Sherif (1935) autokinetic-effect study and the Solomon Asch (1955) line-length study. Other studies have focused on the conditions—for example, group size and member status—under which conformity pressures increase or decrease (Latané, 1981). Perhaps the most dramatic demonstration of conformity is the Zimbardo (1975) prison study, in which ordinary young men turned into brutal guards or passive prisoners in response to the role they were assigned.

Obedience happens when you go along with a direct request because you were ordered to do so by someone who has authority over you (as in the earlier example of lying to a customer because your supervisor told you to do so). The topic of obedience, and the studies focusing on it, have raised provocative philosophical, ethical, moral, and theoretical questions. The most famous study on this topic is the classic research by Stanley Milgram (1965, 1974). In this experiment, participants were faced with the dilemma of obeying an authority figure who ordered them to hurt another person or risking disobedience by refusing to continue the experiment. The majority of participants choose to hurt another person rather than disobey the authority figure. Sadly, history is filled with examples of ordinary people who prove unable to resist the overpowering social influences of obedience and conformity—with tragic results (Pratkanis & Aronson, 1992; see Cohen, 1993, for a personal account).

Conformity and obedience differ in the degree of choice the individual feels he or she has regarding pressure to conform or to obey a direct command. With conformity, people generally feel that they have a choice about their actions; with obedience, people feel that they have little choice (Milgram, 1974). Conformity and obedience also differ in the degree of responsibility the person is willing to accept for his or her actions. In situations of conformity, people like to think that they acted out of their own volition. They will often deny that they were influenced by others, and they claim responsibility for their own actions (Milgram, 1974). With obedience, people tend to deny responsibility for their actions and claim that they were merely "following orders" (see Milgram, 1974, for a discussion of other differences between obedience and conformity).

People may also outwardly conform to what others are doing, without believing in the value of the behavior. Or they may follow a direct command while inwardly disagreeing with the command. In such cases, the behavior is called *compliance*, or compliance without acceptance. If the person truly believes in his or her actions, we call the behavior *acceptance* or *internalization*.

❧ COMPLIANCE TECHNIQUES

There is a second use of the word *compliance* in social psychology. The phrase *compliance techniques* refers to a group of "tricks" that people can use to get others to obey them. While obedience is generally granted to a person with authority, compliance techniques let someone of equal status gain a perceived "upper hand" so that others feel obligated to go along with his or her request. Compliance techniques are used by salespeople, for example, to get others to buy their products. The best clue that you have fallen victim to one of these compliance techniques is that, *afterward*, you regret your action and wonder why you went along with it. This is because compliance techniques are very hard to spot.

According to Robert Cialdini, compliance techniques work much like the Japanese martial art of jujitsu (Cialdini, 1993). Jujitsu allows a physically smaller or weaker person to beat a larger, stronger opponent by taking advantage of the principles of physics—such as gravity, momentum, leverage and inertia—that operate naturally in any situation. Instead of physical principles, a person using compliance techniques takes advantage of normal *social* principles in order to influence others. There's nothing inherently wrong with these compliance techniques. However, when people end up agreeing to do things under conditions in which they would not *ordinarily* agree, then we could say that such a technique has been used unfairly.

Reciprocity. For example, take the *norm of reciprocity,* which states that you should repay in kind what another has done for you (Gouldner, 1960). This norm works well to regulate behaviors such as the sending of holiday cards, baby-sitting between neighbors, or shift-swapping among coworkers. However, when the norm is invoked in a manipulative way, reciprocity becomes a compliance technique (Cialdini, 1993). Think about supermarkets that give out free food or product samples. Generally the norm of reciprocity will make a customer feel somewhat obligated to return the "favor." And what better way to show your appreciation than by buying the product you have just sampled thanks to the "generosity" of the asker!

Door-in-the-Face. The *door-in-the-face technique*, also called *reciprocal concessions*, derives from the norm of reciprocity. In this case, a person makes a large request that they are pretty sure their target will refuse. Once the target says no (i.e., slams the door in the asker's face), the asker counteroffers with a second request—smaller than the first one, but generally the one he or she wanted all along. Saying no to the first request increases the likelihood that the target will say yes to the second request (Cialdini et al., 1975). This is because the target perceives the asker as having "given in" and so feels pressure to reciprocate by also "giving in" and saying "yes." In one experiment, people agreed to chaperone delinquent children on one trip to the zoo after first turning down the much larger request to volunteer as a Big Brother or Big Sister (Cialdini et al., 1975).

Foot-in-the-Door. The use of multiple requests, as with the door-in-the-face technique, prolongs the interaction between the asker and the target. Lengthening the exchange makes it more likely that the target will ultimately go along with the asker. This is the principle behind the *foot-in-the-door* technique. Here the asker starts with a small request. Saying yes to a small request makes it more likely that the target will then agree to a larger request. This is because committing to a public behavior and perceiving it as being their own doing makes people believe more strongly in what they have done, and makes them more likely do more in the future (Myers, 1999). In one experiment, people were about four and a half times more likely to comply with a large request (putting a big sign on their lawn), after first having agreed to the smaller request (putting a small sign in their window) (Freedman & Fraser, 1966).

The Low-Ball Technique. Public commitment is such a strong force that it can make people stick to their initial agreements even if the terms change unfavorably (Cialdini et al., 1978). This is called the *low-ball technique*. For example, suppose you have agreed to buy a stereo at a certain price and have signed the sales contract. While the salesperson is confirming the sale with the manager, you are probably thinking about how great the stereo will sound in your apartment. You might even be dreaming about how much more fun your party will be tonight with a really good sound system instead of your old one. But what if the salesperson returns and says, "I'm sorry, but there was a miscalculation, the real price is actually $300 higher." Most people, having made a public commitment to "purchase," will agree to the new "price" even though they have every legal right not to go through with the transaction. In one study, twice as many students showed up for an experiment at 7:00 A.M. if they first agreed to be in the experiment without knowing the starting time than the number who arrived "on time" who were asked up-front to appear at 7:00 A.M. (Cialdini et al., 1978).

That's Not All. Yet another compliance technique works because it seems too good a deal to pass up. In the *That's Not All* technique, an interested customer asks the price of an item. The seller states the price, but before the customer has a chance to respond the seller says something like, "Wait, that's not all." The seller then proceeds to either lower the price or to add in other items so that suddenly the deal looks too good to refuse (Burger, 1986). In a clever series of studies using bake sales to raise money for the local chapter of a psychology club, Berger found that when the initial deal was changed for the better, such as through lowering the price of a cupcake or adding a small bag of cookies, more people agreed to it than if the final deal—discounts and cookies and all—was offered up-front.

Even a Penny. In the *Even a Penny* technique, the target is asked for a contribution so low that it would be difficult to refuse without feeling inexcusably cheap. To employ this technique, an asker will request a donation for his or her cause and then add "Even a penny will help" (Cialdini & Schroeder, 1976). This usually evokes aid from even the most hardened target, because nobody wants to admit publicly that they are cheap. As a bonus, people will often give more than the penny. In fact, the amount collected through this compliance technique often exceeds what would have been collected without it.

Other compliance techniques. As you might imagine, there are many other compliance techniques used by salespeople, marketers, legitimate charities, and ordinary people. Marwell and Schmitt (1967) identified 16 such additional techniques, including promises, threats, claims of expertise, liking, and punishment. Robert Cialdini, the social psychologist who has done the most research in this area, admits that he became interested in the subject of compliance because "All my life I've been a patsy. For as long as I can recall, I've been an easy mark for the pitches of peddlers, fund-raisers, and operators of one sort or another" (Cialdini, 1993, p. xiii). Cialdini conducts research in both the laboratory and the field, and often combines controlled experiments with naturalistic field studies. He has even participated in sales training programs and has worked in advertising and fund-raising in order to get an inside look at these techniques. His goal is to help people understand the kinds of compliance techniques in use so that they can protect themselves from unwanted requests.

❧ Is Social Influence Really That Bad?

Many of the examples we've just explored may have made you conclude that social influence is generally a bad thing. But, there are actually numerous situations where compliance, conformity, obedience, and perhaps even deindividuation are appropriate and can actually help society to function smoothly. It's *blind*, or unthinking, submission to social influence that is worrisome. Perhaps being vulnerable to the influence of others is the price we pay for being social animals. Certainly we can see social influence as a kind of "double-edged sword." However, by understanding the many kinds of social influence, we can protect ourselves from undue influence and—equally important—become aware of our own impact on those around us.

REFERENCES

Asch, S. E., (1955). Opinions and social pressures. *Scientific American, 193*(5), 31–35.

Burger, J. M. (1986). Increasing compliance by improving the deal: The that's-not-all technique. *Journal of Personality and Social Psychology, 51,* 277–283.

Cialdini, R. B. (1993). *Influence: Science and practice* (3rd ed.). New York: HarperCollins.

Cialdini, R. B., Cacioppo, J. T., Bassett, R., & Miller, J. A. (1978). Low-ball procedure for producing compliance: Commitment then cost. *Journal of Personality and Social Psychology, 36,* 463–476.

Cialdini, R. B., & Schroeder, D. A. (1976). Increasing compliance by legitimizing paltry contributions: When even a penny helps. *Journal of Personality and Social Psychology, 34,* 599–604.

Cialdini, R. B., Vincent, J. E., Lewis, S. K., Catalan, J., Wheeler, D., & Danby, B. L. (1975). Reciprocal concessions procedure for inducing compliance: The door-in-the-face-technique. *Journal of Personality and Social Psychology, 31,* 206–215.

Cohen, A. (1993, March 3). From the very first, the things that were me, that comprised my very soul, began to die. *Chronicle of Higher Education,* p. B2.

Dashiel, J. F. (1930). An explanatory analysis of some group effects. *Journal of Abnormal and Social Psychology, 25,* 190–199.

DeAngelis, T. (1994, December). Perceptions influence student drinking. *APA Monitor,* p. 35.

deCastro, J. M., & Brewer, M. (1991). The amount eaten in meals by humans is a power function of the people present. *Physiology and Behavior, 51,* 121–125.

Dennis, A. R., & Valacich, J. S. (1993). Computer brainstorms: More heads are better than one. *Journal of Applied Psychology, 78,* 531–537.

Festinger, L., Pepitone, A., & Newcomb, T. (1952). Some consequences of deindividuation in a group. *Journal of Abnormal and Social Psychology, 47,* 382–389.

Freedman, J. L., & Fraser, S. C. (1966). Compliance without pressure: The foot-in-the-door technique. *Journal of Personality and Social Psychology, 4,* 195–202.

Gouldner, A. W. (1960). The norm of reciprocity. *American Sociological Review, 25,* 161–178.

Hall, J. (1971, November). Decisions, decisions, decisions. *Psychology Today,* 51–54, 86–87.

Janis, I. L. (1971, November). Groupthink. *Psychology Today,* 43–46.

Karau, S. J., & Williams, K. D. (1993). Social loafing: A meta-analytic review and theoretical integration. *Journal of Personality and Social Psychology, 65,* 681–706.

Latané, B. (1981). The psychology of social impact. *American Psychologist, 36,* 343–356.

Marwell, G., & Schmitt, D. R. (1967). Dimensions of compliance gaining behavior: An empirical analysis. *Sociometry, 30,* 350–364.

Milgram, S. (1965). Some conditions of obedience and disobedience to authority. *Human Relations, 18*(1), 57–75.

Milgram, S. (1974). *Obedience to authority.* New York: Harper & Row.

Mitchell, M. (1995, October 1). Ms. Demeanor: Rules can irritate but they serve a purpose. *The Philadelphia Inquirer,* p. G4.

Moorehead, G., Ference, R., & Neck, C. P. (1991). Group decision fiascoes continue: Space shuttle *Challenger* and a revised groupthink framework. *Human Relations, 44*(6), 539–550.

Myers, D. G. (1999). *Social psychology* (6th ed.). Boston, MA: McGraw Hill.

Pratkanis, A., & Aronson, E. (1992). How to become a cult leader. In *Age of propaganda: The everyday use and abuse of persuasion.* New York: W. H. Freeman.

Prentice, D. A., & Miller, D. T. (1993). Pluralistic ignorance and alcohol use on campus: Some consequences of misperceiving the social norm. *Journal of Personality and Social Psychology, 64,* 243–256.

Sherif, M. (1935). A study of some social factors in perception. *Archives of Psychology, 27*(187), 1-60.

Sommer, R., Wynes, M., & Brinkley, G. (1992). Social facilitation effects in shopping behavior. *Environment and Behavior, 24,* 285–297.

Travis, L. E. (1925). The effect of a small audience on eye-hand coordination. *Journal of Abnormal and Social Psychology, 20,* 142–146.

Triplett, N. (1898). The dynamogenic factors in pacemaking and competition. *American Journal of Psychology, 9,* 507–533.

Zajonc, R. B. (1965). Social facilitation. *Science, 149,* 269–274.

Zimbardo, P. G. (1975). Transforming experimental research into advocacy for social change. In M. Deutsch & H. A. Hornstein (Eds.), *Applying social psychology.* Hillsdale, NJ: Erlbaum.

SUGGESTED READINGS

Cialdini, R. B. (1993). *Influence: Science and practice* (3rd ed.). New York: HarperCollins.

Cialdini, R. B. (1995). A full-cycle approach to social psychology. In G. G. Brannigan & M. R. Merrens (Eds.), *The social psychologists: Research adventures.* New York: McGraw-Hill.

Janis, I. L. (1971, November). Groupthink. *Psychology Today,* 43–46.

Kelman, H. C., & Hamilton, V. L. (1989). *Crimes of obedience.* New Haven, CT: Yale University Press.

Milgram, S. (1974). *Obedience to authority.* New York: Harper & Row.

Milgram, S. (1993). *The individual in a social world* (2nd ed.). New York: McGraw-Hill.

PROPAGANDA IN THE THIRD REICH: A CASE FOR UNCERTAINTY

From Theory to Application

Anthony Pratkanis and Elliot Aronson

It is one thing to study social influence in the laboratory and quite another to study it in the real world. The implications of social psychological theory for the betterment of society are no clearer than in this case study by Anthony Pratkanis and Elliot Aronson. These researchers explored the successful use of propaganda by the government of Adolf Hitler in World War II.

According to Pratkanis and Aronson, the young but recently defeated Hitler blamed Germany's failure in the first world war on the skillful use of propaganda by the British and American governments. When he rose to power, Hitler determined to use these same powerful tools of persuasion and social influence to help Germany win World War II. As his first step, he appointed Joseph Goebbels to Minister of Popular Enlightenment and Propaganda.

The propaganda campaign that Goebbels masterminded was both frightening and impressive. As such, it provides a chilling illustration of many principles of social influence—including persuasion, conformity, compliance, and obedience. Pratkanis and Aronson want you to take two lessons from this reading. The first is to understand the power of social influence. The second is to allow uncertainty into your judgments, rather than holding a totalitarian belief in your own correctness. With these lessons in mind, Pratkanis and Aronson hope that you will become wary of the dangers of propaganda and so become neither a victim nor a perpetrator of evil.

The year was 1924 and a young aspiring artist named Adolf Hitler sat thinking in his jail cell. Like many of his generation, he had found it painful to accept German's defeat in the World War, a war in which he had served in vain as a combat soldier. He shared his country's humiliation over the punishments dictated by the Treaty of Versailles. Adolf Hitler considered just how it all came about.

Hitler believed that one of the key factors in Germany's defeat was the skillful use of propaganda by British and American governments. As Hitler put it:

> But it was not until the War that it became evident what immense results could be obtained by a correct application of propaganda. Here again, unfortunately, all our studying had to be done on the enemy side, for the activity on our side was modest, to say the least. . . . For what we failed to do, the enemy did, with amazing skill and really brilliant calculation. I, myself, learned enormously from this enemy war propaganda.[1]

What did Hitler learn from Allied war propaganda? Both the British and Americans established steering committees and organizations to develop and disseminate propaganda. For example, in the United States the Committee on Public Information (CPI), dubbed the Creel Committee after its chair, newspaper editor George Creel, assisted in training "Four-Minute Men," volunteers who would speak at local gatherings on behalf of the war effort. The CPI encouraged the film industry to make pro-war films and saw to it that "facts" about the war were disseminated widely to the press.

The most striking aspect of British and American propaganda, however, was the "atrocity story"—reports of alleged cruelty performed by the enemy on innocent civilians or captured soldiers. The purpose of such tales was to stiffen the resolve to fight (we can't let this cruel monster win) and to convince citizens of the morality of the war. For example, rumors circulated that the Germans boiled the corpses of enemy soldiers to make soap and that they mistreated the citizens of occupied Belgium. Much was made of the execution of an English nurse serving in Brussels for helping Allied soldiers return to the war and the German sinking of the luxury liner *Lusitania*, which, incidentally, happened to be carrying arms and war supplies. Although some of these atrocity sto-

"Propaganda in the Third Reich: A Case for Uncertainty," by A. Pratkanis and E. Aronson, reprintd from *Age of Propaganda: The Everyday Use and Abuse of Persuasion*, 1992. pp. 249–259.

ries contained a grain of truth, some were greatly exaggerated and others were pure fiction.[2]

Hitler realized that if Germany was ever to regain its dignity and win the next war, it would have to go the Allies one better in the war called persuasion.[3] He outlined his plan of attack in two chapters of the book he wrote in jail, *Mein Kampf (My Struggle)*. For Hitler, propaganda was a means to an end—in this case, the promotion of the German state and the establishment and maintenance of the rule of the Nazi party. As such, there were no ethics that governed persuasion; there was only the rule of success or failure. As Hitler put it when talking about propaganda, "the most cruel weapons were humane if they brought about a quicker victory."[4]

Hitler was contemptuous of the ability of the masses to understand events. If he were alive today, he might remark that the people can operate only in the peripheral route to persuasion and that they use simple heuristics to guide their thinking. Effective propaganda relies on heuristics and appeals to the emotions. Hitler wrote in *Mein Kampf:*

> Its [propaganda's] effect for the most part must be aimed at the emotions and only to a very limited degree at the so-called intellect. We must avoid excessive intellectual demands on our public. The receptivity of the great masses is very limited, their intelligence is small, but their power of forgetting is enormous. In consequence of these facts, all effective propaganda must be limited to a very few points and must harp on these slogans until the last member of the public understands what you want him to understand by your slogan.[5]

Having learned from the Allied efforts in World War I the value of an organization capable of coordinating and delivering effective propaganda, Hitler established an apparatus of his own. This organization was privy to all the dealings of the Reich and had the responsibility of selling the government's actions to the masses. To head up this organization, Hitler selected as his Minister of Popular Enlightenment and Propaganda Joseph Goebbels, the son of a lower-middle-class Catholic family from a small town in the Rhineland. Goebbels served as minister of propaganda for the time the Nazis came to power in 1933 until he committed suicide (after first poisoning his six children) near the end of the war. To get a flavor of what Nazi propaganda was really like, let's look at a few of the persuasion tactics used.

One of the first, and most important, tasks of the Ministry of Popular Enlightenment and Propaganda was to gain control of the mass media and to attract the attention of the masses. Hitler and Goebbels controlled journalists and filmmakers through a mixture of punishments and rewards. The Nazi regime made certain that it was the primary source of news and easily accessible to certain journalists. Most importantly, the Nazis gained the attention of the masses by making their propaganda entertaining. For example, the 1936 Olympics, which were held in Berlin, were used as a vehicle to promote the image of a strong "Aryan" nation and to build the self-esteem of the German people. Nazi posters used eye-catching graphics such as bold print and slashing, violent lines as well as attention-getting headlines. Radio news programs were often packaged as entertainment, featuring famous singers and celebrities. With such complete control of the press, radio, theater, cinema, music, and the arts, the essential themes of the Nazi party were repeated and repeated. It was nearly impossible in Germany during the 1930s to read a book or newspaper, listen to a radio broadcast, or see a film without coming into contact with the Nazi picture of the world.

Goebbels masterfully spread the agenda of the German nation by labeling events with easily learned slogans or terms that captured Germans' attention and directed their thinking. For example, he insisted that the word *Führer* (leader) be used only to refer to Hitler. To link the Russians and British as enemies of Germany, he labeled an aborted British raid as the "Maisky Offensive," after the Russian envoy to London, thereby creating the impression that the raid was conducted to appease the Soviets. To provide hope in 1942, Goebbels coined the phrase *schleichende Krise* (creeping crisis) to suggest economic, social, and political unrest in England. Although in hindsight these phrases may seem contrived, they did create a "picture of the head" of world reality: "The Russians and the British are in cahoots to get us; fortunately, there is unrest in England and we have our leader."

Goebbels also established "pictures in the head" through the use of innuendo and rumor. In the years of the Nazi party's rise to power, Goebbels would denigrate the character of members of the "opposition" by circulating rumors of scandals involving them. Toward the end of the war, as Germany suffered defeats on the battlefield, rumors were circulated the German scientists were nearing the completion of two new weapons—a U-boat capable of traveling underwater at high speeds and an anti-aircraft gun whose missiles were magnetically drawn to aircraft in the sky. The purpose of such rumors was to instill the belief that Germany could still win the war and should continue the struggle, despite a rash of defeats.

Nazi propaganda used heuristics extensively to secure agreement with its message. For example, rallies and propaganda films always showed masses of cheering, applauding, saluting Nazi supporters. We know this as the social consensus heuristic—if everyone else agrees, so should I.

Nazi slogans expressed an air of confidence: "Join Our Struggle;" "Fight With Us;" "Adolf Hitler Is Victory." Whenever Hitler spoke, he spoke with confidence and certainty of the Nazi purpose and the ability of the German people to accomplish this purpose. As we saw earlier, a speaker's confidence serves to increase the likelihood that a message will be accepted.

Hitler and Goebbels used historical symbols and monuments extensively to package the regime. As Hitler was coming to power, he announced his "25 Theses," reminiscent of the 95 Theses that German religious leader Martin Luther had tacked to a church door in Wittenberg. Nazi artwork and posters often employed the style of Albrecht Dürer to suggest the historical roots of the regime. A popular genre of Nazi film was the historical biography. In such films, the life of a national historic hero such as Friedrich Schiller or Otto von Bismark was described with an emphasis on parallels (often irrelevant) to the life and times of Adolf Hitler.

Architecture was also used to package the Third Reich. Under the direction of Albert Speer, the Nazis planned an extensive effort to erect public buildings of a special nature. Due to the war effort, few were built. Those that were served Nazi purposes. For example, priority was given to erecting sports arenas, gigantic assembly halls, cinemas, and theaters—all of which could be used for political purposes. The Nazi style, which might best be termed "Nordic Hellenism," was classical in design, but on a gigantic scale. Public buildings were designed to look like enlarged Greek temples with towering steps and row upon row of columns. The design reinforced the image of the Nazis as heir to the great cultures of the past. An individual who entered such an edifice would feel his or her own stature dwarfed by the power of the state as represented by the building. In contrast, the original Greek temples were always built to human proportions, leaving the visitor with the feeling that, as Protagoras said, "humans are the measure of all things."

Another concern of Nazi propaganda was the creation of a band of supporters loyal to the Nazi party. As he was gaining power, Hitler dressed his supporters in brown shirts. Wearing the Nazi brown shirt in public became an act of commitment to the cause. The response of other Germans, at first, was one of ridicule. For many supporters, such a response likely produced even more commitment to the cause. As a means of reducing cognitive dissonance, the young brown-shirted Nazi would likely think *"This ridicule is just a small price to pay for the noble Nazi cause,"* rather than admit that brown shirts and Nazi fanaticism were rather silly. He would undoubtedly turn to fellow brown-shirters for social support, and Hitler would have added another loyal member to his band of cohesive followers.

Goebbels also employed the inoculation technique. One problem faced by any war propagandist is what to do when your side suffers a defeat in a major battle. Such a defeat could lower morale and the credibility of the regime. Goebbels anticipated this possibility by frequently issuing warnings about false hopes and illusions and by portraying the enemy as formidable, but defeatable. Thus, when the Allied forces achieved a victory, Germans were prepared to think *"This is a difficult struggle; we must try harder,"* not *"What has Hitler gotten us into?"*

Perhaps the most demonic and elusive Nazi propaganda ploy combined the fear appeal with the granfalloon tactic. After World War I, Germany's economy was in ruins, partly as a result of the demands of the Treaty of Versailles. The result was devastating for German citizens. A high rate of inflation coupled with high rates of unemployment disrupted families and left many in poverty. Many men felt humiliated because they could not support their families.

Hitler and Goebbels were able to take advantage of the nation's fears by proposing a granfalloon solution. A single theme was echoed in most if not all Nazi propaganda: The Jews were to blame for al the nation's problems. Couched as a documentary about the role of Jews in history, the 1940 film *The Eternal Jew,* for example, portrayed the Jew as a money-grabbing villain who not only is a drain on society but also carries diseases and lacks proper values. Scenes from the film showed "kosher-style" ritual animal slaughter embellished to create the illusion of sadistic practices in the Jewish religion. In a similar vein, the film *The Jew Süss* vividly tells the story of a Jewish man raping a German maiden. The image of a Jew as despicable, inferior, and menacing was repeated over and over again in speeches, posters, films, newspapers, and even academic treatises.

What was the solution to this Jewish menace? The German people were once a proud nation; under the leadership of Adolf Hitler Germany can put an end to the Jewish threat and once again return to its past grandeur. To get this message across, Nazi propaganda first demonstrated that the party supported traditional German values. Nazi posters often featured scenes of traditional family life—a woman breast-feeding her child, children happily staring off into a distant future with the Nazi banner waving in the background, a father proudly standing next to his family.

Next, Nazi propaganda showed that a unified Germany could achieve its goals. This theme was powerfully expressed in the 1934 film *The Triumph of Will.* The film opens with scenes of handsome young men in preparation to become soldiers. Hitler oversees their training. By the film's end, these young men have been turned into a powerful Nazi war machine. The message: By working together we can be strong again.

Finally, Nazi propaganda located the source of this new-found achievement in one man—Adolf Hitler. As one campaign poster put it—"Hitler, our last hope." Goebbels's goal was to portray Hitler as a kind father whose nation had called him to serve in its time of greatest need. Propaganda thus needed to present two sides of Hitler. On the one hand, posters showed Hitler smiling and shaking the hands of children; newsreels showed him awkwardly accepting the praises of his nation. As Goebbels once wrote in a magazine article, "The simplest people approach him with confidence because they feel he is their friend and protector."[6] The other side of Hitler was that of Führer. To capture this side of the image, posters portrayed Hitler in military garb standing erect and confident in purpose; newsreels presented endless scenes of Hitler reviewing the nation's troops.

The success of the Nazi propaganda machine, however, was based on more than just the use of some clever persuasion tactics. It was also due to a nearly wholesale acceptance of the idea that persuasion was to start at the top of society and be directed downward toward the masses. It was the responsibility of the ruling elite to make the decisions and then inform the masses of the wisdom of those decisions through propaganda; the responsibility of the masses was to follow. And what better role for the masses?—since, by and large, they are ignorant and cannot think. We have seen this model of the role of persuasion in society before. Aristotle argued that persuasion was needed to instruct those who could not reason fully. Propaganda is a means to communicate the "truth" to the ignorant.

Although such a model of persuasion may more or less describe any society at a given time, it is not an inevitable outcome. The Greek sophist Protagoras saw a different role for persuasion—through argument, the advantages and disadvantages of any course of action can be made clearer. The early founders of the U.S. government recognized that no party could be privy to the total truth; a society consists of competing interests. The U.S. Constitution, with its system of checks and balances, was one attempt to prevent any given group from gaining absolute control and to provide a forum for resolving differences of opinion.

The most dangerous aspect of Nazi propaganda, however, is its assumption that there is an absolute truth and the ruling elite alone are privileged to know this truth. In his film series *The Ascent of Man,* the eminent scholar and humanist Jacob Bronowski catalogs the dangers of believing in this myth of absolute truth.[7] In one of the films, Bronowski looks at the culture and thought of Germany just before World War II and finds that there were two radically different philosophies, two fundamentally different ways of looking at the world—one represented by some of the scientists of the time and the other by the Nazi party.

These scientists were coming to the realization that human knowledge could never be absolute. There was no "God's-eye view." Based on their scientific findings, physicists such as Albert Einstein, Werner Heisenberg, and Max Born were proposing such ideas as the theory of relativity and the uncertainty principle, which led to the recognition that there is no absolute fixed point of reference and that human knowledge is limited. In the social sciences, the exploration of other cultures and other peoples was fast leading to the conclusion that habits and beliefs differed widely and that it was becoming increasingly difficult to say which is "best."

In the infancy of social psychology, Kurt Lewin was developing his theory of the psychological field. His theory emphasized how an individual's psychological needs and tasks influence his or her perception of the world. According to Lewin, different individual with differing needs and tasks would come to perceive the same event differently. Ironically, the inspiration for Lewin's theory came from his experiences as a soldier in World War I, where Lewin noticed that, as he approached the battlefield, his perception of the environment changed: No longer did he see beautiful gullies and interesting rock formations, but rather places to hide and things that could kill. Just before World War II, Lewin, who

was Jewish, was forced to flee Nazi Germany. He came to America, where he trained many of the first generation of American social psychologists. The irony is that Kurt Lewin and Adolf Hitler fought on the same side in World War I. Both men experienced the same event; each reached a different conclusion.

The alternative position was one of dogma. The Nazi party embodied the truth; there was no need to tolerate other points of view. Hitler expressed this alternative philosophy succinctly:

> The function of propaganda is, for example, not to weigh and ponder the rights of different people, but exclusively to emphasize the one right which it has set out to argue for. Its task is not to make an objective study of the truth, in so far as it favors the enemy, and then set it before the masses with academic fairness; it's task is to serve our own right, always and unflinchingly . . . As soon as our own propaganda admits so much as a glimmer of right on the other side, the foundation of doubt in our own right has been laid.[8]

What are the fruits of the myth of absolute dogma? Six million of the 9.5 million Jews living in Europe were killed. The Allied forces lost more than 11 million soldiers in battle, including 7.5 million Russian, 2.2 million Chinese, and a quarter of a million American soldiers. The Axis powers lost more than 5 million soldiers in battle, including 3.5 million German and 1.2 million Japanese soldiers. Civilian casualties are harder to estimate. Direct civilian casualties as a result of the war include 2.5 million Russian, 860,000 Japanese, 300,000 German, and 60,595 British citizens. Another estimated 10 million Russians lost their lives through indirect causes, such as famine and disease. In all, over 36.5 million persons lost their lives. And for what reason?

At the end of his film, Bronowski offers an antidote to this "itch for absolute knowledge and power." There is a shallow pond just outside the concentration camp and crematorium at Auschwitz. The ashes of some 2 million people were flushed into this pond—an act caused by arrogance, by ignorance, by dogma. In one of the most dramatic moments on film, Jacob Bronowski walked out into this pond, bent down and scooped up a handful of the ashes of some of these 2 million people. He made a simple request taken from Oliver Cromwell, "I beseech you, in the bowels of Christ, think it possible you may be mistaken."

If there is one thing to be learned from our study of persuasion, it is that we can be mistaken and misled. We have seen how information about our world can be selectively edited by news and entertainment organizations or managed by experienced political consultants. The picture of the world that emerges, mistaken as it may be, serves to guide our thinking and our actions. We have also seen that it is possible for a propagandist to play on our emotions and to take advantage of our decision-making processes by invoking simple heuristics. All of this leads to a single conclusion: *As human beings, we can be wrong.* Let us keep this fact in mind whenever we make decisions—especially those that cause damage to others.

One cannot study Nazi propaganda without passion and emotion. Both of the authors of this article lost friends and relatives during World War II, either in combat or in the Holocaust. We are sure that most readers of this article have suffered similar losses or have felt pain and anguish when watching footage of Nazi concentration or death camps. Joseph Goebbels once boasted, "Nothing is easier than leading the people on a leash. I just hold up a dazzling campaign poster and they jump through it."[9] We owe it to the memory of his victims and to ourselves to learn as much as we can about the ways of propaganda so that we may prove Herr Goebbels false.

ENDNOTES

[1]Hitler, A. (1925), *Mein kampf.* Boston: Houghton Mifflin, p. 176.

[2]Jowett, G. S., & O'Donnell, V. (1986). *Persuasion and propaganda.* Beverly Hills, CA: Sage; Peterson, H. C. (1939). *Propaganda for war: The campaign against American neutrality, 1914–1917.* Norman, OK: University of Oklahoma Press.

[3]For excellent discussions of Nazi and World War II propaganda, see Childers, T. (1983). *The Nazi voter.* Chapel Hill, NC: University of North Carolina Press; Doob, L. W. (1950). Goebbel's principles of propaganda. *Public Opinion Quarterly, 14,* 419–422; Hale, O. J. (1964). *The captive press in the Third Reich.* Princeton, NJ: Princeton University Press; Herzstein, R. E. (1978). *The war that Hitler won.* New York: Paragon House; Rhodes, A. (1987). *Propaganda: The art of persuasion: World War II.* Secaucus, NJ: Wellfleet Press; Rutherford, W. (1978). *Hitler's propaganda machine.* London: Bison Books; Welch, D. (1983). *Nazi propaganda.* Beckenham, Kent, UK: Croom Helm; Zeman, Z. A. B. (1964). *Nazi propaganda.* London: Oxford University Press.

[4]Hitler. See note 1, p. 178.

[5]Ibid, pp. 180–181.

[6]Quoted in Rhodes, A. (1987). See note 3, p. 13.

[7]Bronowski, J. (1973). *The ascent of man.* Boston: Little, Brown.

[8]Hitler. See note 1, pp. 182–183.

[9]Quoted in Rhodes, A. (1987). See note 3, p. 90.

↭ Questions

1. What kinds of social influence did Goebbels use? How? With what results? What was the purpose of Nazi propaganda? Did Goebbels succeed?

2. What do Pratkanis and Aronson mean when they say, "Propaganda is a means to communicate the 'truth' to the ignorant"? Why do they say that the most dangerous aspect of Nazi propaganda is its assumption "that there is an absolute truth and the ruling elite are privileged to know this truth"? Why is this assumption so dangerous? How does this assumption relate to Pratkanis' and Aronson's definition of propaganda?

3. What is the difference between the propaganda used by the British and American governments in World War I and that used by the German government in World War II? Is this difference important? Why or why not?

4. Did the German people recognize the propaganda tactics that Goebbels used? Why or why not? How does one tell if something is propaganda? Could this kind of propaganda happen in the United States today? Why or why not? If so, what could you do to protect yourself from it?

PREJUDICE

Do you remember when the Crayola™ crayon box contained a "flesh-colored" crayon? What color was it? What color of ladies' hosiery is "nude"? What color of make-up is called "natural"? If banks and governmental offices are closed on the "Sabbath," why are they open on Fridays and Saturdays? If an employer offers health coverage for a worker's significant other, why does that apply only to married people? Why are airline seats narrow? What is the official title for the spouse of the president of the United States?

Prejudice and discrimination can be more subtle than you think. While most of us would agree that people should not be treated unfairly because of their race, gender, nationality, religion, or sexual orientation, do we always recognize discrimination when we see it? Did you recognize that the above questions highlight examples of prejudice and discrimination? That "flesh," "nude," and "natural" apply only to *white* skin; that Sunday is the *Christian* Sabbath; that most employers don't give benefits for *gay or lesbian* couples, no matter how long they have been together; and that airplane seats are not designed for *overweight* people? These are all examples of *institutionalized* discrimination. And if you thought that the spouse of a U.S. president is called "the First *Lady*," you have your own prejudgments of who can—and can't—be president.

PREJUDICE, STEREOTYPING, AND DISCRIMINATION

Prejudice is an attitude you have toward a person who's a member of a group that you perceive to be significantly different from your own (Fiske, 1998). A *prejudicial attitude*, like other attitudes, has three components: affect (emotion), behavior, and cognitions (thoughts) (Fiske, 1998). The emotional component of prejudice is almost always negative and may include fear, hate, suspicion, or contempt. The behavioral component of prejudice takes the form of *discrimination*, where we act differently toward someone as a result of their perceived group membership. Finally, the cognitive component—a *stereotype*—consists of beliefs about what people from certain groups are like.

Prejudice Today. It's tempting to think that things are better today for groups that have formally suffered overt prejudice, such as African-Americans, women, Jews, gays and lesbians, and people with AIDS (Taylor, Peplau, & Sears, 2000). However, a lack of blatant racism or sexism does not necessarily mean that people fully endorse equality (see Solomon,

1994, for a first-hand account). For example, while "old-fashioned" racism has decreased, a "new-fashioned" prejudice called *modern racism* (McConahay, 1986), *symbolic racism* (Kinder & Sears, 1981), or *racial resentment* (Kinder & Sanders, 1996) has taken its place. Rather than lessening, it seems that prejudices have merely changed shape with the shifting political and social tide from the 1960s to the 1990s.

What does this new-fashioned racism look like? Although few people today endorse white supremacy, racial segregation, or formal discrimination, many believe that blacks have not been unfairly disadvantaged by discrimination, should do more to help themselves, and should not receive "special treatment" in hiring or college admissions (Taylor, Peplau, & Sears, 2000). Researchers have also documented similar sexist beliefs, called *neosexism*, where people do not believe that women have been unfairly disadvantaged and should not receive special consideration in hiring, promotion, or salary decisions (Swim, Aikin, Hall, & Hunter, 1995; Tougas, Brown, Beaton, & Joly, 1995).

Symbolic racism is a stronger predictor than traditional racism of a person's views toward busing, affirmative action, and African-American political leaders (Sears, Van Laar, Carrillo, & Kosterman, 1997). New-fashioned prejudices are also strong predictors of negative attitudes and discrimination toward many other groups. For example, some people today oppose affirmative action for women (Swim et al., 1995) and AIDS-related policies (Haddock, Zanna, & Esses, 1993; Price & Hsu, 1992), discriminate against overweight people (Crandall, 1994), and oppose immigration (Pettigrew & Meertens, 1995).

Other social psychologists have theorized that many people today feel *racial ambivalence*; they believe in racial equality but also support the traditional American value of self-reliance. As a result, they see victims of prejudice as responsible for their own condition. They thus "blame the victim" and become unsympathetic to those who have suffered from prejudice and discrimination in general (Katz, Wackenhut, & Hass, 1986). As a result of this ambivalence, such people may avoid interactions with persons of other races because of the negative feelings these interactions evoke (Gaertner & Dovidio, 1986). The problem is that by avoiding such situations, they never confront their prejudices. They therefore can preserve their self-image of being unprejudiced people. Such ambivalence occurs with sexism as well: There is evidence that men may hold similar ambivalent attitudes toward feminist women (MacDonald & Zanna, 1998).

In light of this work on new forms of prejudice, many wonder whether the apparent declines in sexism and racism are merely illusory changes (Taylor, Peplau, & Sears, 2000). Again, while few would seriously endorse formalizing racial segregation, there is still much resistance to the smaller social changes necessary for true racial equality in the United States today (Jackman & Muha, 1984). For example, evidence suggests that while people endorse racial equality and would readily work or live in an integrated setting, many do not have cross-race friendships and would feel uncomfortable if a member of their immediate family married interracially (Myers, 1999). As a result, social psychologists have become especially sensitive to the way racial attitudes are measured. They have developed new, indirect measures of prejudice and

Table 1 *Changes over Time in Racial Prejudices of Whites (In Percentages)*

Changes Over Time in the Racial Attitudes of Whites (in Percentages)

	Before 1986	After 1986	Percentage Change
White and black students should go to same, not separate schools	32 (1942)	96 (1995)	+64
Would vote for well-qualified black person for president if nominated by own party	37 (1958)	92 (1996)	+55
Oppose laws against intermarriage	38 (1963)	87 (1996)	+49%
Whites do not have the right to keep blacks out of their neighborhoods	39 (1963)	86 (1996)	+47
Federal government should ensure that white and black children go to same schools	47 (1964)	38 (1994)	-9
Preference in hiring and promotion should be given to blacks	33 (1985)	23 (1996)	-10
Government should provide special aid to minorities	22 (1970)	22 (1988)	0

Note: The year of each survey is in parentheses.
Source: Survey data given by Schuman, Steeh, Bobo, and Krysan (1997)
From Taylor, Peplau, & Sears, 2000, p. 193.

stereotyping in order to study these issues more effectively (e.g., Crosby, Bromley, & Saxe, 1980).

◁ WHAT CAUSES PREJUDICE?

Social psychologists have studied four major causes of prejudice (see Table 2). Let's consider each of them in turn.

Table 2 *Four Causes of Prejudice*

Social cognition	The way we think
Attributional biases	The way we assign meaning
Resource allocation	The way we allocate resources
Social learning, conformity, and institutionalization	The way we conform

From Aronson, Wilson, & Akert, 1999.

1. Social Cognition. Might stereotyping and prejudice be unfortunate byproducts of the way we process information? According to the social cognition view, the way we think about our social world may inadvertently lead us to stereotyping and prejudice. For example, we often use schemas or stereotypes to organize information and classify people (Fiske & Taylor, 1991). In doing so, we also tend to make lots of errors, hold biases, and take shortcuts (Fiske & Taylor, 1991). Let's take a closer look at how social cognition works.

Social categorization. Perhaps we take the first step down the path to prejudice when we categorize people into groups. No matter how trivial, arbitrary, or downright random this process is, the moment we do it, some strange things happen (Tajfel, Billig, Bundy, & Flament, 1971). According to *social identity theory*, we begin to identify with people in our own group (called our *ingroup*) and contrast ourselves with people in other groups (called *outgroups*). Eventually, we evaluate ourselves and others primarily by group membership (Turner, 1984, 1987, 1991; Tajfel, 1981, 1982; see the poem "We and They" for an amusing perspective on social categorization). For example, in addition to individual identities such as wife or mother, a woman might also see herself as having social identities, such as Jew, black, or woman.

We and They
by Rudyard Kipling

Father, Mother and Me,
    Sister and Auntie say
All the people like us are We,
    And everyone else is They.
And They live over the sea
    While we live over the way,
But—would you believe it?—They look upon We

As only a sort of They!

We eat pork and beef
    With cow-horn-handled knives.
They who gobble Their rice off a leaf
    Are horrified out of Their lives;
While They who live up a tree,
    Feast on grubs and clay,
(Isn't it scandalous?) look upon We
    As a simply disgusting They!

We eat kitcheny food.
    We have doors that latch.
They drink milk and blood
    Under an open thatch.
We have doctors to fee.
    They have wizards to pay.
And (impudent heathen!) they look upon We
    As a quite impossible They!

All good people agree,
    And all good people say,
All nice people, like us, are We
    And everyone else is They:
But if you cross over the sea,
    Instead of over the way,
You may end by (think of it!) looking on We
    As only a sort of They!

As a result of social categorization, we often exaggerate the similarities within groups and the differences between groups (Taylor, 1981). We view members of our own group as unique individuals but perceive people in an outgroup as more similar to one another—*the outgroup homogeneity effect* (Ostrom & Sedikides, 1992). Because we like people who we think are similar to us and dislike people we think are different from us, we favor our own group—an *ingroup bias*—and believe that it is better than other groups (Byrne & Wong, 1962). You can see how the simple cognitive act of categorization quickly sets the stage for prejudice and discrimination (Dovidio & Gaertner, 1999).

Stereotype activation. Because the social categories we use to identify ourselves and classify others have specific meanings in our society, categorization inevitably leads to evaluation. Every categorization—especially the most salient ones of race and gender—has beliefs or stereotypes (many of which are derogatory) attached to it. As a result, putting people in categories activates stereotypical beliefs about them.

Once activated, stereotypes cause us to think ill of others (e.g., Greenberg & Pyszczynski, 1985). However, the news is not all bad. We *can* choose to ignore or refute the stereotype (Devine, 1989; Devine, Monteith, Zuwerink, & Elliot, 1991). There appear to be two steps to the cognitive processing of stereotypes: an automatic and a controlled process. The automatic process activates stereotypes, often without our awareness, while the controlled process can refute or ignore them.

This implies that people who are not prejudiced take actions to prevent an activated stereotype from influencing their judgments—for example, to consciously refute the stereotype—while prejudiced people mindlessly go along with the activated stereotype (Devine, 1989). A similar automatic process appears to operate with gender stereotypes as well (Bargh, Raymond, Pryor, & Strack, 1995).

Illusory correlation. Stereotypes may influence our judgments of others in yet another way. Consider the idea that, to make sense of the world, we look for or impose order on random events (Fiske & Taylor, 1991). We might thus see a relationship between two events that are, in reality, unrelated or related only slightly. We make this *illusory correlation* when we have strong expectations or when events are unusual (Chapman, 1967).

For example, consider the position of minority group members. Because they are in the minority, they are seen as unusual. We know that distinctive, or salient, stimuli draw a disproportionate amount of our attention (Fiske & Taylor, 1991). As a result, we are likely to see or impose a relationship between a minority person's characteristics (e.g., race) and some event or behavior (e.g., a particularly violent crime committed by a person of that race, or an outstanding sports play we might see on the news) (Hamilton & Gifford, 1976). Through this process, we might believe the illusory correlations that African-Americans are responsible for violent crime or that the best athletes are African-American.

This tendency to see an illusory correlation is exacerbated if we already have in our mind some stereotype about a group member. Once the stereotype has been activated—for example, by hearing someone make a derogatory remark about people from that group—we will likely notice events that fit the stereotype more than events that contradict it. This tendency only reinforces the stereotype (Hamilton & Sherman, 1989). Illusory correlations may also be created or reinforced by the media through depictions of minority members in stereotypical roles (Busby, 1975, Deaux & LaFrance, 1998).

Revising stereotypes. Is it possible to change our stereotypes? It *is*—but it's very difficult. When presented with only a single piece of information that disconfirms a stereotype, people will try to rationalize the inconsistent information (e.g., create a subtype within the stereotype) rather than modify or discard the stereotype (Webber & Crocker, 1983). Thus a person who doesn't fit the stereotype becomes the "exception to the rule." With many contradictions to a stereotype, people eventually will modify their beliefs (Webber & Crocker, 1983). But such modification happens only if the "exceptions" occur frequently and counteract many different aspects of the stereotype. Of course, strongly prejudiced people, who may be highly emotionally invested in their prejudicial attitudes, may never be able to change (Aronson, Wilson, & Akert, 1999).

2. *Attributional Biases.* Once we have categorized people, we quickly try to determine why they act the way they do (Fiske & Taylor, 1991). When we make judgments about people against whom we hold prejudicial attitudes, the usual errors and biases that arise during any judgment process increase. We refer to these errors as attributional biases, three of which are discussed below.

The ultimate attribution error. In explaining why someone behaved as he or she did, we tend to identify the person more than the situation as the cause of the behavior. This is called the fundamental attribution error (Ross, 1977). Through this form of error, we make dispositional attributions; that is, we decide that a person's disposition or character is the reason behind his or her behavior. Stereotypes are another highly negative form of dispositional attributions (Aronson, Wilson, & Akert, 1999). The tendency to attribute events to the dispositions of an entire group of people—clearly a result of prejudice—is called the *ultimate attribution error* (Pettigrew, 1979). As a result of this error, any stereotype about a group of people quickly turns into false beliefs about their personalities. Entire cultures have thus been labeled as aggressive, conniving, dumb, lazy, and so forth (Aronson, Wilson, & Akert, 1999).

Group-serving bias. While blaming undesirable behaviors on the personality of an outgroup, prejudiced people will make excuses for such behavior in their own ingroup ("They are violent. We were just protecting ourselves"). Similarly, people readily dismiss positive behaviors of an outgroup as due to luck, high effort, special advantage, or the one-time demands of a situation (Myers, 1999). This reaction is called the *group-serving bias* (Jackson, Sullivan, & Hodge, 1993).

Blaming the victim. Our desire to see the world as a fair and just place where people get what they deserve may also cause us to blame victims for their own misfortunes (Lerner, 1980). We are especially likely to think this way about members of an outgroup. As a result, we "blame the victims" for their joblessness, low wages, low-quality housing, poor education, lack of opportunities, etc., without acknowledging the situations or institutions that may have played a direct role in their plight. Sadly, blaming the victim is so comforting because it lets us believe that such misfortunes wouldn't happen to us (Jones & Aronson, 1973). Of course, the irony in all this is that we then fail to take precautions to protect ourselves from those very misfortunes. We may also fail to sympathize with those who have been actively discriminated against (Aronson, Wilson, & Akert, 1999).

3. *Resource Allocation.* When combined with competition for scarce resources, our natural tendency to use stereotypes leads to particularly negative prejudicial attitudes and virulent discrimination. Perhaps you've heard the phrase, "If you want peace, work for justice," which speaks to this principle.

Below, we summarize three theories about the connection between prejudice and the desire for resources.

Realistic conflict theory. According to realistic conflict theory, prejudice and discrimination occur when conflict over limited resources erupts (Jackson, 1993; Levine & Campbell, 1972). People feel threatened by members of outgroups when vital resources such as jobs, housing, and food are in scarce supply. For example, during a recession, people may blame immigrants for taking jobs away from citizens. Indeed, many studies have documented this phenomenon in the United States and other countries (e.g., Palmer, 1996), and in our own time (e.g., Greeley & Sheatsley, 1971) as well as in earlier eras (e.g., Dollard, 1938; Jacobs & Landau, 1971).

Frustration-aggression theory. When frustrated, people are likely to act aggressively. The pain and frustration of not being able to achieve a goal evokes hostility (Miller & Bugelski, 1948). A typical response is retaliation against the person who has "caused" the frustration—such as an individual who is perceived as competition for scarce resources. However, if an actual competitor for precious resources does not exist, or if it is not possible to attack the person directly responsible for the frustration, people will find a "scapegoat" for their aggression (Allport, 1954). In particular, people displace their aggression onto groups that are already visible, disliked, and relatively powerless (Berkowitz, 1962). For example, scapegoating may explain the link between the price of cotton and the number of lynchings in the American South between 1882 and 1930: As the price dropped (and economic hardship struck), the number of lynchings increased (Hovland & Sears, 1940). Similarly, Jews have been used as scapegoats throughout history, but particularly in Nazi Germany, when government leaders publicly blamed them for Germany's post-World War I economic crisis. These accusations culminated in the wave of mass murder known as the Holocaust (Berkowitz, 1962).

The authoritarian personality. An early explanation of prejudice claimed that a certain kind of person—the authoritarian personality—was particularly prone to holding prejudicial attitudes (Adorno, Frenkl-Brunswik, Levinson, & Sanford, 1950). According to this theory, the authoritarian personality shows exaggerated obedience to authority, high conformity to conventional standards of behavior, self-righteous hostility, and aggression toward those who are "different." Such people believe in a hierarchical "pecking order," in which people higher up are entitled to more rewards and resources than people at the bottom. They blame their own lack of resources on outgroup members who are not entitled to such things—in the eyes of the authoritarian personality—because of their low status.

More recent work has updated this original description and has found right-wing authoritarianism among political conservatives (Altemeyer, 1988). Just as they did over 50 years ago, conservative attitudes today are also correlated with prejudice toward minorities, including certain races and ethnicities, gays and lesbians, AIDS victims, drug users, and the homeless (Taylor, Peplau, & Sears, 2000; e.g., Peterson, Doty, & Winter, 1993).

4. Social Learning, Conformity, and Institutionalization. The final cause of prejudice is the most simple and yet the most pervasive. According to social learning theory, we learn both directly and by observation from our social environment; that is, from the actions and statements of our parents, peers, teachers, and the media (Bandura, 1997). We learn not only from what our parents tell us, but also from what they show us. Moreover, we pick up society's views from the media, including TV, radio, advertisements, magazines, newspapers, and the Internet.

We may develop stereotypes and prejudices because we find ourselves conforming to the dominant values of our culture. We may also look to others to determine what is correct (informational social influence) or acceptable (normative social influence) in a given situation. Our tendency to conform to others or to our culture may even cause us to perpetuate stereotypes without realizing it. For example, we might laugh at ethnic jokes without thinking about their true meaning.

Further, these stereotypes and prejudices may become institutionalized. That is, political leaders and lawmakers may legitimize and reinforce the prevailing attitudes of society through their communications to the public and their policy decisions. As a result, we may find ourselves victims of racism or sexism—through discriminatory institutional practices that are no longer overtly motivated by prejudice (Myers, 1999). The opening paragraph of this chapter listed just a few examples of institutionalized prejudice.

❧ THE IMPACT OF PREJUDICE

How does it feel to be treated differently from others? To be actively persecuted or discriminated against? An early study addressing this question is the classic white/black doll study by Kenneth and Maimie Clark (1947). The two researchers wondered how growing up during racial segregation and playing with white dolls would affect the self-concept and self-esteem of African-American children. They discovered that, by age three, these children had internalized the cultural value that the white doll was better and prettier than the black doll.

More recent studies have not found differences in doll choice of African-American children (Porter, 1971; Porter & Washington, 1979; Gopaul-McNicol, 1987). But this does not mean that prejudice and discrimination has disappeared or has no impact on people. There are at least two ways in which people are directly harmed by prejudice, stereotyping, and discrimination

Self-Fulfilling Prophecy. When we hold unfounded expectations about what another person is like, we act differently toward that person than we might otherwise. As a result, we may actually cause the person to behave in accord with our beliefs. This is called a *self-fulfilling prophecy* (Rosenthal, 1985, 1991; Rosenthal & Jacobson, 1968; Snyder, Tanke, & Berscheid, 1977). This phenomenon was vividly demonstrated in a study involving job interviews (Word, Zanna, & Cooper, 1974). Not only did the researchers find that interviewers treated black applicants differently than white applicants—for example, by sitting farther away from the applicant and avoiding eye contact—but that their behavior had a negative impact on the applicants. Specifically, in a second part of the experiment in which all the applicants were treated in the same way that the black applicants were originally treated, both black and white applicants were rated by observers as less qualified for the position in question. This study suggests that poor performance of outgroup members might be due primarily to low expectations or discriminatory behavior on the part of judges.

Stereotype threat. Imagine going into a situation knowing that people expect you to do poorly simply because you have, say, blue eyes. Imagine the apprehension you would feel, knowing that not only is your own performance on the line, but so is the reputation of *people like you.* This phenomenon is called *stereotype threat* and has been demonstrated in African-American (Steele, 1997; Steele & Aronson, 1995) and women students in testing situations (Spencer & Steele, 1997, in Aronson, Wilson, & Akert, 1999). Stereotype threat is a major problem; for example, it may cause African-American adolescents to "disidentify" with school and seek out other activities, such as playing basketball or hanging out with friends, that feel safer to them (Steele, 1997).

❧ HOW CAN WE REDUCE PREJUDICE?

Given the harm that prejudice and discrimination inflict on their victims as well as on our society as a whole, social psychologists have actively been seeking ways to reduce these tendencies. Some researchers believe that contact between groups may lessen or even eliminate prejudice; however, experiments have shown that this does not work unless six conditions are met (see Table 3).

With *mutual interdependence,* two or more groups need each other in order to achieve a *common goal* that is important to each of them. In the classic "Robber's Cave" study of competition and prejudice between two groups of boys at a summer camp, the experimenters arranged for a series of "problems" to occur—a water shortage, a truck that broke down on a camping trip—which could be solved only if both groups of boys cooperated (Sherif, 1956). In the "jigsaw classroom," students had to learn a history lesson by working

Table 3 *Six Conditions of Contact That Reduce Prejudice*

Mutual interdependence
Common goal
Equal status
Friendly and informal setting
Interactions with multiple members of each group
Social norms promoting equality

From Aronson, Wilson, & Akert, 1999.

together with children who were different from them (Aronson & Bridgeman, 1979). In each of these studies, animosity between groups lessened.

Such contact between antagonistic groups also needs to occur in a *friendly, informal setting,* in which the groups have *equal status* and the prevailing *social norms promote equality,* as in the camping trip in the Robber's Cave experiment. Further, the groups should have an opportunity to mix so as to get to know one another by *interacting with many members of the other group.* Prejudices will not be reduced if the groups stay on separate sides of the room while at a dance or while watching a movie (a failed intervention of the Robber's Cave experiment). In the jigsaw classroom, children were allowed to talk quietly with one another during the lesson. Over many weeks, Anglo, African-American, and Mexican-American children got to know each other quite well, got along better, and showed more empathy for their former "enemies" (Aronson & Bridgeman, 1979).

Unfortunately, the way we process and organize information about our social world may cause us to stereotype. However, this process is not inevitable. Nor must stereotyping always lead to prejudice and discrimination. There are plenty of things that we as individuals can do to rid our society of discrimination and conflict, and to promote peace and justice. Understanding how prejudice happens in the first place is an excellent first step.

REFERENCES

Adorno, T. W., Frenkl-Brunswik, E., Levinson, D. J., & Sanford, R. N. (1950). *The authoritarian personality.* New York: Harper & Row.

Allport, G. (1954). *The nature of prejudice.* Reading, MA: Addison-Wesley.

Altemeyer, B. (1988). *Enemies of freedom: Understanding right-wing authoritarianism.* San Francisco: Jossey-Bass.

Aronson, E., & Bridgeman, D. (1979). Jigsaw groups and the desegregated classroom: In pursuit of common goals. *Personality and Social Psychology Bulletin, 5,* 438–446.

Aronson, E., Wilson, T. D., & Akert, R. M. (1999). *Social psychology* (3rd ed.). New York: Longman.

Bandura, A. (1997). *Self-efficacy: The exercise of control*. New York: Freeman.

Bargh, J. A., Raymond, P., Pryor, J. B., & Strack, F. (1995). Attractiveness of the underling: An automatic power-sex association and its consequences for sexual harassment and aggression. *Journal of Personality and Social Psychology, 68*, 768–781.

Berkowitz, L. (1962). *Aggression: A social psychological analysis*. New York: McGraw-Hill.

Busby, L. J. (1975). Defining the sex-role standard in commercial network television programming directed at children. *Journalism Quarterly, 51*, 690–696.

Byrne, D., & Wong, T. J. (1962). Racial prejudice, interpersonal attraction, and assumed dissimilarity of attitudes. *Journal of Abnormal and Social Psychology, 65*, 246–253.

Chapman, L. J. (1967). Illusory correlation in observational report. *Journal of Verbal Learning and Verbal Behavior, 5*, 151–155.

Clark, K., & Clark, M. (1947). Racial identification and preference in Negro children. In T. M. Newcomb & E. L. Hartley (Eds.), *Readings in social psychology* (pp. 169–178). New York: Holt.

Crandall, C. S. (1994). Prejudice against fat people: Ideology and self-interest. *Journal of Personality and Social Psychology, 66*, 882–894.

Crosby, F., Bromley, S., & Saxe, L. (1980). Recent unobtrusive studies of black and white discrimination and prejudice: A literature review. *Psychological Bulletin, 87*, 546–563.

Deaux, K., & LaFrance, M. (1998). Gender. In D. T. Gilbert, S. T. Fiske, & G. Lindzey (Eds.), *The handbook of social psychology* (4th ed., Vol. 1, pp. 788–828). New York: McGraw-Hill.

Devine, P. G. (1989). Stereotypes and prejudice: Their automatic and controlled components. *Journal of Personality and Social Psychology, 56*, 5–18.

Devine, P. G., Monteith, M. J., Zuwerink, J. R., & Elliot, A. J. (1991). Prejudice with and without compunction. *Journal of Personality and Social Psychology, 60*, 817–830.

Dollard, J. (1938). Hostility and fear in social life. *Social Forces, 17*, 15–26.

Dovidio, J. F., & Gaertner, S. L. (1999). Reducing prejudice: Combating intergroup bias. *Current Directions in Psychological Science, 8*, 101–105.

Fiske, S. T. (1998). Prejudice, stereotyping and discrimination. In D. Gilbert, S. T. Fiske, & G. Lindzey (Eds.), *The handbook of social psychology* (4th ed., Vol. 2, pp. 357–414). New York: McGraw-Hill.

Fiske, S. T., & Taylor, S. E. (1991). *Social cognition* (2nd ed.). New York: McGraw-Hill.

Gaertner, S. L., & Dovidio, J. F. (1986). The aversive form of racism. In J. F. Dovidio & S. L. Gaertner (Eds.), *Prejudice, discrimination, and racism: Theory and research* (pp. 61–89). New York: Academic Press.

Gopaul-McNicol, S.-A. A. (1987). A cross-cultural study of the effects of modeling, reinforcement, and color-meaning word association on doll color preference of Black preschool children and White preschool children in New York and Trinidad. *Dissertation Abstracts International, 48*, 340–341.

Greeley, A., & Sheatsley, P. (1971). The acceptance of desegregation continues to advance. *Scientific American, 225*(6), 13–19.

Greenberg, J., & Pyszczynski, T. (1985). The effect of an overheard slur on evaluations of the target: How to spread a social disease. *Journal of Experimental Social Psychology, 21*, 61–72.

Haddock, G., Zanna, M. P., & Esses, V. M. (1993). Assessing the structure of prejudicial attitudes: The case of attitudes toward homosexuals. *Journal of Personality and Social Psychology, 65*, 1105–1118.

Hamilton, D. L., & Gifford, R. K. (1976). Illusory correlation in interpersonal perception: A cognitive basis of stereotypic judgments. *Journal of Experimental Social Psychology, 12*, 392–407.

Hamilton, D. L., & Sherman, S. J. (1989). Illusory correlations: Implications for stereotype theory and research. In D. Bar-Tal, C. F. Graumann, A. W. Kruglanski, & W. Stroebe (Eds.), *Stereotypes and prejudice: Changing conceptions* (pp. 59–82). New York: Springer-Verlag.

Hovland, C. I., & Sears, R. R. (1940). Minor studies in aggression: 6. Correlation of lynchings with economic indices. *Journal of Psychology, 9*, 301–310.

Jackman, M. R., & Muha, M. J. (1984). Education and intergroup attitudes: Moral enlightenment, superficial democratic commitment, or ideological refinement? *American Sociological Review, 49*, 751–769.

Jackson, J. W. (1993). Realistic group conflict theory: A review and evaluation of the theoretical and empirical literature. *Psychological Record, 43*, 395–413.

Jackson, L. A., Sullivan, L. A., & Hodge, C. N. (1993). Stereotype effects on attributions, predictions, and evaluations: No social judgments are quite alike. *Journal of Personality and Social Psychology, 65*, 69–84.

Jacobs, P., & Landau, S. (1971). *To serve the devil* (Vol. 2, p. 71). New York: Vintage Books.

Jones, C., & Aronson, E. (1973). Attribution of fault to a rape victim as a function of the respectability of the victim. *Journal of Personality and Social Psychology, 26*, 415–419.

Katz, I., Wackenhut, J., & Hass, R. G. (1986). Racial ambivalence, value duality, and behavior. In J. F. Dovidio & S. L. Gaertner (Eds.), *Prejudice, discrimination, and racism: Theory and research* (pp. 35–60). New York: Academic Press.

Kinder, D. R., & Sanders, L. N. (1996). *Divided by color: Racial politics and democratic ideals*. Chicago, IL: University of Chicago Press.

Kinder, D. R., & Sears, S. O. (1981). Prejudice and politics: Symbolic racism versus racial threats to the good life. *Journal of Personality and Social Psychology, 40*, 414–431.

Lerner, M. J. (1980). *The belief in a just world: A fundamental decision*. New York: Plenum.

Levine, R. A., & Campbell, D. T. (1972). *Ethnocentrism: Theories of conflict, ethnic attitudes, and group behavior*. New York: Wiley.

MacDonald, T. K., & Zanna, M. P. (1998). Cross-dimension ambivalence toward feminists: Can cross-dimension ambivalence affect hiring decisions? *Personality and Social Psychology Bulletin, 24*, 427–441.

McConahay, J. B. (1986). Modern racism, ambivalence, and the Modern Racism Scale. In J. F. Dovidio & S. L. Gaertner (Eds.), *Prejudice, discrimination, and racism: Theory and research* (pp. 91–125). New York: Academic Press.

Miller, N., & Bugelski, R. (1948). Minor studies in aggression: The influence of frustrations imposed by the ingroup on attitudes expressed by the outgroup. *Journal of Psychology, 25,* 437–442.

Myers, D. G. (1999). *Social psychology* (6th ed.). Boston: McGraw-Hill.

Ostrom, T., & Sedikides, C. (1992). Outgroup homogeneity effects in natural and minimal groups. *Psychological Bulletin, 112,* 536–552.

Palmer, D. L. (1996). Determinants of Canadian attitudes towards immigration: More than just racism? *Canadian Journal of Behavioural Science, 28,* 180–192.

Peterson, B. E., Doty, R. M., & Winter, D. G. (1993). Authoritarianism and attitudes toward contemporary social issues. *Personality and Social Psychology Bulletin, 19,* 174–184.

Pettigrew, T. F. (1979). The ultimate attribution error: Extending Allport's cognitive analysis of prejudice. *Personality and Social Psychology Bulletin, 55,* 461–476.

Pettigrew, T. F., & Meertens, R. W. (1995). Subtle and blatant prejudice in western Europe. *European Journal of Social Psychology, 25,* 57–75.

Porter, J. R. (1971). *Black child, white child: The development of racial attitudes.* Cambridge, MA: Harvard University Press.

Porter, J. R., & Washington, R. E. (1979). Black identity and self-esteem, 1968–1978. *Annual Review of Sociology.* Stanford, CA: Annual Reviews.

Price, V., & Hsu, M. (1992). Public opinion about AIDS policies: The role of misinformation and attitudes toward homosexuals. *Public Opinion Quarterly, 56,* 29–52.

Rosenthal, R. (1985). From unconscious experimenter bias to teacher expectancy effects. In J. B. Dusek, V. C. Hall, & W. J. Meyer, (Eds.), *Teacher expectancies.* Hillsdale, NJ: Erlbaum.

Rosenthal, R. (1991). Teacher expectancy effects: A brief update 25 years after the Pygmalion experiment. *Journal of Research in Education, 1,* 3–12.

Rosenthal, R., & Jacobson, L. (1968). Pygmalion in the classroom: Teacher expectation and student intellectual development. New York: Holt, Rinehart, & Winston.

Ross, L. (1977). The intuitive psychologist and his shortcomings: Distortions in the attribution process. In L. Berkowitz (Ed.), *Advances in experimental social psychology.* (Vol. 10, pp. 173–220). New York: Academic Press.

Sears, D. O., Van Laar, C., Carrillo, M., & Kosterman, R. (1997). Is it really racism? The origins of white Americans' opposition to race-targeted policies. *Public Opinion Quarterly, 61,* 16–53.

Sherif, M. (1956, November). Experiments in group conflict. *Scientific American, 195,* 54–58.

Snyder, M., Tanke, E. D., & Berscheid, E. (1977). Social perception and interpersonal behavior: On the self-fulfilling nature of social stereotypes. *Journal of Personality and Social Psychology, 35,* 656–666.

Solomon, J. (1994, October 30). Reliving "Black Like Me": My own journey into the heart of race-conscious America. *The Washington Post,* p. c1.

Steele, C. M. (1997). A threat in the air: How stereotypes shape intellectual identity and performance. *American Psychologist, 52,* 613–629.

Steele, C. M., & Aronson, J. (1995). Stereotype threat and the intellectual test performance of African Americans. *Journal of Personality and Social Psychology, 69,* 797–811.

Swim, J. K, Aikin, K. J., Hall, W. S., & Hunter, B. A. (1995). Sexism and racism: Old-fashioned and modern prejudices. *Journal of Personality and Social Psychology, 68,* 199–214.

Tajfel, H. (1981). *Human groups and social categories: Studies in social psychology.* London: Cambridge University Press.

Tajfel, H. (1982). Social psychology of intergroup relations. *Annual Review of Psychology, 33,* 1–39.

Tajfel, H., Billig, M. G., Bundy, F. P., & Flament, C. (1971). Social categorization and intergroup behavior. *European Journal of Social Psychology, 1,* 149–178.

Taylor, S. E. (1981). A categorization approach to stereotyping. In D. L. Hamilton (Ed.), *Cognitive processes in stereotyping and intergroup behavior.* Hillsdale, NJ: Erlbaum.

Taylor, S. E., Peplau, L. A., & Sears, D. O. (2000). *Social psychology* (10th ed.). Upper Saddle River, NJ: Prentice-Hall.

Tougas, F., Brown, R., Beaton, A. M., & Joly, S. (1995). Neosexism: *Plus ça change, plus c'est pareil. Personality and Social Psychology Bulletin, 21,* 842–849.

Turner, J. C. (1984). Social identification and psychological group formation. In H. Tajfel (Ed.), *The social dimensions: European developments in social psychology* (Vol. 2). London: Cambridge University Press.

Turner, J. C. (1987). *Rediscovering the social group: A self-categorization theory.* New York: Basil Blackwell.

Turner, J. C. (1991). *Social influence.* Milton Keynes, England: Open University Press.

Webber, R., & Crocker, J. (1983). Cognitive processes in the revision of stereotypic beliefs. *Journal of Personality and Social Psychology, 45,* 961–977.

Word, C. O, Zanna, M. P., & Cooper, J. (1974). The nonverbal mediation of self-fulfilling prophecies in interracial interaction. *Journal of Experimental Social Psychology, 10,* 109–120.

SUGGESTED READINGS

Aronson, E., & Patnoe, S. (1997). *Cooperation in the classroom: The jigsaw method.* New York: Longman.

Brewer, M., & Brown, R. (1998). Intergroup relations. In D. Gilbert, S. Fiske, & G. Lindzey (Eds.), *The handbook of social psychology* (4th ed., Vol. 2, pp. 554–594). New York: McGraw-Hill.

Dovidio, J. F., & Gaertner, S. L. (Eds.). (1986). *Prejudice, discrimination, and racism.* New York: Academic Press.

Ponterotlo, J., & Pedersen, P. (1993). *Preventing prejudice: A guide for counselors and educators.* New York: Sage.

Williams, G. H. (1995). *Life on the color line.*

REDUCING PREJUDICE:
COMBATING INTERGROUP BIASES

John F. Dovidio, Colgate University
Samuel L. Gaertner, University of Delaware

Here's something to think about: How is it that major league baseball players can play fiercely all season against each other and then suddenly become cooperative teammates during the all-star game? It's all in the categorization, you might say.

This simple example illustrates the power behind the work of John Dovidio and Samuel Gaertner. In this review article, they summarize the traditional approach to prejudice: using persuasion, education, and socialization to change the false beliefs that perpetuate prejudice. They note that today there are fewer overt expressions of prejudice. Instead, we see what's called "modern" racism, which involves nonconscious or unintentional forms of prejudice. To combat these forms, Dovidio and Gaertner suggest that psychologists get people to change their cognitive categories through changing conditions of contact. Much as the baseball player has to stop thinking of his new teammates and his former enemies as them *and instead think of* them *as* us *in order to play in the all-star game, prejudice could lessen if people* decategorized *or* recategorized *others by emphasizing similarity or solidarity rather than differences.*

What Dovidio and Gaertner suggest challenges people's innermost identities and group loyalties. However, their work is rich and exciting and provides a new way of understanding why techniques like the "jigsaw classroom" and superordinate goals help reduce prejudice. When it comes to reducing prejudice, you might say that everybody wins through these researchers' work.

Prejudice is commonly defined as an unfair negative attitude toward a social group or a member of that group. Stereotypes, which are overgeneralizations about a group or its members that are factually incorrect and inordinately rigid, are a set of beliefs that can accompany the negative feelings associated with prejudice. Traditional approaches consider prejudice, like other attitudes, to be acquired through socialization and supported by the beliefs, attitudes, and values of friends and peer groups (see Jones, 1977). We consider the nature of traditional and contemporary forms of prejudice, particularly racial prejudice, and review a range of techniques that have been demonstrated empirically to reduce prejudice and other forms of intergroup bias. Bias can occur in many forms, and thus it has been assessed by a range of measures. These measures include standardized tests of prejudice toward another social group, stereotypes, evaluations of and feelings about specific group members and about the group in general, support for policies and individual actions benefiting the other group, and interaction and friendship patterns.

In part because of changing norms and the Civil Rights Act and other legislative interventions that made discrimination not simply immoral but also illegal, overt expressions of prejudice have declined significantly over the past 35 years. Contemporary forms of prejudice, however, continue to exist and affect the lives of people in subtle but significant ways (Dovidio & Gaertner, 1998; Gaertner & Dovidio, 1986). The negative feelings and beliefs that underlie contemporary forms of prejudice may be rooted in either individual processes (such as cognitive and motivational biases and socialization) or intergroup processes (such as realistic group conflict or biases associated with the mere categorization of people into in-groups and out-groups). These negative biases may occur spontaneously, automatically, and without full awareness.

Many contemporary approaches to prejudice based on race, ethnicity, or sex acknowledge the persistence of overt, intentional forms of prejudice but also consider the role of these automatic or unconscious processes and the consequent indirect expressions of bias. With respect to the racial prejudice of white Americans toward blacks, for example, in contrast to "old-fashioned" racism, which is blatant, aversive racism represents a subtle, often unintentional, form of bias that characterizes many white Americans who possess strong egalitarian values and who believe that they are nonprejudiced. Aversive racists also possess negative racial feelings and beliefs (which develop through normal socialization or reflect social-categorization biases) that they are unaware of or that they try to dissociate from their nonprejudiced self-images. Because aversive racists consciously endorse egalitarian values, they will not discriminate directly and openly in ways that can be attributed to racism; however, because of their negative feelings, they will discriminate, often unintentionally, when their behavior can be justified on the basis of some factor other than race (e.g., questionable qualifications for a position). Thus aversive racists may regularly engage in discrimination while they maintain self-images of being nonprejudiced. According to symbolic racism theory, a related perspective that has emphasized the role of politically conservative rather than liberal ideology (Sears, 1988), negative feelings toward blacks that whites acquire early in life persist into adulthood but are expressed indirectly and symbolically, in terms of opposition to busing or resistance to preferential treatment, rather than directly or overtly, as in support for segregation.

Contemporary expressions of bias may also reflect a dissociation between cultural stereotypes, which develop through common socialization experiences and because of repeated exposure generally become automatically activated, and individual differences in prejudicial motivations. Although whites both high and low in prejudice may be equally aware of cultural stereotypes and show similar levels of automatic activation, only those low in prejudice make a conscious attempt to prevent those negative stereotypes from influencing their behavior (Devine & Monteith, 1993).

❧ INDIVIDUAL PROCESSES AND PREJUDICE REDUCTION

Attempts to reduce the direct, traditional form of racial prejudice typically involve educational strategies to enhance knowledge and appreciation of other groups (e.g., multicultural education programs), emphasize norms that prejudice is wrong, and involve direct persuasive strategies (e.g., mass media appeals) or indirect attitude-change techniques that make people aware of inconsistencies in their attitudes and behaviors (Stephan & Stephan, 1984). Other techniques are aimed at changing or diluting stereotypes by presenting counter-stereotypic or nonstereotypic information about group members. Providing stereotype-disconfirming information is more effective when the information concerns a broad range of group members who are otherwise typical of their group rather than when the information concerns a sin-

gle person who is not a prototypical representative of the group. In the latter case, people are likely to maintain their overall stereotype of the group while subtyping, with another stereotype, group members who disconfirm the general group stereotype (e.g., black athletes; Hewstone, 1996). The effectiveness of multicultural education programs is supported by the results of controlled intervention programs in the real world; evidence of the effectiveness of attitude- and stereotype-change approaches, and the hypothesized underlying processes, comes largely (but not exclusively) from experimental laboratory research.

Approaches for dealing with the traditional form of prejudice are generally less effective for combating the contemporary forms. With respect to contemporary racism, for example, whites already consciously endorse egalitarian, nonprejudiced views and disavow traditional stereotypes. Instead, indirect strategies that benefit from people's genuine motivation to be nonprejudiced may be more effective for reducing contemporary forms of prejudice. For example, techniques that lead people who possess contemporary prejudices to discover inconsistencies among their self-images, values, and behaviors may arouse feelings of guilt, tension about the inconsistencies, or other negative emotional states that can motivate the development of more favorable racial attitudes and produce more favorable intergroup behaviors (even nonverbal behaviors) several months later. Also, people who consciously endorse nonprejudiced attitudes, but whose behaviors may reflect racial bias, commonly experience feelings of guilt and compunction when they become aware of discrepancies between their potential behavior toward minorities (i.e., what they *would* do) and their personal standards (i.e, what they *should* do) during laboratory interventions. These emotional reactions, in turn, can motivate people to control subsequent spontaneous stereotypical responses and behave more favorably in the future (Devine & Monteith, 1993). People's conscious efforts to suppress stereotypically biased reactions can inhibit even the immediate activation of normally automatic associations, and with sufficient practice, these efforts can eliminate automatic stereotype activation over the long term.

Approaches oriented toward the individual, however, are not the only way to combat contemporary forms of prejudice. Strategies that emphasize intergroup processes, such as intergroup contact and social categorization and identity, are alternative, complementary approaches.

❧ INTERGROUP CONTACT

Real-world interventions, laboratory studies, and survey studies have demonstrated that intergroup contact under specified conditions (including equal status between the groups, cooperative intergroup interactions, opportunities for personal acquaintance, and supportive egalitarian norms) is a powerful technique for reducing intergroup bias and conflict (Pettigrew, 1998). Drawing on these principles cooperative learning and "jigsaw" classroom interventions (Aronson & Patnoe, 1997) are designed to increase interdependence between members of different groups working on a designated problem-solving task and to enhance appreciation for the resources they bring to the task. Cooperation is effective for reducing subsequent intergroup bias when the task is completed successfully, group contributions to solving the problem are seen as different or complementary, and the interaction among participants during the task is friendly, personal, and supportive.

Recent research has attempted to elucidate how the different factors of intergroup contact (e.g., cooperation, personal interaction) operate to reduce bias. Engaging in activities to achieve common, superordinate goals for instance, changes the functional relations between groups from actual or symbolic competition to cooperation. Through psychological processes to restore cognitive balance or reduce inconsistency between actions and attitudes, attitudes toward members of the other group and toward the group as a whole may improve to be consistent with the positive nature of the interaction. Also, the rewarding properties of achieving success may become associated with members of other groups, thereby increasing attraction.

❧ SOCIAL CATEGORIZATION AND IDENTITY

Factors of intergroup contact, such as cooperation, may also reduce bias through reducing the salience of the intergroup boundaries, that is, through *decategorization*. According to this perspective, interaction during intergroup contact can individuate members of the out-group by revealing variability in their opinions (Wilder, 1986) or can produce interactions in which people are seen as unique individuals (personalization), with the exchange of intimate information (Brewer & Miller, 1984). Alternatively, intergroup contact may be structured to maintain but alter the nature of group boundaries, that is, to produce *recategorization*. One recategorization approach involves either creating or increasing the salience of crosscutting group memberships. Making interactants aware that members of another group are also members of one's own group when groups are defined by a different dimension can improve intergroup attitudes (Urban & Miller, 1998). Another recategorization strategy, represented by our own work on the Common In-Group Identity Model, involves interventions to change people's conceptions of groups, so that they think of membership not in terms of several different groups, but in terms of one, more inclusive group (Gaertner, Dovidio, Anastasio, Bachman, & Rust, 1993).

The Common In-Group Identity Model recognizes the central role of social categorization in reducing as well as in creating intergroup bias (Tajfel & Turner, 1979). Specifically, if members of different groups are induced to conceive of themselves more as members of a single, super-ordinate group rather than as members of two separate groups, attitudes toward former out-group members will become more positive through processes involving pro-in-group bias. Thus, changing the basis of categorization from race to an alternative dimension can alter who is a "we" and who is a "they," undermining a contributing force to contemporary forms of racism, such as aversive racism. The development of a superordinate identity does not always require people to abandon their previous group identities; they may possess dual identities, conceiving of themselves as belonging both to the superordinate group and to one of the original two groups included within the new, larger group. The model also recognizes that decategorization (seeing people as separate individuals) can also reduce bias. In contrast, perceptions of the groups as different entities (we/they) maintains and reinforces bias. The Common In-Group Identity Model is presented schematically in Figure 1.

In experiments in the laboratory and in the field, and in surveys in natural settings (a multi-ethnic high school, banking mergers, and blended families), we have found evidence consistent with the Common In-Group Identity Model and hypothesis that intergroup contact can reduce prejudice. Specifically, we have found that key aspects of intergroup contact, such as cooperation, decrease intergroup bias in part through changing cognitive representations of the groups. The development of a common in-group identity also facilitates helping behaviors and self-disclosing interactions that can produce reciprocally positive responses and that can further reduce intergroup prejudices through other mechanisms such as personalization.

Moreover, the development of a common in-group identity does not necessarily require groups to forsake their original identities. Threats to important personal identities or the "positive distinctiveness" of one's group can, in fact, exacerbate intergroup prejudices. The development of a dual identity (two subgroups in one group; see Fig. 1), in which original and superordinate group memberships are simultaneously salient, is explicitly considered in the model. Even when racial or ethnic identity is strong, perceptions of a superordinate connection enhance interracial trust and acceptance. Indeed, the development of a dual identity, in terms of a bicultural or multicultural identity, not only is possible but can contribute to the social adjustment, psychological adaptation, and overall well-being of minority-group members (LaFromboise, Coleman, & Gerton, 1993). Recognizing both different and common group membership, a more complex form of a common in-group identity, may also increase the generalizability of the benefits of intergroup contact for prejudice reduction. The development of a common in-group identity contributes to more positive attitudes toward members of other groups present in the contact situation, whereas recognition of the separate group memberships provides the associative link by which these more positive attitudes may generalize to other members of the groups not directly involved in the contact situation.

Figure 1. *The Common I-Group Identity Model. In this model, elements of an intergroup contact situation (e.g., intergroup independence) influence cognitive representations of the groups as one superordinate group (recategorization), as two sub-groups in one group (recategorization involving a dual identity), as two groups (categorization), or as separate individuals (decategorization). Recategorization and decategorization, in turn, can both reduce cognitive, effective, and behavioral biases, but in different ways. Recategorization reduces bias by extending the benefits of in-group favoritism to former out-group members. Attitudes and behavior toward these former out-group members thus become more favorable, approaching attitudes and behaviors toward in-group members. Decategorization, in contrast, reduces favoritism toward original in-group members as they become perceived as separate individuals rather than members of one's own group.*

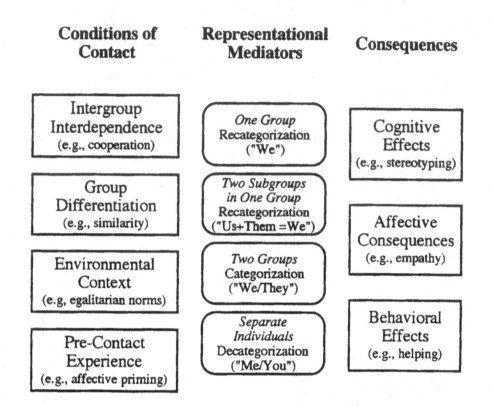

❦ CONCLUSION

Prejudice can occur in its blatant, traditional form, or it may be rooted in unconscious and automatic negative feelings and beliefs that characterize contemporary forms. Whereas the traditional form of prejudice may be combated by using direct techniques involving attitude change and education, addressing contemporary forms requires alternative strategies. Individual-level strategies engage in genuine motivations of people to be nonprejudiced. Intergroup approaches focus on realistic group conflict or the psychological effects of categorizing people into in-groups and out-groups. The benefits of intergroup contact can occur through many routes, such as producing more individuated perceptions of out-group members and more personalized relationships. Intergroup contact can also produce more inclusive, superordinate representations of the groups, which can harness the psychological forces that contribute to intergroup bias and redirect them to improve attitudes toward people who would otherwise be recognized only as out-group members. Understanding the processes involved in the nature and development of prejudice can thus guide, both theoretically and pragmatically, interventions that can effectively reduce both traditional and contemporary forms of prejudice.

RECOMMENDED READING

Brewer, M. B., & Miller, N. (1996). *Intergroup relations.* Pacific Grove, CA: Brooks/Cole.

Brown, R. J. (1995). *Prejudice.* Cambridge, MA: Blackwell.

Hawley, W. D., & Jackson, A. W. (Eds.). (1995). *Toward a common destiny: Improving race and ethnic relations in America.* San Francisco: Jossey-Bass.

Landis, D., & Bhagat, R. S. (Eds.). (1996). *Handbook of intercultural training.* Thousand Oaks, CA: Sage.

Stephan, W. G., & Stephan, C. W. (1996). *Intergroup relations.* Boulder, CO: Westview Press.

❧ Questions

1. Dovidio and Gaertner discuss individual and intergroup processes behind stereotyping and prejudice. Which set of processes should be targeted in order to reduce traditional forms of racism? Why? Which set of processes should be targeted in order to reduce current forms of racism? Why?

2. Thing about groups to which you belong (race, sex, nationality, sexual orientation, sports teams, clubs, fraternities, sororities, etc.). Using these groups, give examples of categorization, decategorization, and recategorization. Which of these three would be most effective at reducing group tensions among these various groups?

3. Dovidio and Gaertner claim that recategorization can change cognitive beliefs, affective consequences, and behavioral effects. If this is true, which one should we reduce to have the greatest impact on lessening prejudice?

4. In a diverse world both within the United States and globally, which technique, individual processes or intergroup process, is more likely to help increase peace? Why?

AGGRESSION

Everybody talks about aggression. We are quick to point out incidents in the news that show just how bad the problem of violence has gotten in our society. But here's a challenge: Take a look at your own behavior. What movies have you seen recently? Were there any violent scenes in them? What TV shows do you watch regularly? Are there any violent scenes in them? What kinds of music do you listen to? What are the lyrics saying? Do you call people names when they make you angry? How often do you joke around by saying things like "I could've died," "I could just kill her," "I hate it when that happens," or "I'll smack you for that." What are your favorite sports? Do you joke around with your friends by punching or hitting them or putting them down with sarcastic remarks?

If you think about it, are you surprised by the amount of aggressive and violent images you expose yourself—and people around you—to in a given day? What impact do you think these images have on us as a society? Why do we act aggressively and become drawn to aggressive images?

ᦉ WHAT IS AGGRESSION?

The definitions of human aggression used by social psychologists vary. However, most would agree with something like, "Aggression is any form of behavior directed toward the goal of harming or injuring another living being who is motivated to avoid such treatment" (Baron & Richardson, 1994, p. 5; Geen, 1998).

Dissenting social psychologists point out that this definition leaves out the intention of the aggressor and whether the aggressive act violates or supports social norms (Taylor, Peplau, & Sears, 2000). Aggressive acts generally are intentional. If pain or injury to another person occurs by accident, psychologists would not label the act as aggression.

Some aggressive acts go along with accepted norms for behavior, such as when people use aggression to defend themselves (Taylor, Peplau, & Sears, 2000). At times, society even officially approves acts of aggression—called *sanctioned aggression*. Examples include behavior required by those in law enforcement and the military in order to do their jobs (Taylor, Peplau, & Sears, 2000). But antisocial aggressive acts that clearly violate social norms—as with criminal acts of violence—create severe problems for society and individuals alike.

Other psychologists have made a distinction between hostile and instrumental aggression. *Hostile aggression* is done with the sole purpose of inflicting pain or injury (Berkowitz, 1983). In *instrumental aggression*, pain or injury is not the immediate goal. Rather, the aggression is used in order to achieve some other goal. For instance, in football, a defensive lineman will do what he can to block his opponent and tackle the ball carrier in order to help his team win (Aronson, Wilson, & Akert, 1999). This is instrumental aggression. However, if he believes that his opponent is "playing dirty," he may purposefully try to hurt him, even if doing so will *not* directly help his team. This is hostile aggression.

☙ IS AGGRESSION INBORN?

Many people wonder whether aggression is somehow part of our nature. These people point to aggressive behavior in other species in order to justify aggression in humans. This reasoning is misguided (Seville statement on violence, 1994). Among human beings, inborn or biologically determined behaviors are not inevitable. Also, "natural" behavior is not necessarily healthier than controlled behavior (e.g., Geen, 1998; Lore & Schultz, 1993).

A recent review of animal research finds that aggressive behavior in animals has evolved because it has survival value. Yet at the same time, animals have also evolved mechanisms to control aggression (Lore & Schultz, 1993). Researchers have concluded that aggression in animals is an *optional* strategy for survival. Whether animals—including humans—act on their aggressive impulses depends on previous experiences and the social situation (Lore & Schultz, 1993).

Instinct. Sigmund Freud (1930) claimed that humans had *Eros*, or life instincts, and *Thanatos*, or death instincts. In his view, death instincts are responsible for aggression. Freud felt that aggressive impulses build up inside us and occasionally need to be released in a safe and controlled manner through *catharsis*. Without this catharsis, aggressive energy "explodes" in unacceptable or dangerous ways. While this aggressive instinct can be controlled, it can never be eliminated. These beliefs led Freud to have a pessimistic outlook toward the idea that international warfare could be prevented (Einstein & Freud, 1933/1964).

The biologist Konrad Lorenz (1976) echoed Freud's concerns. He agreed that humans, like other animals, do have instincts for aggressive behavior, but he also believed that we have instincts for inhibiting aggression. Yet Lorenz feared that through the development and widespread use of weapons, we are arming our "fighting instinct" without similarly arming our "inhibitions instinct."

Today, psychologists know that "naming is not explaining"; that is, imagining an instinct behind a behavior does not explain why the behavior actually occurs (Myers, 1999). In addition, if all humans have aggressive instincts, then why is there such variation in aggressiveness among different cultures? This variation suggests that other mechanisms, such as social or cultural structures, play a larger role than instincts do in human aggression.

Temperament. We know that animals such as pit bulls and fighting cocks can be bred for aggressiveness. What about humans? As it turns out, our temperament, or degree of emotional stability and reactivity, can make us more or less reactive to violent cues and therefore prone to aggressive behavior (Rushton, Fulker, Neale, Nias, & Eysenck, 1986) . Because our temperament is determined by both our genetic makeup and by our nervous system's reactivity, it remains fairly consistent throughout our lives (Kagan, 1989). A child who is impulsive, fearless, and prone to temper-tantrums is thus at risk for violent behavior as an adolescent (American Psychological Association [APA], 1993). By "at risk," we mean that there are other factors involved, such as culture and social context, that may determine whether the adolescent *actually* behaves aggressively. In addition, people can be taught how to manage their reactions so as *not* to act aggressively.

☙ IS AGGRESSION BIOLOGICAL?

While little evidence exists that aggression is inborn, there are, in fact, biological and chemical influences on aggressiveness. However, even these are best viewed as triggers for aggression only under certain circumstances. For example, blood chemistry influences neural sensitivity to aggressive cues in a situation. People who have been drinking *alcohol*, for instance, are more likely to act aggressively, especially when provoked (Taylor & Leonard, 1983). It seems that alcohol lowers inhibitions against aggressive behavior. The hormone *testosterone* (found predominantly in males) is also correlated with violent criminal behavior, aggression, and the apparently universal tendency of men to act more aggressively than women (Geen, 1998). While many people take this as evidence that testosterone *causes* aggressive behavior, the relationship between testosterone and aggression is complex. Some studies, for instance, find that aggressive behavior is *followed* by an increase in testosterone in males. Other studies find that testosterone levels also increase after nonviolent competition and achievement (e.g., playing tennis or winning a lottery). The best conclusion we can draw at this time is that testosterone is related to competition, dominance, and achievement, which in turn are often associated with conflict and aggression (Geen, 1998). Hormonal activity also appears to predict aggression when the social context allows or even encourages aggressive behavior; for example, when people are playing aggressive sports like boxing, or when they belong to a street gang (Geen, 1998). Note that these effects are for males only. Judging from the few studies that have been done, the impact of testosterone and other hormones in females is even less clear (Geen, 1998).

☙ IS AGGRESSION LEARNED?

If aggression is not inborn and not strongly biologically determined, is it learned social behavior? The answer to this question appears to be yes.

Reinforcement. When a behavior is rewarded, we are more likely to repeat that behavior. At a very simple level, people act aggressively because it pays. Children who get what they want from other children through bullying, for example, continue to act aggressively (Patterson, Littman, & Bricker, 1967). Aggressive hockey players score the most goals (McCarthy & Kelly, 1978), and people who riot and protest often get what they want (Dyers, 1999). Even terrorism seems to increase and feed on publicity (Rubin, 1986, in Aronson, Wilson, & Akert, 1999).

Norms. Aggression also varies with culture. In fact, it varies *within* a culture depending on social conditions. For example, the Iroquois Indians lived peacefully in northern New York and southern Canada with surrounding Huron Indians until the arrival of Europeans, which initiated competition over furs for trading (Hunt, 1940).

Today, in the United States, we can find regional differences in aggression. For example, one researcher describes the American South as a "culture of honor," in which people feel the need to use aggression for protection and in response to insults (Nisbett, 1993). This culture probably developed during the early economic and occupational settlement of the south. In one experiment, Southern men were more upset, offended, and primed for aggression than were Northern men by an accidental bump and insult of an experimental confederate.

Social Learning. According to *social learning theory*, we not only learn first-hand that aggression pays, we also learn this lesson by watching others (Bandura, 1997). Family, culture, and the mass media all expose us to aggressive models on a daily basis (Bandura, 1979). From observing others, we learn what to do, and we learn what consequences to expect from our actions. In a classic study, children watched an adult hit a giant inflatable clown named "Bobo" (Bandura, Ross, & Ross, 1961). Later, when the children were frustrated by not being able to play with the toys they wanted, they attacked "Bobo" in the same manner as the adult they had witnessed earlier. They used the same actions and even the same exclamations. Children who did not see the hitting adult stayed calm when faced with the same frustrating experience as the other children. Children most often imitate powerful, important, successful, and liked individuals (Taylor, Peplau, & Sears, 2000).

❧ CAN SOCIAL SITUATIONS PROVOKE AGGRESSION?

By now you may have seen a theme emerge: that aggression can be provoked by the social situation. Here are a few more social situations that are likely to evoke aggression.

Frustration. According to the *frustration-aggression theory*, we are likely to act aggressively when we have been frustrated or prevented from obtaining a goal (Dollard, Doob, Miller, Mowrer, Sears 1939). Frustration—and aggression—intensify when the frustration is unexpected and particularly

unpleasant, and when we are close to achieving the goal (Aronson, Wilson, & Akert, 1999). Frustration doesn't always increase aggression, as more recent research has demonstrated (Berkowitz, 1989). But it does make us feel angry or annoyed—two emotions that can prompt us to attack under the right conditions.

What *are* the conditions that make us act aggressively after a frustrating experience? The size, strength, and availability of the person who frustrated us all play a role (Aronson, Wilson, & Akert, 1999). Clearly, we won't strike out against someone who is much stronger or larger than we are or who is physically unreachable at the moment of our frustration. Second, we are more likely to lash out when the cause of our frustration is incomprehensible, illegitimate, or intentional (Aronson, Wilson, & Akert, 1999); for example, when the car ahead of you at a traffic light doesn't move after the light turns green because the driver is distracted.

People who have come to expect things, like jobs, good housing, safe neighborhoods, and fair pay—but have missed out on these things—may feel particularly frustrated when they see others enjoying such benefits. This is an example of *relative deprivation*. Paradoxically, it is not people who are totally deprived who feel the most frustration, but rather those who do have some nice things and have come to expect more. The most vivid example of this principle are the race riots of the 1960s in America. The violence proved most intense not in the areas of the worst poverty but in areas such as Watts in Los Angeles and Detroit, Michigan. In these regions, conditions were particularly bad for African-Americans relative to whites living in the same areas—and relative to the gains that African-Americans elsewhere had won (Frank, 1978).

Cognitive Neoassociation. Why does frustration, or any aversive condition, lead to aggression? According to the *cognitive neoassociation theory*, unpleasant situations trigger a series of negative thoughts and emotions (Berkowitz, 1989). These thoughts and emotions in turn catalyze a "flight or fight" response. Which response we make (escape the situation or fight) depends on our temperament, prior learning, and other aspects of the situation (Berkowitz, 1993; see Figure 1). However, our thoughts, actions, and emotions are all connected. Therefore, once fleeing or fighting has been activated in our thoughts, actions, or emotions, then the other two become activated as well (Geen, 1998). The bottom line is that once any unpleasant stimulus, such as frustration, temperature, crowding, makes us angry, we are likely to become aggressive (see Table 1).

Aggressive Stimuli. The presence of an object that is associated with aggression can also bring hostile thoughts to mind (Anderson, Anderson, & Deuser, 1996). These thoughts then make it more likely that we will act aggressively. Negative attitudes, unpleasant physical characteristics, incendiary names, and weapons all can bring to mind aggressive thoughts (Franzoi, 2000). For example, names that remind people of bullies or villains (e.g., "Adolf" [Hitler] or

Figure 1 *Cognitive neoassociation theory. According to Leonard Berkowitz, unpleasant stimulation leads to negative feelings and negative thoughts. The negative thoughts follow the negative feelings but can also feed back into increased negative feelings. Other cues in the situation, such as the presence of guns, may tilt these negative thoughts toward the consideration of aggressive behavior.*

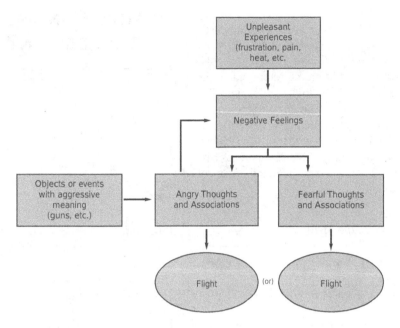

From Kenrick, Neuberg, & Cialdini, 1999, p. 363.

"Arnold" [Schwarzenegger]) may cue aggression (Berkowitz & Geen, 1966).

In particular, the sight of a weapon—whether an actual one or a picture of one—is a powerful aggressive cue (Berkowitz & LePage, 1967; but see also Anderson, Benjamin, & Bartholow, 1998). This is called, simply, the *weapons effect.* Interestingly, countries that ban handguns have lower murder rates (Sloan et al., 1988), and when the District of Columbia in the United States adopted hand-gun restrictions, gun-related murders and suicides dropped 25 percent (Loftin, McDowall, Wiersema, & Cottey, 1991).

Direct Provocation and Reciprocation. Finally, and not surprisingly, we are likely to act aggressively when another person has directly provoked or angered us (Baron, 1988). As we saw with frustrating events, lack of malignant intention on the part of the other person, or extenuating circumstances (such as an accident blocking traffic at an intersection), can avert aggressive behavior (Kremer & Stephens, 1983).

❧ WHAT KINDS OF SITUATIONS MAKE US ANGRY?

Many kinds of unpleasant stimuli other than interpersonal conflict are likely to make us uncomfortable. As we have

seen, according to the cognitive neoassociation theory, discomfort causes us to experience hostile thoughts, angry feelings, and a readiness to act aggressively (Geen, 1998). While many things can make us angry, Table 1 shows stressors that have been specifically linked to aggression.

Table 1 *Stressors Linked to Aggression*

Stressor
Pain
Extremely high temperatures
Extremely low temperatures
High humidity
Crowding
Air pollution
Unpleasant odors

From Aronson, Wilson, & Akert, 1999; Geen, 1998.

❧ AGGRESSION IN THE MEDIA: A TRIGGER FOR ACTUAL BEHAVIOR?

We've seen that people can learn to behave aggressively by watching others. We've also seen that witnessing aggression can cue aggressive thoughts, feelings, or behaviors. You might well be wondering what impact violence on TV, movies, and computer and video games has on us as a society. Considerable evidence collected in over 30 years of laboratory and naturalistic field research supports the idea that watching violence in the media is associated with increased physical and verbal aggression in the viewer (Geen, 1998; but see Friedrich-Cofer & Huston, 1986, and Freedman, 1984, for criticisms of this work). In addition, children and adults prone to aggression are more likely to watch violent TV shows than other kinds of programs (Gunter, 1985; Singer & Singer, 1981, 1986). Children are particularly vulnerable to the effects of watching violence in the media. Those who view a lot of violence end up acting violently as teens and adults (Geen, 1998). Table 2 summarizes the many effects of watching violence in the media.

Table 2 *Watching Violence in the Media . . .*

Increases our arousal: Arousal or minor irritations may then be interpreted as anger.

Weakens our inhibitions: We become more willing to engage in violence.

Primes violence: We experience hostile thoughts, angry feelings, and a readiness to act aggressively.

Models violent actions: We learn new techniques, weapons, and targets of violence.

Desensitizes us to violence: We feel less empathy for victims.

Extinguishes our aversion to violence: We end up enjoying watching violence.

Adapts us to violence: We need to see more to get the same thrill as before.

Defines normative behavior: Violence is seen as acceptable.

Legitimizes violence: Violence is seen as good.

Violent Pornography. What is the effect of watching films that depict sexual violence toward women? So-called slasher or "snuff" films and other kinds of violent pornography are a particularly dangerous form of media. Many studies have shown that viewing explicit sexual material, called erotica, is not harmful in itself (Aronson, Wilson, & Akert, 1999). The real damage comes when sexual material is paired with violence or force. Men who watch such images experience an increase in sexual fantasies involving aggression and a greater acceptance of sexual violence toward women. They also commit more actual violence against women (Donnerstein, 1980; Donnerstein & Berkowitz, 1981; Malamuth, 1986; Malamuth & Briere, 1986; Malamuth, Linz, Heavey, Barnes, & Acker, 1995). Films depicting violence against women also hurt women viewers. After viewing such images, women reported feeling vulnerable and helpless (Reid & Finchilescu, 1995). Given the powerful effects on both men and women, it is ironic that mutually consenting,

sexually explicit movies earn an X-rating but that violent action-adventure movies are typically given the more lenient R-rating.

❧ HOW CAN WE REDUCE AGGRESSION?

Punishment. Studies have shown that mild but swift punishment can stop aggressive behavior in children without legitimizing it. Indeed, mild punishments can induce the child to internalize a value of nonaggression (Aronson & Carlsmith, 1963; Freedman, 1965; Olweus, 1991, 1995). However, severe punishment for violent crimes is an ineffective deterrent. Finally, consistency of punishment works better to deter crime than severity of punishment (Berkowitz, 1993).

Catharsis. Despite Freud's notion that instincts such as aggression must be released, there is no evidence that acting aggressively reduces the need for further aggression (Bushman, Baumeister, & Stack, 1999). Expressing emotions in a productive way in order to gain new insights and self-awareness (such as writing) *does* help the emotion to subside (Pennebaker, 1990). However, watching aggression or playing an aggressive sport like football may actually increase aggression by cueing additional aggressive thoughts, emotions, and behaviors (Russell, 1983). Yet despite the lack of evidence, the notion that "getting it out of your system" will reduce aggression persists.

Similarly, acting aggressively against the source of your anger does not reduce hostility (Geen, Stonner, & Shope, 1975). If anything, it works much as watching aggression or acting aggressively does: It reduces inhibitions and provokes further violence. This is because, to justify the retaliation, the aggressor may blame and degrade the victim. It's easy to act aggressively against someone whom we dislike, and so the violence of retaliation tends to escalate (Aronson, Wilson, & Akert, 1999).

Social Learning Theory. If we learn aggression, can we unlearn it? Apparently, there is some hope for this idea. For example, participants in the studies on the effects of viewing violent pornography were interviewed by the experimenters at the end of the experiment. When the experimenters carefully explained to them that the idea that "women want to be raped" is a myth, participants became *less* accepting of rape than participants who had not seen the violent pornography (Check & Malamuth, 1984; Malamuth & Check, 1984; as cited in Myers, 1999). Similar strengthening of such antiviolent attitudes during post-experiment interviews were found by other researchers (Donnerstein & Berkowitz, 1981, as cited in Myers, 1999).

The most direct evidence that we can unlearn aggression comes from a recent study. Highly aggressive boys went through a training session to counteract the usual effects of

TV violence (e.g., modeling, or believing that violence is normal and legitimate). The boys were taught that the violence they saw on TV is unrealistic and unacceptable, and that one should not behave like the people they saw on TV. After two years of this intervention, boys who received this training were less aggressive than a comparable group of highly aggressive boys who did not receive this training (Huesmann, Eron, Klein, Brice, & Ficher, 1983).

What Can You Do to Reduce Aggression? From our discussion so far about the causes and results of aggression, perhaps you have your own thoughts about how aggression can be reduced in our society. Table 3 lists some excellent ideas (see also APA and the American Academy of Pediatrics, 1995; and Nemecek, 1998).

Table 3 *What You Can Do to Reduce Aggression*

Teach norms against aggression (e.g., "We don't settle disagreements by fighting").

Minimize cues for aggression in the environment (e.g., don't display weapons or other aggressive symbols; repair broken objects; replace graffiti with community murals).

Think critically about what you see in the media.

Minimize situational stressors (e.g., temperature, humidity, noise, crowding) that may make people angry.

Reinterpret a situation before you seek retaliation (e.g., don't immediately assume the person meant harm; think about a possible extenuating circumstance).

Acknowledge your anger and explain why you feel angry, in a calm, nonviolent manner.

Take responsibility for times when you have angered another person, and apologize to diffuse the situation.

Model nonaggressive behavior for others.

Improve your communication skills.

Improve your problem-solving skills.

Build empathy toward others.

From Aronson, Wilson, & Akert, 1999; Smith & Mackie, 1995.

As you can see, there is plenty that we can do as individuals and as a society to reduce aggression. Aggression is not inevitable, nor is it part of our biological heritage. It is a learned behavior that may be fostered or inhibited by the social situation. It is therefore up to us to create a society that is free of violence and raw anger. Reducing aggression is hard work, given the powerful trends toward it in our culture. However, doing so is well worth the effort. Our culture is made up of the individual actions that we each take every day. How can *you* contribute to building an aggression-free society?

REFERENCES

American Psychological Association (1993). *Violence and youth: Psychology's response. Vol. 1: Summary report of the American Psychological Association Commission on Violence and Youth.* Washington, DC: Public Interest Directorate, American Psychological Association.

American Psychological Association and the American Academy on Pediatrics. (1995). *Raising children to resist violence: What you can do.* Washington, DC: American Psychological Association.

Anderson, C. A., Anderson, K. B., & Deuser, W. E. (1996). Examining an affective aggression framework: Weapon and temperature effects on aggressive thoughts, affect, and attitudes. *Personality and Social Psychology Bulletin, 22,* 366–376.

Anderson, C. A., Benjamin, A. J., & Bartholow, B. D. (1998). Does the gun pull the trigger? Automatic priming effects of weapon pictures and weapon names. *Psychological Science, 9,* 308-314.

Aronson. E., & Carlsmith, J. M. (1963). Effect of severity of threat in the devaluation of forbidden behavior. *Journal of Abnormal and Social Psychology, 66,* 584–588.

Aronson, E., Wilson, T. D., & Akert, R. M. (1999). *Social psychology* (3rd ed.). New York: Longman.

Bandura, A. (1979). The social learning perspective: Mechanisms of aggression. In H. Toch (Ed.), *Psychology of crime and criminal justice.* New York: Holt, Rinehart, & Winston.

Bandura, A. (1997). *Self-efficacy: The exercise of control.* New York: Freeman.

Bandura, A., Ross, D., & Ross, S. A. (1961). Transmission of aggression through imitation of aggressive models. *Journal of Abnormal and Social Psychology, 63,* 575–582.

Baron, R. A. (1988). Negative effects of destructive criticism: Impact on conflict, self-efficacy, and task performance. *Journal of Applied Psychology, 73,* 199–207.

Baron, R. A., & Richardson, D. R. (1994). *Human aggression* (2nd ed.). New York: Plenum.

Berkowitz, L. (1983). Aversively simulated aggression. *American Psychologist, 38,* 1135–1144.

Berkowitz, L. (1989). The frustration-aggression hypothesis: An examination and reformulation. *Psychological Bulletin, 106,* 59–73.

Berkowitz, L. (1993). *Aggression: Its causes, consequences, and control.* New York: McGraw-Hill.

Berkowitz, L., & Geen, R. G. (1966). Film violence and the cue properties of available targets. *Journal of Personality and Social Psychology, 3,* 525–530.

Berkowitz, L., & LePage, A. (1967). Weapons as aggression-eliciting stimuli. *Journal of Personality and Social Psychology, 7,* 202–207.

Bushman, B. J., Baumeister, R. F., & Stack, A. D. (1999). Catharsis, aggression, and persuasive influence: Self-fulfilling or self-defeating prophecies? *Journal of Personality and Social Psychology, 76,* 367–376.

Check, J., & Malamuth, N. (1984). Can there be positive effects of participation in pornography experiments? *Journal of Sex Research, 20,* 14–31.

Dollard, J., Doob, L., Miller, N., Mowrer, O. H., Sears, R. R. (1939). *Frustration and aggression.* New Haven, CT: Yale University Press.

Donnerstein, E. (1980). Aggressive erotica and violence against women. *Journal of Personality and Social Psychology, 39,* 269–277.

Donnerstein, E., & Berkowitz, L. (1981). Victim reactions in aggressive erotic films as a factor in violence against women. *Journal of Personality and Social Psychology, 41,* 710–724,

Einstein, A., & Freud, S. (1933/1964). Why war? In the standard edition of the *Complete Psychological Works of Sigmund Freud* (Vol. 22, pp. 197–215). London: Hogarth.

Frank, J. D. (1978). *Psychotherapy and the human predicament: A psychosocial approach.* New York: Schocken Books.

Franzoi, S. L. (2000). *Social psychology* (2nd ed.). New York: McGraw-Hill.

Freedman, J. (1965). Long-term behavioral effects of cognitive dissonance. *Journal of Experimental Social Psychology, 1,* 145–155.

Freedman, J. L. (1984). Effect of television violence on aggressiveness. *Psychological Bulletin, 96,* 227–246.

Freud, S. (1930). *Civilization and its discontents* (J. Riviere, trans.). London: Hogarth.

Friedrich-Cofer, L., & Huston, A. C. (1986). Television violence and aggression: The debate continues. *Psychological Bulletin, 100,* 364–371.

Geen, R. G. (1998). Aggression and antisocial behavior. In D. Gilbert, S. T. Fiske, & G. Lindzey (Eds.), *The handbook of social psychology* (4th ed., Vol. 2, pp. 317–356). New York: McGraw-Hill.

Geen, R. G., Stonner, D., & Shope, G. (1975). The facilitation of aggression by aggression: A study in response inhibition and disinhibition. *Journal of Personality and Social Psychology, 31,* 721–726.

Gunter, B. (1985). Determinants of television viewing preferences. In D. Zillmann & J. Bryant (Eds.), *Selective exposure to communication* (pp. 93–112). Hillsdale, NJ: Elrbaum.

Huesmann, L. R, Eron, L. D, Klein, R., Brice, P., & Fischer, P. (1983). Mitigating the imitation of aggressive behaviors by changing children's attitudes about media violence. *Journal of Personality and Social Psychology, 44,* 899–910.

Hunt, G. T. (1940). *The wars of the Iroquois.* Madison, WI: University of Wisconsin Press.

Kagan, J. (1989). Temperamental contributions to social behavior. *American Psychologist, 44,* 668–674.

Kenrick, D. T., Neuberg, S. L., & Cialdini, R. B. (1999). *Social psychology: Unraveling the mystery.* Needham Heights, MA: Allyn & Bacon.

Kremer, J. F., & Stephens, L. (1983). Attributions and arousal as mediators of mitigation's effect on retaliation. *Journal of Personality and Social Psychology, 45,* 335–343.

Loftin, C., McDowall, D., Wiersema, B, & Cottey, T. J. (1991). Effects of restrictive licensing of handguns on homicide and suicide in the District of Columbia. *New England Journal of Medicine, 325,* 1615–1620.

Lore, R. K., & Schultz, L. A. (1993). Control of human aggression. *American Psychologist, 48,* 16–25.

Lorenz, K. (1976). *On aggression.* New York: Bantam Books.

Malamuth, N. M. (1986). Predictors of naturalistic sexual aggression. *Journal of Personality and Social Psychology, 50,* 953–962.

Malamuth, N. M., Linz, D., Heavey, C. L., Barnes, G., & Acker, M., (1995). Using the confluence model of sexual aggression to predict men's conflict with women: A 10-year follow-up study. *Journal of Personality and Social Psychology, 69,* 353–369.

Malamuth, N. M., & Briere, J. (1986). Sexual violence in the media: Indirect effects on aggression against women. *Journal of Social Issues, 42,* 75–92.

Malamuth, N. M., & Check, J. V. P. (1984). Debriefing effectiveness following exposure to pornographic rape depictions. *Journal of Sex Research, 20,* 1–13.

McCarthy, J. F., & Kelly, B. R. (1978). Aggression, performance variables, and anger self-report in ice hockey players. *Journal of Psychology, 99,* 97–101.

Myers, D. G. (1999). *Social psychology* (6th ed.). Boston: McGraw-Hill.

Namecek, S. (1998, September). Forestalling violence. *Scientific American,* 15–16.

Nisbett, R. E. (1993). Violence and U.S. regional culture. *American Psychologist, 48,* 441–449.

Olweus, D. (1991). Bully/victim problems among school children: Basic facts and effects of a school-based intervention program. In D. Peppler & K. Rubin (Eds.), *The development and treatment of childhood aggression* (pp. 411–448). Hillsdale, NJ: Erlbaum.

Olweus, D. (1995). Bullying or peer abuse at school: Facts and interventions. *Current directions in psychological science, 4,* 196–200.

Patterson, G. R., Littman, R. A., & Bricker, W. (1967). Assertive behavior in children: A step toward a theory of aggression. *Monographs of the Society of Research in Child Development (Serial No. 113), 32,* 5.

Pennebaker, J. W. (1990). *Opening up: The healing powers of confiding in others.* New York: William Morrow.

Reid, P., & Finchilescu, G. (1995). Media violence against women: Its effects on women. *Psychology of Women Quarterly, 19,* 397–411.

Rushton, J. P., Fulker, D. W., Neale, M. C., Nias, D. K. B., & Eysenck, H. J. (1986). Altruism and aggression: The heritability of individual differences. *Journal of Personality and Social Psychology, 50,* 1192–1198.

Russell, G. W. (1983). Psychological issues in sports aggression. In J. H. Goldstein (Ed.), *Sports violence.* New York: Springer-Verlag.

Seville Statement (1994). *American Psychologist, 49,* 845–850.

Singer, J. L., & Singer, D. G. (1981). *Television, imagination, and aggression: A study of preschoolers.* Hillsdale, NJ: Erlbaum.

95

Singer, J. L., & Singer, D. G. (1986). Family experiences and television viewing as predictors of children's imagination, restlessness, and aggression. *Journal of Social Issues, 42*, 107–124.

Sloan, J. H., Kellerman, A. L, Reay, D. T., Ferris, J. A., Koepsell, T., Rivera, F. P., Rice, C., Gray, L., & LoGerfo, J. (1988). Handgun regulations, crime, assaults, and homicide: A tale of two cities. *New England Journal of Medicine, 319*, 1256—1261.

Smith, E. R., & Mackie, D. M. (1995). *Social psychology.* New York: Worth Publishers.

Taylor, S. P., & Leonard, K. E. (1983). Alcohol and human physical aggression. In R. Geen & E. Donnerstein (Eds.), *Aggression: Theoretical and empirical reviews.* New York: Academic Press.

Taylor, S. E., Peplau, L. A., & Sears, D. O. (2000). *Social psychology* (10th ed.). Upper Saddle River, NJ: Prentice-Hall.

SUGGESTED READINGS

American Psychological Association and the American Academy on Pediatrics. (1995). *Raising children to resist violence: What you can do.* Washington, DC: American Psychological Association.

Baron, R. A., & Richardson, D. R. (1994). *Human aggression.* New York: Plenum Press.

Berkowitz, L. (1993). *Aggression: Its causes, consequences, and control.* Philadelphia: Temple University Press.

Björkqvist, K., & Niemelä, P. (1992). *Of mice and women: Aspects of female aggression.* San Diego: Academic Press.

Campbell, A. (1993). *Men, women, and aggression.* New York: Basic Books.

Eron, L. D., Gentry, J. H., & Schlegel. P. (Eds.). (1994). *Reason to hope: A psychosocial perspective on violence and youth.* Washington, DC: American Psychological Association.

Huesmann, L. R. (1994). *Aggressive behavior: Current perspectives.* New York: Plenum Press.

Levinson, D. (1994). *Aggression and conflict: A cross-cultural encyclopedia.* Santa Barbara, CA: ABC-CLIO.

Renfrew, J. W. (1997). *Aggression and its causes: A biopsychosocial approach.* New York: Oxford University Press.

Tavris, C. (1989). *Anger: The misunderstood emotion*

CONFLICT &
PEACEMAKING

Imagine doing your laundry on a Monday night in your apartment or residence hall. You throw your clothes and some soap into a washing machine, turn the dial, and scope out several dryers that —although they're in use now— you think might be available by the time your wash is done. You figure you'll take the opportunity to go for a walk while your laundry is being washed. When you return 45 minutes later, you're annoyed to see that someone has taken up all six dryers—and has not yet returned to remove his or her now dry and cold clothes. You wait five, maybe 10 minutes. Then you decide that you have had enough. After all, you've got other things to do tonight. What do you do? Do you remove the offender's clothes and put yours in one of the dryers? Do you nicely fold the offender's laundry? Do you wait a little longer? Do you think the offender has truly forgotten his or her wash? Or, is the offender a selfish jerk who doesn't care about anyone else? On the other hand, is the offender a sly and lazy manipulator who is hoping that someone will save him or her from the arduous task of laundry folding?

This situation illustrates conflict: a perceived incompatibility of goals (Myers, 1999). In this case, you cannot use the dryers as long as another person's clothing occupies them, so your goals and those of the rude dryer user are incompatible. According to Pruitt (1998), the term *conflict* refers to the opposing actions taken by two or more parties *and* the issue that sparks the disagreement. Thus, conflict can refer to *conflict behaviors* (such as arguments, fights, and wars) and to the causes or *sources of conflict behaviors* (such as disagreement, annoyance, or clashing interests). Pick up any daily newspaper or tune into the first 10 minutes of a news broad-

cast and you will see how serious a problem conflict is in many societies around the world. In this chapter, we explore conflict through several models, or simulations, of social dilemmas. We then take a look at common sources of conflict and possible ways to resolve conflicts.

ॐ MODELING SOCIAL CONFLICTS: SOCIAL DILEMMAS

A social dilemma occurs when two or more parties must choose between self-interest and collective interest (Pruitt, 1998). In the above example, leaving clothes in the dryer too long is convenient for the person who did it, but it is inconvenient for others who want to use the dryer. A decision that favors self-interest is called *defection*; a decision that favors the interest of the group or the collective is called *cooperation*. The dilemma is that if all parties choose self-interest, then the outcome is unpleasant for everybody. However, if all parties choose collective interest and forego self-interest, something interesting happens: In the *short term*, the outcome is worse for specific individuals, but in the *long run*, it benefits everybody. Social dilemmas are thus *mixed-motive* situations. That is, there is both a *divergence* of interests (the individual pitted against the collective) and a *convergence* of interests (mutual cooperation benefits all parties). Because many social problems involve choosing between self-interest and collective interest, the study of social dilemmas through modeling (simulating) can help social psychologists understand how conflicts arise and come to resolution (Pruitt, 1998).

The Trucking Game. In an early attempt to model conflict, researchers designed a simulated trucking game (Deutsch & Krauss, 1960). In the game, two participants maneuvered their "trucks" on a gameboard from a starting point to a finishing point. They each had two possible routes: a long, winding two-lane road, and a short road. However, to use the short route, participants had to take a one-lane road that the other participant shared (see Figure 1). Each participant controlled bridges at either end of this one-lane road, which he or she could open and close at will to block the other participant. Participants were told to earn as many points as possible for themselves by getting from start to finish as quickly as possible. Despite participants' realization that cooperation (taking turns driving over the one-lane road) had the biggest payoff for both, they fought for the exclusive use of the road. In other words, instead of cooperation and mutual gain, participants opted for direct competition with each other. The players would close their gate, blocking the other participant's progress, and then retaliate for the same behavior from their opponent. Competition quickly escalated, dashing all hopes of cooperation. As a result, neither participant scored as high as he might have if cooperation had been the strategy of choice.

Prisoner's Dilemma. A similar decision between self-interest and collective interest is illustrated by the *prisoner's dilemma*:

> "Two criminal suspects are questioned separately by the district attorney. They are jointly guilty; how-

Figure 1 *Subject's road Map*

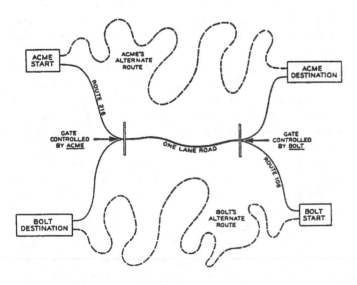

From Deutsch & Krauss, 1960.

ever, the DA has only enough evidence to convict them of a lesser offense. So the DA creates an incentive for each to confess privately: If one confesses and the other doesn't, the DA will grant the confessor immunity (and will use the confession to convict the other of a maximum offense). If both confess, each will receive a moderate sentence. If neither confesses, each will receive a light sentence" (Myers, 1999, p. 517; Rapoport, 1960).

By assigning point values to the different choices and outcomes in this dilemma, we can compare the benefits of each choice (see Table 1). What matters most in this comparison is the *relationship among the outcomes*—i.e. that mutual cooperation (5 points to each suspect) pays off more than mutual competition (2 points to each suspect). (The specific point values are arbitrary and may vary from one version of the game to another. They are chosen by the researcher to model whatever real-life dilemma he or she has in mind.) The dilemma occurs because confessing earns you a sentence but protects you from whatever the other person decides to do. However, defecting (lying about your guilt) may earn you either a maximum sentence or a light sentence, but it also prevents you from gaining the best payoff (immunity) (Dawes, 1991). Many analysts claim that the arms race between the United States and the former Soviet Union poignantly illustrated just this sort of dilemma. Each side chose to build up arms for self-protection—or mutually assured destruction—rather than risk cooperation for the greater collective payoff of world peace (Myers, 1999). Similarly, in a fire emergency, more people will survive if everyone exits the building in an orderly fashion. However, when people panic and try to protect their own self-interests by all running for the exit at the same time, many more people end up dying (Brehm, Kassin, & Fein, 1999).

Table 1 *The Prisoner's Dilemma Payoff Matrix*

		Person B	
		Response I (Defect)	Response II (Cooperate)
Person A	Response I (Defect)	2, **2**	7, **0**
	Response II (Cooperate)	0, **7**	5, **5**

Tragedy of the Commons. A special case of the prisoner's dilemma occurs when two or more parties must share a limited resource. The name of this dilemma derives as follows: Old English towns often had a centrally located pasture (the commons) that all the townspeople could share in grazing their animals. As long as each farmer used the pasture in moderation, then the grass grew back as rapidly as it was eaten and continued to support all of the grazing animals. To see how this works, suppose the commons could sustain the grazing of 100 cows, and there were 100 farmers using it. If each farmer limited himself to one cow, the commons would continue to feed all 100 cows. If one farmer decided to graze *two* cows, he might individually profit without too much hardship to the commons. However, if *each* herder added a cow, then collectively they would overtax—and ultimately destroy—their shared resource (Hardin, 1968).

In this *commons-* or *resource dilemma*, self-interest suggests that each party should take as much as possible. However, if some individuals take too much or if everybody acts on the basis of self-interest, the entire group suffers (Pruitt, 1998). This kind of dilemma crops up in many real-world situations, such as environmental pollution, deforestation, ocean dumping, overfishing, commercial development of wilderness areas (Brehm, Kassin, & Fein, 1999), highway traffic, and even Internet congestion (Myers, 1999).

Public Goods Dilemmas. In resource dilemmas involving public goods, once again self-interest conflicts with the collective good. However, the danger is not that people will *take* too much of a resource from "the commons" but that individuals will not *contribute* enough to the shared resource (Pruitt, 1998). For example, the blood supply, public broadcasting, public schools, libraries, roads, and parks all depend on people giving "their fair share" for the good of all (Brehm, Kassin, & Fein, 1999).

Resolving Social Dilemmas. You can see how important cooperation is—from simply conserving water and electricity in your own home to donating blood or keeping parks clean—in order for all citizens to benefit. What can be done to resolve social dilemmas and foster cooperation? Table 2 lists a few ideas. These suggestions all work by making cooperation for the collective good more appealing than self-interest.

Table 2 *How to Resolve Social Dilemmas*

---

1. Develop regulations (e.g. rules, laws) for the common good.
2. Make the group of resource users small, to increase personal accountability.
3. Foster communication among users to reduce mistrust.
4. Change the payoffs to make cooperation more rewarding than defection.
5. Appeal to users' sense of altruism, social responsibility, and cooperation.

From Gifford & Hine, 1997.

❧ THE ROOTS OF CONFLICT

We have seen that conflict can arise when self-interest is pitted against collective interest. Other factors can spark conflict as well. Some of the most common ones are competition, perceived injustice, and misperceptions.

Competition. According to the *realistic conflict theory*, competition between groups for limited or scarce resources, political power, or social can catalyze conflict (Aronson, Wilson, & Akert, 1999; Jackson, 1993; Levine & Campbell, 1972). Such conflict further spawns prejudice and discrimination, and may even escalate to aggression and violence. For example, in what was called the Robber's Cave study, two groups of boys at a summer camp competed for a trophy and prizes. Their friendly competition through sports and camp activities soon erupted into prejudice and conflict between the groups (Sherif, 1956). Fortunately (as we will see), the researchers figured out how to get matters back in hand.

Perceived Injustice. Similarly, perceived injustice may fuel trouble between groups. Whether we define "justice" as equality (an equal share for each) or equity (a fair share for each), and as based on need or on merit, the feeling that an injustice has been done will likely create conflict. People see injustice when they believe that what they are receiving is not commensurate with what they have contributed (Walster, Walster, & Berscheid, 1978). The result is conflict over perceived "fair share." For example, if you have worked hard for a B in a difficult class and you see somebody who chronically misses class get an A, you will likely feel cheated.

Misperceptions. When parties are in conflict, often there is a small degree of actual incompatibility, accompanied by a large degree of misperception (e.g., Keltner & Robinson, 1996; White, 1996). Put another way, parties who are at odds have distorted images of each other. Interestingly, they often have the *same* distorted images of the other, called *mirror-image perceptions*. That is, people in conflict see the same positive characteristics in themselves and the same negative characteristics in their enemy (Tobin & Eagles, 1992; White, 1996). For example, Catholic and Protestant university students in Northern Ireland were shown videos of a Protestant attack at a Catholic funeral, and a Catholic attack at a Protestant funeral. Each side claimed that the other attacked because they were "bloodthirsty" but that their own side attacked out of self-defense or retaliation (Hunter, Stringer, & Watson, 1991; Myers, 1999). Clearly, mirror-image perceptions only magnify what may have been a manageable conflict.

Alarmingly, even when perceptions are wrong, they tend to be self-confirming, thus instigating a vicious cycle of misinterpretation, mistrust, and threat (Bronfenbrenner, 1961). Table 3 lists some mirror-image perceptions that perpetuated the arms race between the United States and the former Soviet Union (Plous, 1985). Further, misperceptions readily turn into *shifting perceptions*; that is, they intensify as the conflict intensifies and lessens as the conflict lessens (Myers, 1999).

Table 3 *Mirror Image Perceptions that Fed the Arms Race*

Assumption	Sample Statement by the U.S. President	Sample Statement by the Soviet General Secretary
1: "We prefer mutual disarmament.'	"We want more than anything else to join with them in reducing the number of weapons." (*New York Times*, 6/15/84)	"We do not strive . . . for military superiority over them; we want termination, not continuation of the arms race." (*New York Times*, 3/12/85)
2: "We must avoid disarming while the other side arms."	"We refuse to become weaker while potential adversaries remain committed to their imperialist adventures." (*New York Times*, 6/1/82)	"Our country does not seek [nuclear] superiority, but it also will not allow superiority to be gained over it." (*Pravda*, 4/9/84)
3: "Unlike us, the other side aims for military superiority."	"For the [former] Soviet leaders peace is not the real issue; rather, the issue is the attempt to spread their dominance using military power." (*New York Times*, 6/28/84)	"The main obstacle—and the entire course of the Geneva talks is persuasive evidence of this—is the attempts by the U.S. and its allies to achieve military superiority." (*Pravda*, 1/3/84)

Adapted from Plous (1985, 1993)

From Myers, 1999, p. 530. Note: Despite each side claiming that they wanted disarmament, each continued to arm itself based on misperceptions of the other.

❧ THE FOUR C'S OF PEACEMAKING

Can anything be done to resolve a conflict? Research both in the laboratory and in the field suggests that the following four steps can help.

Contact. Parties who are in conflict and who want to resolve the tension must try to have *contact* with each other. But to *lessen* the conflict, such contact must occur in informal and friendly settings where the groups come together as equals (Aronson, Wilson, & Akert, 1999; Myers, 1999). For example, the Robber's Case experiment took place in the relaxed setting of a summer camp for boys (Sherif, 1956). Another study, the "jigsaw classroom" experiment, took place in school without the teacher's direct supervision (Aronson & Bridgeman, 1979).

Cooperation. Mere contact is not enough to resolve conflicts. Both sides also need to come together with the aim of cooperating. In order to do this, both sides should agree on a goal that is more important to each of them than their conflict. Further, in order to achieve this larger goal the conflicting parties must work together (Aronson, Wilson, & Akert, 1999; Myers, 1999).

A threat from an outside source often effectively serves this purpose by uniting the conflicting parties. For example, in many inner-city neighborhoods, black, white, and Hispanic families unite to rid their community of drug dealers and crack houses. There is also an economic collective of Arabs and Jews who make and market food products together for mutual economic gain (Marter, 1995). In the Robber's Cave study, the researchers reduced the conflict by having the boys work together to pull a truck that had broken down during an outing (Sherif, 1956). Similarly, a mutual learning effort, such as in the jigsaw classroom study, can establish higher goals that foster cooperation among people from different backgrounds (Aronson & Bridgeman, 1979).

Communication. Communication and trust are crucial to resolving conflicts *before* they escalate—for once conflicts have reached a flashpoint, communication may only fan the flames (Deutsch, 1973). The first step is for the parties in question to try to understand, and reduce or eliminate, misperceptions (especially self-confirming ones) through communication. Then, each side must present its needs and concerns. Conflicting parties may communicate directly through *bargaining* or *negotiation*. However, when the opposing sides are unable to communicate or do not trust each other, then structured workshops or a third-party mediator may help (e.g., Paul, 1998; Kelman, 1997; Ross & Ward, 1995; Sleek, 1996).

A third-party mediator might play several roles. He or she can *mediate* by facilitating communication and offering suggestions (Pruitt, 1998). Examples of mediators include marriage counselors, labor mediators, and diplomats (Myers, 1999). Mediation may facilitate the negotiation process because it helps each side to feel that it is not caving in to the other's demands (Myers, 1999). Mediation and negotiation work best when the conflict is moderate, the disputants are highly motivated to resolve the conflict, and there is no severe resource shortage involved, no general principle at stake, and no divisiveness *within* any of the parties (Pruitt, 1998).

The next step is to get each side to rethink its demands. In contrast to a win-lose solution, where one side must capitulate to the other, the ideal solution to a conflict is a win-win or *integrative solution,* where each side gets much of what it wants. For example, suppose your roommate likes to listen to rock music on his stereo while you are trying to study. You don't mind quiet music while studying, but rock music just makes it impossible for you to concentrate. You could handle this conflict by establishing "no stereo" quiet hours, or you could just go to the library to study. In both of these solutions, one party has "won" at the expense of the other. However, agreeing on the *kind* of music to play while you are trying to study—like light jazz or Sara McLaughlan—is an integrative solution that gives each of you something you want or find acceptable. To help find an integrative solution, each side should clearly identify its goals and rank-order them. Using these goals, experienced negotiators can then offer mutually beneficial trade-offs of higher goals for lesser goals that will lead to integrative solutions (Thompson, 1990).

Sometimes when the conflict is so difficult or the positions of the disputants are so divergent, disputants may resort to an arbitrator, who will impose a settlement. *Arbitration* occurs when a neutral, outside person studies the conflict and makes recommendations that each side must agree to (Pruitt, 1998). While arbitration guarantees that the combatants will reach a settlement, it is unlikely to produce valuable mutual benefits and compliance by both parties (McEwen & Maiman, 1989). In fact, the threat of arbitration often motivates disputants to try harder to solve their conflicts on their own (McGillicuddy, Welton, & Pruitt, 1987). The danger with arbitration is that, if the conflict seems irreconcilable, both parties may insist on unreasonable offers from the other side. In this way, they try to secure an advantage when the arbitrator seeks a compromise (Pruitt, 1986). In such cases, "final-offer arbitration"—in which each party makes an offer from which the arbitrator chooses—may encourage the disputants to suggest more reasonable solutions (Myers, 1999).

Conciliation. Suppose a conflict has escalated to the point where misperceptions and mistrust are so high that the disputants cannot communicate, much less reconcile their positions. What can be done? A strategy known as GRIT (an acronym for *g*raduated and *r*eciprocated *i*nitiatives in *t*ension *r*eduction) may help to ease tensions (Osgood, 1962). First, one side announces its intent to appease or reconcile with the other side by publicly declaring its intention to enact a conciliatory act. This helps the other side to correctly interpret the act as genuine, and publicly pressures the other side to reciprocate. Next, the first side implements a few easily verifiable conciliatory acts. These are most successful if they are costly or risky, because they demonstrate the sincerity and seriousness behind them (Pruitt, 1998). Finally, while taking conciliatory action, each side retains retaliatory capability in order to avoid being taken unfair advantage of by the other side. The GRIT strategy has been used to resolve conflicts in both the social psychology laboratory and in the real world (Lindskold, 1978; Lindskold, Han, & Betz, 1986; Lindskold & Collins, 1978).

For example, many particularly worrisome conflicts between the United States and the former Soviet Union—including standoffs between President John F. Kennedy and Premier Nikita Khrushchev in the early 1960s (Etzioni, 1967), and between President George Bush and President Mikhail Gorbachev in the early 1990s (Myers, 1999)—were de-escalated by the GRIT strategy. GRIT also helped to reduce tensions between Israel and Egypt in 1975, allowing the reopening of the Suez Canal to Egyptian ships (Rubin, 1981).

Returning to our example of the laundry room dilemma, what would you do about the "dryer hog"? Before you answer, think about a major theme in social psychology—that we often underestimate the impact of the situation on individual behavior. When it comes to conflict and peacemaking, we should also take care not to underestimate our own power to *create* situations. We can choose between defection and cooperation, and between conflict and peace, by our perceptions, our actions, and our *reactions.*

REFERENCES

Aronson, E., & Bridgeman, D. (1979). Jigsaw groups and the desegregated classroom: In pursuit of common goals. *Personality and Social Psychology Bulletin, 5,* 438–446.

Aronson, E., Wilson, T. D., & Akert, R. M. (1999). *Social psychology* (3rd ed.). New York: Longman.

Brehm, S. S., Kassin, S. M., & Fein, S. (1999). *Social psychology* (4th ed.). Boston: Houghton-Mifflin.

Bronfenbrenner, U. (1961). The mirror image in Soviet-American relations. *Journal of Social Issues, 17*(3), 45–56.

Dawes, R. M. (1991). Social dilemmas, economic self-interest, and evolutionary theory. In D. R. Brown & J. E. Keith Smith (Eds.), *Frontiers of mathematical psychology: Essays in honor of Clyde Coombs.* Chicago: University of Chicago Press.

Deutsch, M. (1973). *The resolution of conflict.* New Haven, CT: Yale University Press.

Deutsch, M., & Krauss, R. M. (1960). The effect of threat upon interpersonal bargaining. *Journal of Abnormal and Social Psychology, 61,* 181–189.

Etzioni, A. (1967). The Kennedy experiment. *The Western Political Quarterly, 20,* 361–380.

Gifford, R., & Hine, D. W. (1997). Toward cooperation in commons dilemmas. *Canadian Journal of Behavioural Science, 29,* 167–179.

Hardin, G. (1968). The tragedy of the commons. *Science, 162,* 1243–1248.

Hunter, J. A., Stringer, M., & Watson, R. P. (1991). Intergroup violence and intergroup attributions. *British Journal of Social Psychology, 30,* 261–266.

Jackson, J. W. (1993). Realistic group conflict theory: A review and evaluation of the theoretical and empirical literature. *Psychological Record, 43,* 395–413.

Kelman, H. C. (1997). Group processes in the resolution of international conflicts: Experiences from the Israeli-Palestinian case. *American Psychologist, 52,* 212–220.

Keltner, D., & Robinson, R. J. (1996). Extremism, power, and the imagined biases of social conflict. *Current Directions In Psychological Science, 4,* 101–105.

Levine, R. A., & Campbell, D. T. (1972). *Ethnocentrism: Theories of conflict, ethnic attitudes, and group behavior.* New York: Wiley.

Lindskold, S. (1978). Trust development, the GRIT proposal, and the effects of conciliatory acts on conflict and cooperation. *Psychological Bulletin, 85,* 772–793.

Lindskold, S., Han, G., & Betz, B. (1986). The essential elements of communication in the GRIT strategy. *Personality and Social Psychology Bulletin, 12,* 179–186.

Lindskold, S., & Collins, M. G. (1978). Inducing cooperation by groups and individuals. *Journal of Conflict Resolution, 22,* 679–690.

Marter, M. (1995, March 22). Arabs and Jews join to make a saucy line. *The Philadelphia Inquirer,* pp. E1, E4.

McEwen, C. A., & Maiman, R. J. (1989). Mediation in small claims court: Consensual processes and outcomes. In K. Kressel & D. G. Pruitt (Eds.), *Mediation research* (pp. 53–67). San Francisco: Jossey-Bass.

McGillicuddy, N. B., Welton, G. L., & Pruitt, D. G. (1987). Third-party intervention: A field experiment comparing three different models. *Journal of Personality and Social Psychology, 53,* 104–112.

Myers, D. G. (1999). *Social psychology* (6th ed.). Boston: McGraw-Hill.

Osgood, C. E. (1962). *An alternative to war or surrender.* Urbana, IL: University of Illinois Press.

Paul, M. (1998, July/August). Psychology's own peace corps. *Psychology Today,* 56–60.

Plous, S. (1985). Perceptual illusions and military realities: A social-psychological analysis of the nuclear arms race. *Journal of Conflict Resolution, 29,* 363–389.

Pruitt, D. G. (1998). Social conflict. In D. Gilbert, S. T. Fiske, & G. Lindzey (Eds.), *The handbook of social psychology* (4th ed., Vol. 2, pp. 470–503). New York: McGraw-Hill.

Rapoport, A. (1960). *Fights, games, and debates.* Ann Arbor, MI: University of Michigan Press.

Ross, L., & Ward, A. (1995). Psychological barriers to dispute resolution. In M. P. Zanna (Ed.), *Advances in experimental social psychology* (Vol. 27, pp. 255–304). New York: Academic Press.

Rubin, J. Z. (1981). *Dynamics of third-party interventions: Kissinger in the Middle East.* New York: Praeger.

Sherif, M. (1956, November). Experiments in group conflict. *Scientific American, 195,* 54–58.

Sleek, S. (1996). Psychologists build a culture of peace. *APA Monitor, 27*(1), 1, 33.

Thompson, L. (1990). The influence of experience on negotiation performance. *Journal of Experimental Social Psychology, 26,* 528–544.

Tobin, R. J., & Eagles, M. (1992). U. S. and Canadian attitudes toward international international A cross national test of the double-standard hypothesis. *Basic and Applied Social Psychology, 13,* 447–459.

Walster, E., Walster, G. W., & Berscheid, E. (1978). *Equity: Theory and research.* Boston: Allyn & Bacon.

White, R. K. (1996). Why the Serbs fought: Motives and misperceptions. *Peace and Conflict: Journal of Peace Psychology, 2*(2), 109–128.

SUGGESTED READINGS

Fisher, R. (1989). *The social psychology of intergroup relations and international conflict resolution.* New York: Springer.

Jessup, J. E. (1998). *An encyclopedic dictionary of conflict and conflict resolution, 1945-1996.* Westport, CT: Greenwood Press.

Rubin, J. Z., Pruitt, D. G., & Kim, S. H. (1994). *Social conflict: Escalation, stalemate, and settlement.* New York: McGraw-Hill.

Sandole, D. J. D., & van der Merwe, H. (Eds.). (1993). *Conflict resolution theory and practice: Integration and application*

Attraction & Relationships

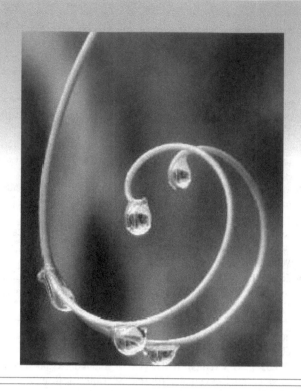

Imagine that you are at a large campus party. You look around the room to find a person to dance with. What kind of person do you look for? Someone who is attractive? Someone with a nice smile? Someone who's laughing and looks like they're having fun?

Suppose you spot someone and dance with him or her. Will the one dance lead to a second dance? How do you know? Now suppose you go to the bar for a cold drink, and the two of you start talking. After a while you decide that you would like to see this person again. What is it about him or her that attracts you? Should you broach the subject of getting together again the following week? What answer are you likely to receive? How do you know?

Is this a person you could marry? Why or why not? Would you marry someone you have only just met? Would you marry someone whom your parents have picked out for you? Why or why not?

This little "thought experiment" gives you a taste of the kinds of questions that social psychologists explore under the topic of attraction and relationships. The basic questions are: What makes us attracted to another person? How do we form intimate relationships and friendships with other people? What is love? What happens when close relationships end?

Table 1 *What Makes Us Attracted to Another Person?*

Aspects of the Situation	Aspects of the Other Person
Familiarity	Similarity
Reciprocal liking	Physical attractiveness

✑ What Makes Someone Attractive?

Social psychologists have studied a number of variables, or antecedents, that lead us to be interested in, curious about, or drawn to others (see Table 1). The predisposition to respond to another person in a positive way—with positive thoughts, feelings, or actions—is called attraction (Berscheid & Reis, 1998). Some variables of attraction—similarity, reciprocity, and physical attractiveness—have to do with the persons involved. Others have to do with the situation—which is in keeping with a major theme of social psychology. These antecedents of attraction explain how we come to initiate interactions with strangers, and they apply to potential romantic relationships as well as friendships.

Familiarity. Much research on attractiveness has demonstrated that we prefer people who are familiar to us (Bornstein, 1989; Harrison, 1977). As a result of this *mere exposure effect* (Zajonc, 1968), we are likely to become attracted to people who live in close *proximity* to us—such as neighbors, roommates, or classmates (Segal, 1974). Even the *anticipation* of a future interaction makes a person just familiar enough to be likable (Darley & Berscheid, 1967). This tendency may stem from a belief that the unfamiliar is possibly harmful (Berscheid & Reis, 1998).

Reciprocal Liking. Remember junior high school, when friends teased you by saying that so-and-so liked you?

Nothing is quite so attractive as another person's attraction for us (Backman & Secord, 1959). Indeed, one of the strongest determinants of whether we will like someone is whether we believe that they like us (Berscheid & Walster, 1978).

However, among married couples, self-esteem also plays a role in reciprocity. In experiments, people with moderate or high self-esteem reciprocated a lab partner's liking for them. By contrast, people with low self-esteem preferred to interact with a person who had criticized them ("She's right; I'm no good at this"), thus verifying their own low opinion of themselves (Swann, Stein-Seroussi, & McNulty, 1992). This preference for a partner who shares one's low opinion of oneself also holds even when the partner is one's own spouse. People with low self-esteem showed as much commitment to their marriages as those with high self-esteem when their spouses' views of them were unfavorable or moderate—again, when their partners' views agreed with their own views. But when a spouse's appraisal was favorable, people with low self-esteem showed a lower commitment to their marriage than people with high self-esteem ("How can she like me; I'm no good for her") (Swann, Hixon, De La Ronde, 1992). Finally, people with low self-esteem would rather have a spouse who shares their negative view of themselves ("He's right; I'm no good"). They reported less marital satisfaction than people with high self-esteem whose partners idealized them. Such idealization ("You're wonderful, honey, I want to make you so happy") no doubt led to a self-fulfilling prophecy, in which spouses with high self-esteem reciprocated their liking for and commitment to each other when they held favorable views of one another (Murray, Holmes, & Griffin, 1996).

Similarity. In addition to familiarity and reciprocity, similarity also fosters liking—whether it's similarity in attractiveness (Berscheid, Dion, Walster, & Walster, 1971), personality traits (Neimeyer & Mitchell, 1988), attitudes (Byrne, 1971), or values (Newcomb, 1961). In addition, people tend to marry others of a similar demographic background, such as in age, race, education, and religion (Qian & Preston, 1993). This tendency toward *homogamy* was first noted almost 90 years ago (Harris, 1912). Clearly, it is more often true that "birds of a feather flock together" than "opposites attract" when it comes to choosing our partners (Boyden, Carroll, & Maier, 1984) *and* our friends (Berscheid & Reis, 1998).

Physical Attractiveness. Think again about finding somebody to dance with at a party. Like most people, you probably imagine trying to find somebody "attractive." To a great extent in our society today, what makes people attractive is more often their looks than their personalities.

For example, a young woman's physical attractiveness is a good predictor of how often she dates (Reis, Nezlek, & Wheeler, 1980). This is not only because people want to be with a physically attractive person but also because we tend to believe that beautiful people have all sorts of other desirable characteristics as well (Dion, Berscheid, & Walster, 1972). Specifically, we tend to believe that attractive people are also happy, extroverted, sexually warm, and responsive, among other things ("What is beautiful is good"). Indeed, people treat attractive people more pleasantly than they do unattractive people. In the process, they actually elicit warm and responsive behaviors—so that the *physical attractiveness stereotype* becomes a self-fulfilling prophecy (Snyder, Tanke, & Berscheid, 1977).

This stereotype is pervasive in American culture (e.g., Eagly, Ashmore, Makhijani, & Longo, 1991). Moreover, its basic elements are shared in both individualistic and collectivistic cultures (Wheeler & Kim, 1997). However, each culture defines "desirable characteristics" differently. For example, in addition to seeing attractive persons as being happy, extroverted, sexually warm, and responsive, Korean college students rated an attractive person as being sensitive, generous, empathetic, and honest. American and Canadian college students rated such a person as also being strong, dominant, and assertive (Wheeler & Kim, 1997).

By now you might be asking yourself, "What about those of us who are not among the beautiful people of this world? Whom will we end up coupled with?" Through the *matching phenomenon*, many people end up marrying someone who is similar to them in physical attractiveness (Berscheid et al., 1971; White, 1980). This phenomenon occurs even among friends: In one study, members of one fraternity matched each other in physical attractiveness (Feingold, 1988). When married couples are not so perfectly matched in physical attractiveness, the less attractive partner usually has other qualities—such as a special talent or a highly successful career—that create an equitable match (Myers, 1999).

But who is physically attractive? Given the consensus in our society on what attractive people are presumed to be like, it should not surprise you that we also tend to agree on what makes a person attractive (Cunningham, Barbee, & Pike, 1990). Women rated men as attractive if they had large eyes, prominent cheekbones, a big smile, and a large chin (Cunningham, Barbee, & Pike, 1990). Men found photographs of women attractive if they too had large eyes, prominent cheekbones, and a large smile. However, men also found a small nose, small chin, narrow cheeks, high eyebrows, and large pupils particularly attractive in women (Cunningham, Barbee, & Pike, 1990). These same qualities of women's faces are also considered attractive among Asian and Hispanic men (Cunningham, Roberts, Barbee, Druen, & Wu, 1995). Men and women both appear to find the "babyface" quality of large eyes attractive. However, they also found the more mature quality of prominent cheekbones attractive (Aronson, Wilson, & Akert, 1999). Babyface qualities are thought to be attractive because of the feelings of warmth and nurturance they elicit (McArthur & Berry, 1987).

Other studies have found that common facial features—as opposed to unusual ones—in both men and women are viewed as attractive. This suggests that attractiveness is not so much a result of uniqueness than of averageness. For example, people of average stature, as opposed to too short or too tall, are rated as attractive (Beck, Ward-Hull, & McLear, 1976; Graziano, Brothen, & Berscheid, 1978). Similarly, computer-generated composite photographs that average facial features (such as size of eyes, length of nose, width of eyes, and size of forehead) are seen as more attractive than the real faces that went into the composite (Langlois & Roggman, 1990; Langlois, Roggman, & Musselman, 1994). Perhaps "averageness" is just another way in which people show their preference for familiarity (Aronson, Wilson, & Akert, 1999).

Despite the strong relationship between physical attractiveness and attraction, there is no reason to bemoan your own looks. First, a person's attractiveness at age 17 is a poor predictor of his or her attractiveness at ages 30 and 50 (Zebrowitz et al., 1993). Second, not only do we perceive attractive people as likable, but we also perceive people we like as more attractive (Gross & Crofton, 1977). So, if you can get someone to like you, then he or she will probably think you're attractive! Third, we also perceive people who are similar to us as attractive (Klentz, Beaman, Mapelli, & Ullrich, 1987). Finally, if you want a quick way to make yourself look instantly appealing . . . just smile (Reis et al., 1980)!

❦ FORMING A RELATIONSHIP

How do we form relationships with other people? The defining quality of a close relationship seems to be mutual influence (Berscheid & Reis, 1998). That is, we say that two people are "involved" when they affect or have an impact on each other.

Social psychologists have identified at least six theories for describing this involvement. Some of these theories focus on the reasons we find certain people attractive (Aronson, Wilson, & Akert, 1999). Others describe how relationships are developed (Berscheid & Reis, 1998) or maintained (Myers, 1999). Yet others stress the features of relationships (Taylor, Peplau, & Sears, 2000).

Interdependence Theory. One way to think about relationships is to focus on the *mutuality* of the influence. People in relationships strongly influence each others' thoughts, emotions, behaviors, and desires in many different situations, and in a consistent manner over time (Kelley et al., 1983). According to interdependence theory, people in a relationship are highly dependent upon each other—for both positive and negative outcomes (Kelley & Thibaut, 1978; Kelley, 1979). In other words, people will remain in a relationship as long as they continue to get positive outcomes from the relationship and *not* get better outcomes in other relationships. If either one decides that they could do better outside the relationship, then the connection will ultimately dissolve.

Two people involved in a relationship will also coordinate their efforts in order to ensure that the relationship is rewarding for each of them. Over time, they will each shift from an individualistic "I" orientation to a mutual "we" orientation (Borden & Levinger, 1991; Aron, Aron, & Smollan, 1992). Further, such couples may come to internalize each others' values, preferences, and interests. In this way, the couple as a whole enjoy greater positive outcomes.

Social Exchange. The transformation in a relationship from an individualistic mentality to a "team" mentality has been described by social exchange theory (Clark & Mills, 1979). According to this theory, there are two kinds of relationships: exchange and communal. In an *exchange* relationship, people give benefits to another with the expectation that these will be repaid in the near future. This businesslike quality of exchanges is found in relationships between strangers or casual acquaintances. With friends or family, our relationships are typically more *communal*. That is, we provide benefits to others to show our caring for them—without expecting repayment. Put another way, we feel personal responsibility for taking care of the needs of loved ones.

Equity Theory. According to equity theory, people are happiest in relationships when the rewards and costs they experience are roughly equivalent to what they put into the relationship (Walster, Walster, & Berscheid, 1978). That is, people may put a lot of time and energy into the relationship, and may incur a lot of emotional or monetary costs—but as long as they get equitable rewards or benefits back, they may be quite content. Equitable relationships are the most stable and happy.

Inequitable relationships are those in which one person feels that they are receiving either too many benefits *or* not enough benefits relative to what they invest in the relationship. Not surprisingly, underbenefited partners report less satisfaction with the relationship (VanYperen & Buunk, 1990). In inequitable relationships, people will take action to restore the balance, either by restoring actual equity (such as giving or withholding attention) or by using cognitive strategies (such as denial or rationalization) to restore psychological equity (Hatfield, Traupmann, Spercher, Utne, & Hay, 1985). As you might guess by having learned about social exchange theory, equity concerns are most likely to emerge in the early stages of a relationship (Cate, Lloyd, & Long, 1988) and may not apply at all in close relationships (Berscheid & Reis, 1998).

Adult Romantic Attachment. Close relationships are also marked by feelings of attachment or bonding (Bowlby, 1969). By our very nature, we need to connect with other people (e.g., Hill, 1987). Without such connections with others, we feel lonely and depressed (e.g., Cutrona, 1982).

Early research on attachment theory in infancy found that infants show varying degrees of attachment to their mothers, ranging from secure to avoidant to anxious or ambivalent (Ainsworth, Blehar, Waters, & Wall, 1978). As it turns out, the kinds of bonds we experienced with a parent or caregiver as an infant predispose us to form similar bonds in our adult love relationships (Hazan & Shaver, 1987; Collins & Read, 1990). Adults with a *secure attachment style* report that they readily trust others, connect easily with others, and have satisfying love relationships. Adults with an *avoidant attachment style* report that they have trouble trusting others, are uncomfortable becoming close to others, and have less satisfying love relationships. Adults with an *anxious attachment style* become preoccupied or obsessed with their partners. They report that they are not as close with their partners as they would like to be, and are less satisfied in their relationships than people from the other attachment styles (Hazan & Shaver, 1987).

Adults with a secure style also reported having the most enduring long-term relationships. Those with an anxious style reported the shortest, and those with an avoidant style were most likely to report never having been in love (Feeney & Noller, 1990). In such studies, people's recollections of their attachment history are correlated with their choice of romantic partner and the outcome of the relationship (Collins & Read, 1990).

Finally, adult attachment style also influences how a person supports or "leans on" a loved one during times of distress (Simpson, Rholes, & Nelligan, 1992). Specifically, a secure person will tend to seek out the company and aid of others, while avoidants are more likely to go it alone.

Self-Disclosure. An important part of any close relationship—whether with friends, family, or romantic partners—is the sharing of information and feelings. Relationships develop and strengthen as the people involved reveal more and more about themselves. Self-disclosure increases—both in the range of topics disclosed and the depth of feelings shared—as partners become better acquainted (Altman & Taylor, 1973). The greatest amount of self-disclosure occurs in the most intimate of relationships (Hornstein & Truesdell, 1988) and tends to plateau at a high level as early as six weeks after the start of the relationship (Hays, 1984, 1985).

Self-disclosure is generally reciprocated, especially at the beginning of relationships (Altman & Taylor, 1973). But after the partners have established a bond, the need to reciprocate every instance of self-disclosure lessens (Derlega, Wilson, & Chaikin, 1976). In general, women self-disclose more than men, and both men and women disclose more with other women (Derlega, Metts, Petronio, & Margulis, 1993).

Intimacy. The sharing of personal information is crucial to the development and maintenance of close relationships, but it is not enough to create *intimacy*. True intimacy emerges when both partners feel understood, validated, and cared for as a result of the interactions between them (Reis & Shaver, 1988). An intimate interaction involves three major steps.

First, one person expresses personal feelings or information—either verbally or nonverbally or both. Second, the other person responds in a warm, caring, concerned, sympathetic way that indicates that he or she understands the first person's thoughts and feelings. Finally, the first person senses and appreciates the other person's caring and understanding and feels connected and close. In a relationship, intimacy builds and deepens as a result of many such interactions (Reis & Shaver, 1988; see Table 2). Intimacy in turn builds trust between partners and fosters relationship satisfaction (Reis & Berscheid, 1998).

Table 2 *How Partners Form Relationships*

The partners interact with each other more frequently and for longer periods of time in an increasing variety of settings.
The two individuals increasingly seek out each other's company.
They open up to each other more and more, disclosing secrets and sharing physical intimacies. They are more willing to share both positive and negative feelings, and they are more apt to offer criticism as well as praise.
Their goals for the relationship become compatible, and they show greater similarity in their reactions to situations.
They begin to sense that their own psychological well-being is tied to the success of the relationship, and view their bond as unique, precious, and irreplaceable.
They begin to act as a couple, rather than as two separate individuals.

From Feldman, 1998, p. 232.

❧ WHAT IS LOVE?

Social psychologists define and describe love in many ways. Here, we review five of the most common meanings. These views all have two assumptions in common: (1) There are various *kinds* of love and (2) the most important difference between love for friends and family and love for a romantic partner is passion. Yet, despite the vast amount of research on love, the reasons *why* we feel intense passion or romantic love for a special person remain a mystery. It seems that love is qualitatively different from liking (Berscheid & Walster, 1974). In fact, as researchers have discovered, attraction and liking typically lead to more liking—not necessarily to passionate or romantic love (Berscheid & Reis, 1998).

Love as an Attitude. According to Rubin (1970, 1973), love is an attitude. If this is so, then we should be able to identify the "ABC's"—affect (feelings), behavior, and cognitions (thoughts)—of love (Breckler, 1984).

Affect. Maybe you know how love feels: Your heart skips a beat; you feel as though you are floating on a cloud; you become giddy and carefree; and you want to run, jump, and scream. You might even experience cold hands, "butterflies in the stomach," or a tingling sensation up and down your spine. In one study, college students reported that they feel all of these things—what we might classify as emotional experiences—when they are in love (Kanin, Davidson, & Scheck, 1970).

Table 3 *Behaviors of Love*

---

1. Saying "I love you" and making other verbal statements of affection.
2. Physically expressing love, such as through hugging or kissing.
3. Engaging in verbal self-disclosure.
4. Nonverbally communicating feelings such as happiness and relaxation when the loved one is present.
5. Giving presents or doing tasks to help the beloved.
6. Showing interest in the loved one's activities, respecting his or her opinions, or giving encouragement.
7. Showing a willingness to tolerate the other person and to make sacrifices to maintain the relationship.

From Swensen, 1972, as cited in Taylor, Peplau, & Sears, 2000, p. 251–252.

Behaviors. When you love someone, you want to show them how much you care for them though your actions (see Table 3). People who are in love will verbally state their feelings to their loved one, physically express that love, share intimate thoughts, communicate nonverbally, give presents, be helpful, show interest, and make sacrifices for the relationship (Swensen, 1972, as cited in Taylor, Pelau, & Sears, 2000). Of course, we engage in some of these behaviors in caring relationships with friends and family members, too.

Cognitions. Rubin (1970, 1973) identified three themes in people's thoughts about love: attachment, caring, and trust. People in love are aware of their own longing and need for the other person. They also report that they would do almost anything for their loved one, and that they would readily share their intimate thoughts and feelings with him or her.

Passionate and Companionate Love. According to some social psychologists there are two kinds of love: passionate and companionate (Berscheid & Walster, 1978; Hatfield, 1988). When we say that we are "in love" with someone, that is *passionate love* (Meyers & Berscheid, 1997). Passionate love is just that—feelings of great passion or intense emotion for the other person. In passionate love, we feel an intense longing for and physiological arousal in response to the other person (Tennov, 1979). When this love is reciprocated, we

feel fulfillment and ecstasy; when it is not, we suffer despair and depression (Hatfield, 1988). Interestingly, different cultures place varying emphasis on the importance of passion. Typically, young people in Western cultures could not imagine marrying somebody with whom they were not passionately in love. Yet arranged marriages, which initially are lacking in such passion but which often prove successful, are the rule in other parts of the world (e.g., Narayan, 1998).

Companionate love is marked by intimacy, affection, and deep caring for another person, without feelings of passion or arousal. Companionate love develops in nonsexual relationships, such as in friendships, or in an enduring romantic relationship in which original passion has cooled. If passionate love is an all-encompassing burning fire, then companionate love is like the smoldering embers that remain and provide warmth long after the flames die down. In relationships in which the intense emotional passion wanes, solid companionate love often replaces it. Companionate love can be just as strong as passionate love. However, it feels less volatile and more stable (Hatfield, 1988).

The Triangular Theory of Love. According to Sternberg (1986; 1988), love is like a triangle consisting of three points: intimacy, passion, and commitment. Intimacy is the feeling of connectedness between the members of a couple. Passion refers to the arousal, sexual attraction, or intense emotions shared by the couple. Commitment involves both the short-term decision to love the other person and the long-term decision to stay together as a couple. The strength of each of the three parts determines the size and shape of the overall "triangle." As a result, love can come in a number of forms. For example, *consummate love* has all three components. *Passionate love*, described above, consists of passion only, without commitment or intimacy. *Companionate love* has intimacy and commitment, without passion (see Figure 1). In addition, the mix and relative strength of these components can vary over the course of a relationship (Sternberg, 1986).

Figure 1 *According to Sternberg (1986), different types of love reflect different combinations of intimacy, passion, and commitment.*

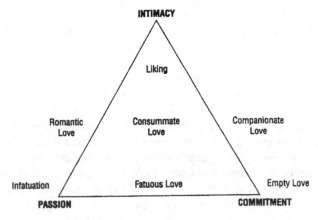

From Taylor, Peplau, & Sears, 2000.

Love Styles. According to some researchers, there are six styles of loving, each of which depends on a lover's goals and aspirations for the relationship (Hendrick & Hendrick, 1986; Lee, 1977; see Table 4). This view likens love styles to the primary and secondary colors of an artist's palette—these six can be blended into entirely new kinds of love (Lee, 1977). In studies, couples in longstanding romantic relationships were more likely to show similarity in their love styles (Hendrick, Hendrick, & Adler, 1988).

Table 4 *Six Love Styles*

Style	Description
Eros	Passionate love
Ludus	Game-Playing love
Storge	Friendship love
Pragma	Practical love
Mania	Possessive love
Agape	Selfless love

From Lee, 1977.

⌇ WHEN RELATIONSHIPS END

Some demographers estimate that 50–66 percent of current first marriages are likely to end in divorce (Berscheid & Reis, 1998). Why some relationships weather conflicts and others dissolve has become a compelling question for social psychologists. Similarly, as we have come to realize the role of relationships in maintaining health and increasing well-being (Berscheid & Reis, 1998), the impact of losing a spouse through death has also become a topic of concern.

Dissatisfaction and Conflict. Satisfied couples generally remain together (Berscheid & Reis, 1998). If dissatisfaction does arise, there are a number of typical reasons (see Table 5). When a conflict occurs, a couple's level of commitment is a good predictor of whether the two will stay together (Rusbult, 1983). Individuals in highly committed relationships tend to overlook their partner's flaws, communicate about their needs, and even change their own behavior in order to help the relationship (Rusbult, Verette, Whitney,

Slovik, & Lipkus, 1991). They also give their partners the benefit of the doubt rather than blame them for problems (Fletcher & Fincham, 1991).

Indeed, a couple can diffuse conflict by engaging in relationship-maintenance activities, such as talking about their feelings, especially in the early stages of a relationship (Cate & Lloyd, 1992; Edwards, 1995). However, many couples in conflict spend less time on such activities. As a result, their love for their partner and commitment to the relationship erode (Cate & Lloyd, 1988). They also begin to blame their partners for problems (Bradbury & Fincham, 1990).

Table 5 *Why Couples Break Up*

Reason for Breakup	Females	Males
Desire for increased autonomy	44%	27%
Dissimilarity	32%	27%
Lack of support	33%	19%
Lack of openness and intimacy	31%	8%
Absence of romance or passion	3%	19%

From Baxter, 1986.

In 115 studies of 45,000 couples, it was shown that unhappy couples consistently disagree, criticize, command, and put each other down, while happy couples more often agree, approve of one another, assent to each other's requests, and laugh together (Myers, 1999). All marriages experience conflicts. The difference between happy and unhappy marriages is that couples in successful marriages are able to reconcile differences, show more affection, and generally have more positive than negative interactions (Gottman, 1994).

When relationship dissatisfaction rears its head, couples can react passively or actively, and in constructive or destructive ways (Rusbult, Yovetick, & Verette, 1996). Troubled couples may show any of the four kinds of behaviors listed in Table 6. Committed couples are more likely to act in one of the two constructive ways. For example, one member of the couple might try to *voice* his or her concerns by talking to the other person, or by attempting to change. Or the couple can decide to go into therapy together. A couple might also try to wait until things improve (*loyalty*). They might be supportive instead of fighting, hold on until a stressful situation at work changes, or pray. Partners can also choose to act in a destructive way and *neglect* the relationship by refusing to deal with

Table 6 *Reactions to Relationship Conflict*

	Active	Passive
Constructive	Voice: Try to improve conditions	Loyalty: Wait for improvement
Destructive	Exit: Harm the partner or terminate the relationship	Neglect: Allow conditions to deteriorate

From Rusbult, Yovetick, & Verette, 1996.

the problem, spending less time with the other person, or investing meager time or energy in the relationship. Perhaps the most destructive thing that any partner can do is to *exit* the relationship by harming the other person, threatening to break up, or actually leaving.

Research has found that when one member of a couple acts destructively, the other partner tends to accommodate by acting in a constructive way (Rusbult, Yovetich, & Verette, 1996). Indeed, committed couples are more likely to both act and react in constructive ways (Rusbalt et al., 1991). However, when both members of a couple act destructively, the relationship often ends (Rusbult, Johnson, & Morrow, 1986), usually after a series of stages (see Figure 2).

Figure 2 *The Stages of Relationship Dissolution*

Intrapsychic Phase:

Personal focus on partner's behavior
Assessing adequacy of partner's behavior
Consider negative aspects of the relationship
Assess positive aspects of alternate relationships

Dyadic Phase:

Confront partner
Negotiate with partner
Decide whether to attempt to repair, redefine, or terminate relationship

Social Phase:

Negotiate postdissolution state with partner
Create public face-saving-blame-placing accounts
Consider effects on other social relationships
Obtain counseling, legal aid

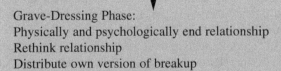

Grave-Dressing Phase:
Physically and psychologically end relationship
Rethink relationship
Distribute own version of breakup

Source: Based on Duck, 1984, p. 16
From Feldman, 1998, p. 255.

Bereavement. The death of a spouse, as with the death of any significant other, engenders profound feelings of loss, sadness, and depression, and disrupts normal behavior and thoughts (Schuchter & Zisook, 1993). The process of bereavement, or coping with the death of a spouse, typically takes two to three years (Stroebe & Stroebe, 1987, 1993).

Psychological distress and physical problems are the worst during the first six months but improve in 12 to 18 months. The surviving spouse faces an increased risk of mortality in the first few months that gradually returns to average by two to three years (Stroebe & Stroebe, 1987, 1993). By 10 years after the death, nearly all surviving spouses have returned to regular psychological functioning (McCrae & Costa, 1993).

Other studies have found that depression is not an inevitable outcome of a spouse's death and that people tend to cope in their own ways with the loss of a loved one. Some may not show distress (Wortman & Silver, 1987). In fact, one study found that 25 percent of widows and widowers experienced personal growth within their first year (Yalom & Lieberman, 1991). However, bereavement is generally more difficult for men than for women, for younger than for older spouses, and when the death is sudden rather than expected (Stroebe & Stroebe, 1983, 1993).

Unrequited Love. Despite "fairy-tale romances" where the prince woos and wins the beautiful princesses, unrequited (or unreciprocated) love is another example of how love can go wrong—before it even begins. As studies of this phenomenon show, this form of love is far from romantic and exciting and is, in fact, doomed from the start. In unrequited love, initial miscommunication and conflict escalate and eventually destroy the relationship.

There are three conditions under which people might find that they love another person who does not love them back (Baumeister & Wotman, 1992). First, there may be a mismatch in attractiveness, in which one person falls for someone far more attractive (in looks, education, or status) than they are. Second, unrequited love happens between two friends when one wants to be "more than friends" but the other wishes to stay "just friends." Third, people may pursue impossible relationships or "fatal attractions" as a result of pathologies, such as ambivalence about intimacy.

An interesting analysis of unrequited love recently characterized the situation for the would-be lover as a "high stakes gamble," in which there is nothing to lose. As the English author William Makepeace Thackeray wrote, "It is best to love wisely, no doubt: But to love foolishly is better than not to be able to love at all" (Baumeister & Wotman, 1992; Baumeister, Wotman, & Stillwell, 1993). The rejector, however, is put in a no-win situation. He or she is forced either to outright spurn the advances of the would-be lover or to play along, which merely prolongs the inevitable pain if the would-be lover's feeling are never returned.

Unrequited love is thus painful for both parties. Each person is trying to be subtle about their attraction or their rejection, so as not to hurt the other person. The situation is therefore ripe for miscommunication and misinterpretation (Baumeister & Wotman, 1992; Baumeister, Wotman, & Stillwell, 1993). The would-be lover tends to believe that the attraction is mutual, that he or she has been led on, and that the rejection was false or not communicated clearly.

Rejectors, who often have done nothing wrong, feel intense guilt. They may also view the would-be lover as intrusive, annoying, unreasonable, and self-deceiving. Even months or years later, the rejector often still feels more pain over spurning someone's love than the would-be lover feels over being spurned (Baumeister & Wotman, 1992). Still, after being rejected, spurned lovers often construct a story that helps them rebuild their self-esteem ("She really loved me. Her parents made her reject me"). Rejectors, for their part, construct a story that reduces the guilt they feel ("I tried, but he just wouldn't take no for an answer") (Baumeister & Wotman, 1992; Baumeister, Wotman, & Stillwell, 1993).

Unrequited love illustrates two important aspects of love and close relationships: A true, healthy relationship is mutual, and clear communication is essential in every kind of relationship.

ஒ

So let's say you *did* find someone to dance with at that campus party. The two of you may end up as friends, as lovers, or perhaps even as a contented old married couple someday. Regardless of the *kind* of relationship involved, our healthy connections with others all start with the basic principles of attraction—and they thrive and endure through sharing, trust, communication, and loving attention.

REFERENCES

Ainsworth, M. D. S., Blehar, M. C., Waters, E., & Wall, S. (1978). *Patterns of attachment: Assessed in the strange situation and at home.* Hillsdale, NJ: Erlbaum.

Altman, I., & Taylor, D. A. (1973). *Social penetration: The development of interpersonal relationships.* New York: Holt, Rinehart, & Winston.

Aron, A., Aron, E. N., & Smollan, D. (1992). Inclusion of other in the self scale and the structure of interpersonal closeness. *Journal of Personality and Social Psychology, 63,* 596–612.

Aronson, E., Wilson, T. D., & Akert, R. M. (1999). *Social psychology* (3rd ed.). New York: Longman.

Backman, C. W., & Secord, P. F. (1959). The effect of perceived liking on interpersonal attraction. *Human Relations, 12,* 379–384.

Baumeister, R. F., & Wotman, S. R. (1992). *Breaking hearts: The two sides of unrequited love.* New York: Guilford.

Baumeister, R. F., Wotman, S. R., & Stillwell, A. M. (1993). Unrequited love: On heartbreak, anger, guilt, scriptlessness and humiliation. *Journal of Personality and Social Psychology,* 377-394.

Baxter, L. (1986). Gender differences in the heterosexual relationship rules embedded in break-up accounts. *Journal of Social and Personal Relationships, 3,* 289–306.

Beck, S. B., Ward-Hull, C. I., & McLear, P. M.(1976). Variables related to women's somatic preferences of the male and female body. *Journal of Personality and Social Psychology, 34,* 1200–1210.

Berscheid, E., Dion, K., Walster, E., & Walster, G. W. (1971). Physical attractiveness and dating choice: A test of the matching hypothesis. *Journal of Experimental Social Psychology, 7,* 173–189.

Berscheid, E., & Reis, H. T. (1998). Attraction and close relationships. In D. Gilbert, S. T. Fiske, & G. Lindzey (Eds.), *The handbook of social psychology* (4th ed., Vol. 2., pp. 193–281). New York: McGraw-Hill.

Berscheid, E., & Walster, E. (1974). A little bit about love. In T. L. Huston (Ed.), *Foundations of interpersonal attraction* (pp. 355–381). New York: Academic Press.

Berscheid, E., & Walster, E. (1978). *Interpersonal attraction* (2nd ed.). Reading, MA: Addison-Wesley.

Borden, V. M. H., & Levinger, G. (1991). Interpersonal transformations in intimate relationships. In W. H. Jones & D. Perlman (Eds.), *Advances in personal relationships* (Vol. 2, pp. 35–56). London: Jessica Kingsley.

Bornstein, R. F. (1989). Exposure and affect: Overview and meta-analysis of research, 1968–1987. *Psychological Bulletin, 106,* 265–289.

Bowlby, J. (1969). *Attachment and loss: Vol. 1. Attachment.* New York: Basic Books.

Boyden, T., Carroll, J. S., & Maier, R. A. (1984). Similarity and attraction in homosexual males: The effects of age and masculinity-femininity. *Sex Roles, 10,* 939–948.

Bradbury, T. N., & Fincham, F. D. (1990). Attributions in marriage: Review and critique. *Psychological Bulletin, 107,* 3–33.

Breckler, S. J. (1984). Empirical validation of affect, behavior, and cognition as distinct components of attitude. *Journal of Personality and Social Psychology, 47,* 1191–1205.

Byrne, D. (1971). *The attraction paradigm.* New York: Academic Press.

Cate, R. M., & Lloyd, S. A. (1992). *Courtship.* Newbury Park, CA: Sage.

Cate, R. M., Lloyd, S. A., & Long, E. (1988). The role of rewards and fairness in developing premarital relationships. *Journal of Marriage and the Family, 50,* 443–452.

Clark, M. S., & Mills, J. (1979). Interpersonal attraction in exchange and communal relationships. *Journal of Personality and Social Psychology, 37,* 12–24.

Collins, N. L., & Read, S. J. (1990). Adult attachment, working models, and relationship quality in dating couples. *Journal of Personality and Social Psychology, 58,* 644–663.

Cunningham, M. R., Barbee, A. B., & Pike, C. L. (1990). What do women want? Facialmetric assessment of multiple motives in the perception of male facial physical attractiveness. *Journal of Personality and Social Psychology, 59,* 61–72.

Cunningham, M. R, Roberts, A. R., Barbee, A. B, Druen, P. B, & Wu, C. (1995). "Their ideas of beauty are, on the whole, the same as ours": Consistency and variability in the cross-cultural perception of female physical attractiveness. *Journal of Personality and Social Psychology, 68,* 261–279.

Cutrona, C. (1982). Transition to college: Loneliness and the process of social adjustment. In L. A. Peplau & D. Perlman (Eds.), *Loneliness: A sourcebook of current theory, research, and therapy* (pp. 291–309). New York: Wiley.

Darley, J. M., & Berscheid, E. (1967). Increased liking as a result of the anticipation of personal contact. *Human Relations, 20,* 29–40.

Derlega, V. J., Metts, S., Petronio, S., & Margulis, S. T. (1993). *Self-disclosure*. Newbury Park, CA: Sage.

Derlega, V. J., Wilson, M., & Chaikin, A. L. (1976). Friendship and disclosure reciprocity. *Journal of Personality and Social Psychology, 34*, 578–587.

Dion, K. K., Berscheid, E., & Walster, E. (1972). What is beautiful is good. *Journal of Personality and Social Psychology, 24*, 285–290.

Eagly, A. H., Ashmore, R. D., Makhijani, M. G., & Longo, L. C. (1991). What is beautiful is good, but . . . : A meta-analytic review of research on the physical attractiveness stereotype. *Psychological Bulletin, 110*, 109–128.

Edwards, R. (1995, February). New tools help gauge marital success. *APA Monitor*, 6.

Feeney, J. A., & Noller, P. (1990). Attachment style as a predictor of adult romantic relationships. *Journal of Personality and Social Psychology, 58*, 281–291.

Feingold, A. (1988). Matching for attractiveness in romantic partners and same-sex friends: A meta-analysis and theoretical critique. *Psychological Bulletin, 104*, 226–235.

Feldman, R. S. (1998). *Social psychology* (2nd ed.). Upper Saddle River, NJ: Prentice-Hall.

Fletcher, G. J. O., & Fincham, F. D. (1991). Attribution processes in close relationships. In G. J. O. Fletcher & F. D. Fincham (Eds.), *Cognition and close relationships* (pp. 7–35). Hillsdale, NJ: Erlbaum.

Gottman, J. M. (1994). *What predicts divorce? The relationship between marital processes and marital outcomes*. Hillsdale, NJ: Erlbaum.

Graziano, W., Brothen, T., & Berscheid, E. (1978). Height and attraction: Do men and women see eye-to-eye? *Journal of Personality, 46*, 128–145.

Gross, A. E., & Crofton, C. (1977). What is good is beautiful. *Sociometry, 40*, 85–90.

Harris, J. A. (1912). Assortative mating in man. *Popular Science Monthly, 80*, 476–492.

Harrison, A. A. (1977). Mere exposure. *Advances in Experimental Social Psychology, 10*, 39–83.

Hatfield, E. (1988). Passionate and companionate love. In R. J. Sternberg & M. L. Barnes (Eds.), *The psychology of love* (pp. 191–217). New Haven, CT: Yale University Press.

Hatfield, E., Traupmann, J., Spercher, S., Utne, M., & Hay, J. (1985). Equity in intimate relations: Recent research. In W. Ickes (Ed.), *Compatible and incompatible relationships* (pp. 91–117). New York: Springer.

Hays, R. B. (1984). The development and maintenance of friendship. *Journal of Social and Personal Relationships, 1*, 75–98.

Hays, R. B. (1985). A longitudinal study of friendship development. *Journal of Personality and Social Psychology, 48*, 909–924.

Hazan, C., & Shaver, P. (1987). Romantic love conceptualized as an attachment process. *Journal of Personality and Social Psychology, 52*, 511–524.

Hendrick, C., & Hendrick, S. S. (1986). A theory and method of love. *Journal of Personality and Social Psychology, 50*, 392–402.

Hendrick, S. S., Hendrick, C., & Adler, N. L. (1988). Romantic relationships: Love, satisfaction, and staying together. *Journal of Personality and Social Psychology, 54*, 980–988.

Hill, C. A. (1987). Affiliation motivation: People who need people, but in different ways. *Journal of Personality and Social Psychology, 52*, 1008—1018.

Hornstein, G. A., & Truesdell, S. C. (1988). Development of intimate conversation in close relationships. *Journal of Social and Clinical Psychology, 7*, 49–64.

Kanin, E. J., Davidson, K. R., & Scheck, S. R. (1970). A research note on male-female differentials in the experience of heterosexual love. *Journal of Sex Research, 6*, 64–72.

Kelley, H. H. (1979). *Personal relationships: The structure and processes*. Hillsdale, NJ: Erlbaum.

Kelley, H. H., Berscheid, E., Christensen, A., Harvey, J. H., Huston, T. L., Levinger, G., McClintock, E., Peplau, L. A., & Peterson, D. R. (1983). Analyzing close relationships. In H. H. Kelley, E. Berscheid, A. Christensen, J. H. Harvey, T. L. Huston, G. Levinger, E. McClintock, L. A. Peplau, & D. R. Peterson, (Eds.), *Close relationships* (pp. 20–67). New York: Freeman.

Kelley, H. H., & Thibaut, J. W. (1978). *Interpersonal relations: A theory of interdependence*. New York, Wiley.

Klentz, B., Beaman, A. L., Mapelli, S. D., & Ullrich, J. R. (1987). Perceived physical attractiveness of supporters and nonsupporters of the women's movement: An attitude-similarity-mediated error. *Personality and Social Psychology Bulletin, 13*, 513–523.

Langlois, J. H., & Roggman, L. A. (1990). Attractive faces are only average. *Psychological Science, 1*, 115–121.

Langlois, J. H., Roggman, L. A., & Musselman, L. (1994). What is average and what is not average about attractive faces? *Psychological Science, 5*, 214–220.

Lee, J. A. (1977). A typology of styles of loving. *Personality and Social Psychology Bulletin, 3*, 173–182.

McArthur, L. Z., & Berry, D. S. (1987) Cross-cultural agreement in perceptions of babyfaced adults. *Journal of Cross-Cultural Psychology, 18*, 165–192.

McCrae, R. R., & Costa, P. T., Jr. (1993). Psychological resilience among widowed men and women: A 10-year follow-up of a national sample. In M. S. Stroebe, W. Stroebe, & R. O. Hansson, (Eds.), *Handbook of bereavement: Theory, research, and intervention* (pp. 196–207). Cambridge: Cambridge University Press.

Meyers, S. A., & Berscheid, E. (1997). The language of love: The difference a preposition makes. *Personality and Social Psychology Bulletin, 23*, 347–362.

Murray, S. L, Holmes, J. G., & Griffin, D. W. (1996). The self-fulfilling nature of positive illusions in romantic relationships: Love is not blind but prescient. *Journal of Personality and Social Psychology, 71*, 1155–1180.

Myers, D. G. (1999). *Social psychology* (6th ed.). Boston: McGraw-Hill.

Narayan, S. (1998, January). Lessons from an arranged marriage. *New Woman*, 79–81, 100.

Neimeyer, R. A., & Mitchell, K, A. (1988). Similarity and attraction: A longitudinal study. *Journal of Social and Personal Relationships, 5*, 131–148.

Newcomb, T. M. (1961). *The acquaintance process*. New York: Holt, Rinehart, & Winston.

Qian, Z., & Preston, S. H. (1993). Changes in American marriage, 1972 to 1987: Availability and forces of attraction by age and education. *American Sociological Review, 58*, 482–495.

Reis, H. T., Nezlek, J., & Wheeler, L. (1980). Physical attractiveness in social interaction. *Journal of Personality and Social Psychology, 38*, 604–617.

Reis, H. T., & Shaver, P. (1988). Intimacy as an interpersonal process. In S. W. Duck (Ed.), *Handbook of personal relationships* (pp. 367–389). Chichester, England: Wiley.

Rubin, Z. (1970). Measurement of romantic love. *Journal of Personality and Social Psychology, 16*, 265–273.

Rubin, Z. (1973). *Liking and loving: An invitation to social psychology.* New York: Holt, Rinehart, & Winston.

Rusbult, C. E. (1983). A longitudinal test of the investment model: The development (and deterioration) of satisfaction and commitment in heterosexual involvements. *Journal of Personality and Social Psychology, 45*, 101–117.

Rusbult, C. E., Johnson, D. J., & Morrow, G. D. (1986). Impact of couple patterns of problem solving on distress and nondistress in dating relationships. *Journal of Personality and Social Psychology, 50*, 744–753.

Rusbult, C. E., Verette, J., Whitney, G. A., Slovik, L. F., & Lipkus, I. (1991). Accommodation processes in close relationships: Theory and preliminary empirical evidence. *Journal of Personality and Social Psychology, 60*, 53–78.

Rusbult, C. E., Yovetick, N. A., & Verette, J. (1996). An interdependence analysis of accommodation processes. In G. J. O. Fletcher & J. Fitness (Eds.), *Knowledge structures in close relationships: A social psychological approach* (pp. 63–90). Mahwah, NJ: Erlbaum.

Schuchter, S. R., & Zisook, S. (1993). The course of normal grief. In M. S. Stroebe, W. Stroebe, & R. O. Hansson (Eds.), *Handbook of bereavement: Theory, research, and intervention* (pp. 23–43). Cambridge: Cambridge University Press.

Segal, M. W. (1974). Alphabet and attraction: An unobtrusive measure of the effect of propinquity in a field setting. *Journal of Personality and Social Psychology, 30*, 654–657.

Simpson, J. A., Rholes, W. S., & Nelligan, J. (1992). Support-seeking and support-giving within couples in anxiety-provoking situations: The role of attachment styles. *Journal of Personality and Social Psychology, 62*, 434–446.

Snyder, M., Tanke, E. D., & Berscheid, E. (1977). Social perception and interpersonal behavior: On the self-fulfilling nature of social stereotypes. *Journal of Personality and Social Psychology, 35*, 656–666.

Sternberg, R. J. (1986). A triangular theory of love. *Psychological Review, 93*, 119–135.

Sternberg, R. J. (1988). Triangulating love. In R. J. Sternberg & M. L. Barnes (Eds.), *The psychology of love* (pp. 119–138). New Haven, CT: Yale University Press.

Stroebe, M. S., & Stroebe, W. (1983). Who suffers more? Sex differences in health risk of the widowed. *Psychological Bulletin, 93*, 297–301.

Stroebe, W., & Stroebe, M. S. (1987). *Bereavement and health.* New York: Cambridge University Health.

Stroebe, M. S., & Stroebe, W. (1993). The mortality of bereavement: A review. In M. S. Stroebe, W. Stroebe, & R. O. Hansson (Eds.), *Handbook of bereavement: Theory, research, and intervention* (pp. 175–195). Cambridge: Cambridge University Press.

Swann, W. B., Jr., Hixon, J. G., & De La Ronde, C. (1992). Embracing the bitter "truth": Negative self-concepts and marital commitment. *Psychological Science, 3*, 118–121.

Swann, W. B., Jr., Stein-Seroussi, A., & McNulty, S. E. (1992). Outcasts in a white-lie society. The enigmatic worlds of people with negative self-conceptions. *Journal of Personality and Social Psychology, 62*, 618–624.

Taylor, S. E., Peplau, L. A., & Sears, D. O. (2000). *Social psychology* (10th ed.). Upper Saddle River, NJ: Prentice-Hall.

Tennov, D. (1979). *Love and limmerence: The experience of being in love.* New York: Stein & Day.

VanYperen, N. W., & Buunk, B. P. (1990). A longitudinal study of equity and satisfaction in intimate relationships. *European Journal of Social Psychology, 20*, 287–309.

Walster, E., Walster, G. W., & Berscheid, E. (1978). *Equity: Theory and research.* Boston: Allyn & Bacon.

Wheeler, L., & Kim, Y. (1997). What is beautiful is culturally good: The physical attractiveness stereotype has different content in collectivistic cultures. *Personality and Social Psychology Bulletin, 23*, 795–800.

White, G. L. (1980). Physical attractiveness and courtship progress. *Journal of Personality and Social Psychology, 39*, 660–668.

Wortman, C. P., & Silver, R. C. (1987). Coping with irrevocable loss. In G. R. VandenBos & B. K. Bryant (Eds.), *Cataclysms, crises, and catastrophes: Psychology in action* (pp. 189–235). Washington, DC: American Psychological Association.

Yalom, I., & Lieberman, M. A. (1991). Spousal bereavement and heightened existential awareness. *Psychiatry, 54*, 334–345.

Zajonc, R. B. (1968). Attitudinal effects of mere exposure. *Journal of Personality and Social Psychology Monograph Supplement, 9*, 1–27.

Zebrowitz, L. A, Olson, K., & Hoffman, K. (1993). The stability of babyfaceness and attractiveness across the lifespan. *Journal of Personality and Social Psychology, 64*, 453–466.

SUGGESTED READINGS

Baumeister, R. F., & Wotman, S. R. (1992). *Breaking hearts: The two sides of unrequited love.* New York: Guilford.

Brehm, S. S. (1992). *Intimate relationships* (2nd ed.). New York: McGraw-Hill.

Duck, S. (1991). *Understanding relationships.* New York: Guilford.

Hatfield, E., & Rapson, R. L. (1993). *Love, sex, and intimacy: Their psychology, biology, and history.*

HELPING BEHAVIOR

ॐ

Imagine that you live in an apartment building. Suddenly, you are awakened from a sound sleep by a loud crash and yelling in a nearby room. You can't quite make out the words, but from the tone of the person's voice you deduce that she is very angry. You hear more noise—it sounds like objects being thrown around—and then you hear someone crying. What do you do?

If you are like most people, you would probably try to figure out what's going on. If you ultimately decided that the problem was a drunken guest who got out of control at the end of a party, what would you do? If you thought that it was a fight between a couple, what would you do? If you figured it was a burglar, what would you do? Or, are you the kind of person who by now has rolled over and gone back to sleep? On the other hand, are you already dressed and headed down the hall to investigate the mayhem?

This scenario illustrates the basic questions that social psychologists ask about helping behavior: Why do we help others? When do we help them? What kinds of people are more likely to help others? In this chapter, we explore social psychologists' answers to each of these questions in turn. But first, let's start with the basic distinction between what we call prosocial behavior and altruism.

ॐ WHAT IS ALTRUISM?

Altruism is part of a larger category of prosocial (helping) behaviors—which include comforting, sharing, and cooperating (Batson, 1998). Though some people think of altruism as an extreme form of self-sacrifice in the absence of obvious

rewards, we can more precisely consider it a motive behind people's decision to help others (Batson, 1998). Altruism is thus the opposite of egoism (or acting solely to benefit ourselves). Social psychologists, along with philosophers, theologians, and biologists, disagree among themselves about whether pure altruism exists; that is, whether helping behavior *always* benefits the helper in some way. As we will see, there are many reasons—both altruistic and egoistic—for why we might help others.

ॐ THEORETICAL PERSPECTIVES: Why Do We Help Others?

Social psychologists have been asking this fundamental question ever since the first textbook in the field was published back in 1908 (Batson, 1998). Today, theories abound about why we help others, many of which you may have already learned about (Batson, 1998; see Table 1). These include *social learning theory, norms and roles,* and *principles of equity.* Still other theories view helping as part of a more general *moral or ethical code* of behavior that we develop as we mature from childhood into adulthood (Gilligan, 1982; Kohlberg, 1976; Piaget, 1932).

Sometimes, our interpretation of a situation can lead us to be unwilling to help. According to *attribution theory,* we try to figure out what caused an event. In deciding whether to assist someone, we try to determine why he or she needs our help. We are more likely to help innocent victims, or victims whom we *perceive* as innocent, than people who we believe caused their own misfortunes (Betancourt, 1990; Weiner, 1980).

Other theories about helping are based on the claim that we generally seek to view ourselves "as decent, competent, likable, honorable, human beings"; thus we help others in order to *maintain or improve our self-esteem* (Aronson, Wilson, & Akert, 1999, p. 19). One study showed that when our self-esteem has been threatened, such as after we receive a bad grade, we are more likely to help others (Fultz, Schaller, & Cialdini, 1988).

In addition to these general social psychological theories, other theories explore helping behavior specifically. According to the *genetic determinism model,* we are preprogrammed by natural selection to want our genetic material to survive (Hamilton, 1964). Therefore, we are more likely to help relatives than friends (Burnstein, Crandall, & Kitayama, 1994; Sime, 1983).

Still, people often go out of their way to assist total strangers (e.g., Associated Press, 1998). What theory can explain this? The *empathy-altruism* hypothesis says that when we empathize with others we will help them without calculating what we have to gain (Batson, 1991). True altruism thus comes from empathy, according to this theory.

However, even when we act out of empathy, there are three kinds of benefits that may still come to us: (1) our discomfort at the sight of another's distress is lessened (*the negative-state relief model*), (2) we avoid our own or others' negative judgments about *not* helping, (3) we get recognition (from ourselves and others) for doing what is seen as right (the *empathetic-joy hypothesis*) (Batson, 1998). While proponents of pure altruism claim that these possible benefits do not motivate altruistic behavior, proponents of egoism disagree (see Kohn, 1990, for a brief summary). In the past 20 years, more than 25 experiments have explored this issue (Batson, 1998).

A review of the evidence from psychology, sociology, economics, political science, and biology suggests that although we may gain the benefits cited above when we help others, none are sufficient in themselves to motivate altruistic helping (Batson, 1998; Piliavin & Charng, 1990). That is, even if our empathy has been aroused by someone else's suffering, we are more likely to help in order to alleviate that person's suffering, rather than simply to make ourselves feel better (Batson, et al., 1991; Smith, Keating, & Stotland, 1989). True altruism thus appears to be a very real part of human nature (Batson, 1998; Piliavin & Charng, 1990).

❦ SITUATIONAL INFLUENCES: WHEN DO WE HELP OTHERS?

One late night in 1964, a young woman named Kitty Genovese was returning to her apartment in the Queens section of New York City when she was brutally attacked and murdered. Thirty-eight of her neighbors witnessed the killing and did nothing, not even call the police, to help her (Rosenthal, 1964). At the time, people generally dismissed the tragedy as just another example of human callousness. Had people living in crowded cities become so apathetic, cold, and indifferent to the plight of others (e.g., Levine, Martinez, Brase, & Sorenson, 1994)? Or, was there something about that particular situation—the darkness, the sheer

Table 1 *Social Psychological Theories of Helping*

Theory	Reason for Helping
1. Social Learning	We have learned, through experience or by watching others, that helping is good.
2. Norms and Roles	The norm of reciprocity requires that we should repay in kind what another has done for us.
	The role of social responsibility requires that we help those who are dependent upon us.
3. Social Exchange or Equity	We help in order to minimize our costs and maximize our benefits, or to maintain equitable or fair relationships with others.
4. Moral Reasoning	Our moral sense of justice or caring prompts us to assist others.
5. Attribution Theory	Our interpretation of another's needs makes us more or less willing to be helpful.
6. Esteem Enhancement and Maintenance	Helping makes us feel better about ourselves.
7. Genetic Determinism Model	Helping maximizes the chances that our own genes will endure.
8. Empathy-Altruism Hypothesis	We understand what it feels like to be in need, so we lend a hand.
9. Negative-State Relief Model	We help alleviate the discomfort of watching someone else in distress.
10. Empathetic-Joy Hypothesis	We assist others to make ourselves feel good.

Items 1-6 from Batson, 1998; 7-10 from Baron & Byrne, 2000.

number of witnesses—that actually *prevented* the bystanders from helping?

In an elaborate program of research, two social psychologists discovered that decisions about whether to help are not simple. Rather, people progress through a series of five intermediary questions, which must all be answered affirmatively before they will give assistance (Darley & Latané, 1968; Latané & Darley, 1969; Latané & Darley, 1970; see Figure 1). To complicate matters, these five decisions must be made quickly. Further, the presence of others strongly influences the decision process at each step, remarkably "tipping the scales toward *inaction*" (Batson, 1998, p. 295).

As Figure 1 implies, the more people who witness an emergency, the less likely it is that any one of them will help the victim. This is called *the bystander effect*. One explanation for this is *pluralistic ignorance*. When people are unsure of what is going on in a situation, they look to other people for guidance. Often, it is not clear that a situation is a genuine emergency. As bystanders stop to see what is happening, they may see other bystanders just standing around. Because nobody else is doing anything, newcomers assume that there is nothing wrong. The presence of others who are "just standing around" makes the situation seem like a nonemergency.

But what about Kitty Genovese? Clearly, this was an emergency. Witnesses reported hearing her cries for help and watching the attack from their windows. Investigators later found out that many witnesses mistakenly assumed that somebody else had already called the police. The phenomenon of *diffusion of responsibility* (Darley & Latané, 1968; Latané & Nida, 1981) may also explain why no one did anything in this case. When there are many witnesses to an event, each person feels less personal obligation for helping. Ironically, *nobody* may call for help.

◆ PERSONALITY INFLUENCES: WHO HELPS OTHERS?

Whether a person helps another depends partly on the aspects of the situation outlined above, as well as on the personality of the bystander. Here are several characteristics that make some people more likely than others to help under certain circumstances.

Gender. Because of the way that many societies teach men and women to behave, it should come as no surprise that there is a gender difference in helping behavior. When the situation requires heroic, chivalrous acts, such as rescuing a person from a car wreck, men are more likely than women to help. However, when the situation requires commitment and nurturance, such as helping an elderly neighbor, then women are more likely than men to help. This difference has been documented in numerous studies (Eagly & Crowley, 1986). Further, in one study, women recalled more times in their

Figure 1 *From an Emergency to a Prosocial Response: Five Essential Steps. Latané and Darley conceptualized prosocial behavior as the end point of a series of five steps: five choice points that lead the individual toward or away from making a helpful response. At each step in the process, the yes/no choices (whether conscious or unconscious, rapid or slow) result in either (1) no-so help will not occur; or (2) yes-so there is progress to the following step and toward a prosocial response.*

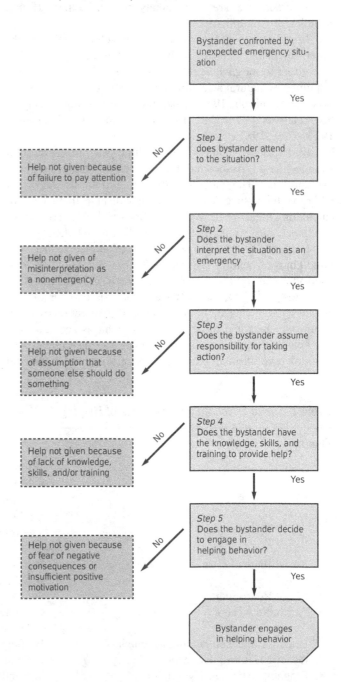

From Baron & Byrne, 2000, p. 400.

recent past when they had helped friends, whereas men recalled more times when they had helped strangers (McGuire, 1994).

Mood. When we are in a good mood, we are more likely to help others than when we are in neutral or bad moods (Isen & Levin, 1972; Salovey, Mayer, & Rosenhan, 1991). This may be because we want to prolong our positive mood by lending a hand, or because when we're feeling good we tend to be more understanding of the plight of others (Aronson, Wilson, & Akert, 1999). In addition, being in a good mood increases our self-awareness. When we are self-aware, we act more in line with our values, which may include helpfulness (Aronson, Wilson, & Akert, 1999).

Yet some researchers have also found that we may be more helpful when we are in a *bad* mood. This can happen particularly if our mood comes from guilt; we help in order to "cancel out" an unsavory deed that we are feeling guilty about (Baumeister, Stillwell, & Heatherton, 1994). We may also be more helpful when in a bad mood in order to make ourselves feel better in general (Salovey, et al., 1991).

Religiosity. Evidence indicates that religious people—those who have faith and regularly attend services or belong to a congregation—give more money, time, thought, and energy toward helping others than people who are not religiously committed (Clary & Snyder, 1991; Omoto, Snyder, & Berghuis, 1993). In particular, religiosity is more predictive of long-term helping than spontaneous helping (Myers, 1999).

Altruistic Personality. Is there a type of person who consistently helps others? Evidence suggests that there is a set of personality characteristics shared by people who risked their own lives to help Jews in Nazi Germany. These so-called rescuers showed empathy toward those in need, belief in a just and fair world, social responsibility to others, a belief that they control what befalls them, and low egocentrism (Oliner & Oliner, 1988).

Rescuers also had a different moral orientation or view of the world than nonrescuers had (Oliner & Oliner, 1988). Those who helped had what's called an *extensive orientation*: They believed it to be their responsibility to help others, even those outside their immediate families. Those people who refused to help Jews had a *constricted orientation*: They gave aid only to a small, exclusive group. In general, people tend to be more helpful to those who are related or close to them (Burnstein, Crandall, & Kitayama, 1994) or who are similar to them in some way (Emswiller, Deaux, & Willits, 1971). Thus it appears that a policy of "brotherly love," whereby we treat *all* people as we would our sister or brother, is the hallmark of the altruistic personality.

The study of helping can certainly expose us to some disturbing events, such as the Kitty Genovese murder and the Holocaust. But perhaps by reading and thinking about the selections in this chapter, you and others will be less likely to fall prey to the bystander effect and more likely to take action in an emergency (Beaman, Barnes, Klentz, & McQuirk, 1978). You may also (if you don't do so already) start reaching out to others beyond your immediate circle of family and friends by volunteering in your community, asking an infirm person if her or she needs your help, or even alerting the police if you hear disturbing noises in a nearby apartment.

REFERENCES

Aronson, E., Wilson, T. D., & Akert, R. M. (1999). *Social psychology* (3rd ed.). New York: Addison-Wesley.

Associated Press (1998, December 16). Grandmothers sit on thief until cops arrive.

Baron, R. A, & Byrne, D. (2000). *Social psychology* (9th ed.). Needham Heights, MA: Allyn & Bacon.

Batson, C. D. (1991). The altruism question: Toward a social-psychological answer. Hillsdale, NJ: Erlbaum.

Batson, C. D. (1998). Altruism and prosocial behavior. In D. Gilbert, S. T. Fiske, & G. Lindzey (Eds.), *The handbook of social psychology* (4th ed., Vol. 2, pp. 282–316). New York: McGraw-Hill.

Batson, C. D., Batson, J. G., Slingsby, J. K., Harrell, K. L., Peekna, H. M., & Todd, R. M. (1991). Empathic joy and the empathy-altruism hypothesis. *Journal of Personality and Social Psychology, 61,* 413–426.

Baumeister, R. F., Stillwell, A. M., & Heatherton, T. F. (1994). Guilt: An interpersonal approach. *Psychological Bulletin, 115,* 243–267.

Beaman, A. L., Barnes, P. J., Klentz, B., & McQuirk, B. (1978). Increasing helping rates through informational dissemination: Teaching pays. *Personality and Social Psychology Bulletin, 4,* 406–411.

Betancourt, H. (1990). An attribution-empathy model of helping behavior: Behavior intentions and judgments of help-giving. *Personality and Social Psychology Bulletin, 16,* 573–591.

Burnstein, E., Crandall, C., & Kitayama, S. (1994). Some neo-Darwinian decision rules for altruism: Weighing cues for inclusive fitness as a function of the biological importance of the decision. *Journal of Personality and Social Psychology, 67,* 773–789.

Clary, E. G., & Snyder, M. (1991). A functional analysis of altruism and prosocial behavior: The case of volunteerism. In M. S. Clark (Ed.), *Prosocial behavior* (pp. 119–148). Newbury Park, CA: Sage.

Darley, J. M., & Latané, B. (1968, December). When will people help in a crisis? *Psychology Today, 2,* 54–57, 70–71.

Eagly, A. H., & Crowley, M. (1986). Gender and helping behavior: A meta-analytic review of the social psychological literature. *Psychological Bulletin, 100,* 283–308.

Emswiller, T., Deaux, K., & Willits, J. E. (1971). Similarity, sex, and requests for small favors. *Journal of Applied Social Psychology, 1,* 284–291.

Fultz, J., Schaller, M., & Cialdini, R. B. (1988). Empathy, sadness, and distress: Three related but distant vicarious affective

❧

responses to another's suffering. *Personality and Social Psychology Bulletin, 14*, 312–325.

Gilligan, C. (1982). *In a different voice: Psychological theory and women's development.* Cambridge, MA: Harvard University Press.

Hamilton, W. D. (1964). The genetical theory of social behavior (I, II). *Journal of Theoretical Biology, 7*, 1–52.

Isen, A. M., & Levin, P. F. (1972). Effect of feeling good on helping: Cookies and kindness. *Journal of Personality and Social Psychology, 21*, 344–348.

Kohlberg, L. (1976). Moral stages and moralization: The cognitive-developmental approach. In T. Lickona (Ed.), *Moral development and behavior: Theory, research, and social issues* (pp. 31–53). New York: Holt, Rinehart, & Winston.

Kohn, A. (1990). *The brighter side of human nature: Empathy and altruism in everyday life.* New York: Basic Books.

Latané, B., & Darley, J. M. (1969). Bystander "apathy." *American Scientist, 57*, 244–268.

Latané, B. & Darley, J. M. (1970). *The unresponsive bystander: Why doesn't he help?* New York: Appleton-Crofts.

Latané, B., & Nida, S. A. (1981). Ten years of research on group size and helping. *Psychological Bulletin, 89*, 308–324.

Levine, R. V., Martinez, T. S., Brase, G., & Sorenson, K. (1994). Helping in 36 U.S. cities. *Journal of Personality and Social Psychology, 67*, 69–82.

McGuire, A. M. (1994). Helping behaviors in the natural environment: Dimensions and correlates of helping. *Personality and Social Psychology Bulletin, 20*, 45–56.

Myers, D. G. (1999). *Social psychology* (6th ed.). Boston: McGraw-Hill.

Oliner, S. P., & Oliner, P. M. (1988). *The altruistic personality.* New York: The Free Press.

Omoto, A. M., Snyder, M., & Berghuis, J. P. (1993). The psychology of volunteerism: A conceptual analysis and a program of action research. In J. B. Pryor & G. D. Reeder (Eds.), *The social psychology of HIV infection.* Hillsdale, NJ: Erlbaum.

Piaget, J. (1932). *The moral judgment of the child.* London: Kegan Paul.

Piliavin, J. A., & Charng, H.-W. (1990). Altruism: A review of recent theory and research. *American Sociological Review, 16*, 27–65.

Rosenthal, A. M. (1964). *Thirty-eight witnesses.* New York: McGraw-Hill.

Salovey, P., Mayer, J. D., & Rosenhan, D. L. (1991). Mood and helping: Mood as a motivator of helping and helping as a regulator of mood. In M. S. Clark (Ed.), *Prosocial behavior: Review of personality and social psychology* (Vol. 12, pp. 215–237). Newbury Park, CA: Sage.

Sime, J. D. (1983). Affiliative behavior during escape to building exits. *Journal of Environmental Psychology, 3*, 21–41.

Smith, K. D., Keating, J. P., & Stotland, E. (1989). Altruism reconsidered: The effect of denying feedback on a victim's status to empathic witnesses. *Journal of Personality and Social Psychology, 57*, 641–650.

Weiner, B. (1980). A cognitive (attribution)-emotion-action model of motivated behavior: An analysis of judgments of help giving. *Journal of Personality and Social Psychology, 39*, 186–200.

SUGGESTED READINGS

Batson, C. D. (1991). *The altruism question: Toward a social-psychological answer.* Hillsdale, NJ: Erlbaum.

Clark, M. S. (Ed.). *Prosocial behavior.* Newbury Park, CA: Sage.

Coles, R. (1997). *The moral intelligence of children.* New York: Random House.

Latané, B., & Darley, J. M. (1970). *The unresponsive bystander: Why doesn't he help?* Englewood Cliffs, NJ: Prentice-Hall.

Schroeder, D. A., Penner, L. A., Dovidio, J. F., & Piliavin, J. A. (1995). *The social psychology of helping and altruism: Problems and puzzles.* New York: McGraw-Hill.

Spacapan, S., & Oscamp, S. (1992). *Helping and being helped: Naturalistic studies.* Newbury Park, CA: Sage.

Wright, R. (1994). *The moral animal: The new science of evolutionary psychology*

Applied Social Psychology

ℰ

Have you ever noticed how riders in buses space themselves out and try not to sit too close to each other?
Have you ever wondered what it would be like to be
a juror? Did you ever notice that the first thing people do who
fall ill or suffer a tragedy is to join a support group? As you
might imagine by now, social psychology has a lot to say
about each of these topics, and many more questions related
to the social and physical environment, law, and health. In
this chapter, we explore each of these areas and see how the
study of social psychology has improved people's everyday
lives through the application of theory and the development
of new research findings.

ℰ Environmental Psychology

By now it's probably obvious to you that, by changing our
own and others' attitudes and behaviors, we can improve both
our social and physical environment. But have you ever
thought that our environment might also have an impact on
us? The basic premise of environmental psychology is that
our environment—our physical and social situation—
strongly shapes our behavior. By changing, manipulating, or
deliberately designing environments, we can affect one
another's attitudes and behaviors, the friends we make
(Festinger, Schachter, & Back, 1950), and even our health
(Elmstahl, Annerstedt, & Ahlund, 1997). Below we take a
closer look at both the environment's impact on us, and our
impact on the environment.

The Social Environment

Personal space. Bus riders who purposefully space themselves
out demonstrate that we each have an area of *personal space*
into which we don't wish others to enter (Hayduk, 1978). The
size of this space determines how closely we approach others
and how we react when others approach us. In intimate relationships people stand close together. Generally, close friends
and family members interact with each other at a distance of
about 18 inches or less (Hall, 1966). We tend to space ourselves a little farther away with casual friends (18 inches to 4
feet), farther away with strangers (4-12 feet), and the farthest
away (12-25 feet) with public or formal events like lectures
and judicial proceedings. However, personal space is determined by culture, and the above-stated ranges hold true
specifically for middle-class Americans (Hall, 1966). People
from Middle Eastern countries, for example, interact with
casual friends at a much closer distance than Americans do,
and are puzzled by what they see as a lack of warmth among
Americans (Watson & Graves, 1966).

Territoriality. To extend their personal space, people also
mark their ownership of areas around them—their territo-
ries—by touching or by leaving personal items (Altman,
1975; Sommer & Becker, 1969). On a campus, for example,
students in the library may define their study area with books
and notebooks. Riders of public transit may claim the seat
next to them by putting their packages or a newspaper on the
seat. While another rider would have every right to sit in such
a seat (after all, people don't "own" seats in public places),

we generally respect a stranger's territory and seek our own place elsewhere.

Crowding. If a bus or train is crowded, people will sit even in "marked" seats. Indeed, part of what makes crowding so uncomfortable is that there are more opportunities for strangers to invade our personal space and fewer opportunities to stake out our own territory. We thus feel a loss of control. We may also experience sensory overload in crowds (Evans & Lepore, 1992). Finally, we may become frustrated if crowds keep us from accomplishing our goals or from escaping the situation (Evans & Lepore, 1992). Crowding, then, is defined more by the psychological experience of the individuals involved than by the actual number of people per spatial unit (Edwards, Fuller, Sermsri, & Vorakitphokatorn, 1994). As with personal space, definitions of crowding vary with culture (Gillis, Richard, & Hagan, 1986).

In crowded conditions, people experience typical stress reactions, such as an increase in blood pressure and adrenaline flow (Evans, 1974, 1980); a higher incidence of illness (Baron, Mandel, Adams, & Griffen, 1976); and, in some situations, even an increase in the death rate (Paulus, McCain, & Cox, 1981). People may also feel more anxious, unhappy, fearful, or angry in such situations (Evans, 1980). As a result of these stresses, people living in crowded environments can even come to dislike each other and to refuse to help one another during times of trouble (Feldman, 1998).

Changing Attitudes and Behaviors Toward the Physical Environment

Energy conservation through vividness. Did you know that the United States consumes more energy per individual than any other nation does (Aronson, Wilson, & Akert, 1999)? This fact, combined with the dwindling of natural resources such as oil, makes conservation imperative. But how can social psychology help us to see the urgency of this problem?

First, let's consider the case of energy conservation within private homes. Simple measures, such as installing insulation, using energy-efficient light bulbs, and maintaining one's furnace, would reduce Americans' energy consumption by 50-75 percent (Williams & Ross, 1980). Yet despite this fact, most homeowners have not taken such steps.

Why? Some researchers have speculated that people do not see energy conservation as a big enough problem to justify a lifestyle change (Gonzales, Aronson, & Costanzo, 1988; Yates & Aronson, 1983). Knowing that people particularly notice vivid information, these experimenters instructed energy auditors to tell homeowners that if all the cracks around their doors and windows were added up, the total would amount to a football-sized hole in their living room wall. Suddenly, a simple act like installing weather stripping seemed more important. Similarly, homeowners were told that living in a house with an uninsulated attic was like going outside without any clothing on (Gonzales, Aronson, & Costanzo, 1988). As a result of the vividness

with which these energy-audit results were presented, the percent of homeowners who enacted the auditor's recommendations jumped from less than 20 percent to 61 percent.

Water conservation through cognitive dissonance. A different tactic was used to get students to conserve water while showering. Using principles of cognitive dissonance theory and a brief survey, researchers made participants mindful of how wasteful they sometimes were with water. Then, the experimenters encouraged the participants to publicly commit to water conservation by asking them to sign a large poster advocating water conservation. Making the participants realize that they were not practicing what they preached caused them to take much shorter showers than they had taken before (Dickerson, Thibodeau, Aronson, & Miller, 1992).

Reducing litter through conformity. While everyone knows that littering is not approved of by society (an *injunctive norm*), many people still try to get away with it in situations in which it seems that "everyone" is doing it (a *descriptive norm*). By focusing people's attention on *either* norm, we can actually reduce littering (Aronson, Wilson, & Akert, 1999).

For example, in one experiment conducted in a parking lot, people watched a research confederate pass by, pick up a fast-food bag from the ground, and throw it in a trash can. When participants arrived at their cars, they found a flyer on the windshield. Only seven percent of the participants who had seen the confederate threw the flyer on the ground, compared to 37 percent of those who had not seen the confederate (Reno, Cialdini, & Kallgren, 1993). Apparently, watching the confederate's behavior made the injunctive norm of not littering visible.

Another experiment made the descriptive norm salient, or noticeable, for participants. In the experimental set-up, a campus mailroom was either (1) perfectly clean, (2) littered with a watermelon rind and handbills, or (3) littered with only a watermelon rind when participants retrieved a flyer from their mailboxes. The greatest amount of littering occurred in the second condition, where the descriptive norm indicated that littering was "the thing to do" (Cialdini, Reno, & Kallgren, 1990). Interestingly, the least amount of littering occurred in the third condition, in which subjects saw that an otherwise clean environment was obviously sullied by one piece of garbage.

Increasing recycling by making it easy to comply. In Fairfax County, Virginia, there were not enough plastic recycling bins available for all of the residents. While it may not seem like a big deal to find your own box for recycling, without a readily available bin, only the most committed people in the county recycled. However, among the people who were issued a bin, a greater percentage of people than before recycled, regardless of their attitudes towards recycling (Guagnano, Stern, & Dietz, 1995). Thus, when it is easy to comply with a norm, people do. When compliance is harder, then only the truly committed will "step up to the plate." The lesson here is that we can persuade each other to act in more environmentally responsible ways either by changing attitudes or by removing barriers to action (Aronson, Wilson, & Akert, 1999).

⳥ SOCIAL PSYCHOLOGY AND LAW

In many areas within our legal system, social psychology theory and research can promote justice and due process. In a typical court case, jurors hear testimony, form impressions of the defendant, evaluate evidence (including research findings), listen to instructions from the judge, discuss the case as a group, and render a verdict (Myers, 1999). The field of social psychology has contributed important knowledge about each of these processes. In fact, social psychological research on stereotyping and prejudice was used as evidence in court in 1954 to abolish school segregation (*Brown v. Board of Education*) and in 1990 to charge a law firm with sexism (*Price Waterhouse v. Hopkins*, in Fiske, Bersoff, Borgida, Deaux, & Heilman, 1991). Specific questions investigated by social psychologists include: How accurate are eyewitnesses? How valid is confession evidence? How are jurors selected? What group processes operate in jury deliberations? Below, we explore the answers to these questions and others.

Eyewitness Testimony. Eyewitness testimony may well be the most compelling kind of evidence in a criminal case (Leippe, 1985). Mock jurors are more likely to vote for conviction when there is an eyewitness—even if the eyewitness's testimony is discredited (Loftus, 1974, 1979a). Indeed, criminal cases that have eyewitnesses are more likely to end in convictions than those without such witnesses (Visher, 1987). The persuasiveness of eyewitness testimony raises two questions (Wells, 1993). First, how accurate are eyewitnesses? Second, how well can jurors judge the reliability of an eyewitness?

How accurate are eyewitnesses? Despite what we may think, our memories are not like videotaped reproductions of what we see. On the contrary, they can be quite fallible (Schacter, 1999) or even false (Loftus, 1997). Problems at all stages of memory creation—from acquisition to storage to recall of information— can erode the accuracy of an eyewitness (Aronson, Wilson, & Akert, 1999).

Think about the conditions at the time of a crime. Generally, a crime is unexpected, occurs quickly, and frightens victims and witnesses. These very conditions make it difficult for people to *encode*, or take in, information (Tollestrup, Turtle, & Yuille, 1994). In particular, the presence of weapons (Loftus, Loftus, & Messo, 1987), poor viewing conditions, or stereotypes of what a crime or criminal is like may prevent a witness from clearly seeing or remembering the features of a perpetrator or the details of a crime (Aronson, Wilson, & Akert, 1999).

Any information that does not get *stored* as memories may become distorted by new information obtained after the actual event (Loftus, 1979a). For example, eyewitnesses are subject to the *misinformation effect*, whereby they may remember information inaccurately after being asked misleading questions or given misleading suggestions by investigators and attorneys (Loftus, 1979a, 1979b). Misleading questions can also cause witnesses to misremember the source of their memories. This *source monitoring error* may lead eyewitnesses to identify innocent people who have become inadvertently associated with the crime in their memories (D. Lindsay & Johnson, 1989).

Finally, problems at the *retrieval* stage (Ellsworth & Mauro, 1998; Koehnken, Malpass, & Wogalter, 1996) can affect how accurately witnesses identify a suspect out of a lineup or out of pictures. For example, when asked to pick a suspect out of a lineup, eyewitnesses are more successful at picking the suspect that most *resembles* the criminal than they are at picking the *actual* criminal (Buckhout, 1974). The constituents of a lineup can thus sway eyewitnesses into making a false identification.

How well can people judge the accuracy of eyewitnesses? Not only are eyewitness accounts not as accurate as we would like them to be (given their extensive use in the legal system) but jurors readily believe eyewitnesses even when the witnesses are inaccurate or mistaken. In particular, jurors—and the legal system—use the confidence of an eyewitness to judge the witness's accuracy (Wells & Murray, 1983). Yet confidence is only modestly related to accuracy of memory (Smith, Kassin, & Ellsworth, 1989). Further, given the way our memory works, a hazy or vague description of a suspect may actually be more accurate than a well-thought-out detailed description (Dunning & Stern, 1994). Similarly, an identification of a suspect from a lineup based on intuition (e.g. how a face stands out) may be more accurate than an identification based on the process of elimination (Dunning & Stern, 1994).

How well can people judge the truthfulness of eyewitnesses? If people are unable to evaluate the accuracy of an eyewitness, can they at least evaluate whether an eyewitness is trying to lie or mislead? Surprisingly (and quite disturbingly, considering who interviews suspects and who must decide verdicts), people are not very good at detecting lies. In fact, in several experiments, experienced and inexperienced law enforcement offers, secret service agents, and even U. S. customs agents were no better at detecting lies than were untrained college students (DePaulo & Pfeiffer, 1986; Ekman & O'Sullivan, 1991).

Nor are so-called lie-detector tests any more accurate. Polygraph tests are notoriously controversial (see Lykken, 1984, and Raskin, 1986) and often yield different results depending on the administrator's experience and the technique used (Ellsworth & Mauro, 1998). While experienced administrators can use the polygraph to detect lies at better than chance, the test is still far from accurate (Ellsworth & Mauro, 1998). One review estimates that the test misidentified about 15 percent of liars as truth-tellers and 15 percent of truth-tellers as liars (Ekman, 1992). Because of its dubious accuracy, most states will not allow polygraph test results to be used in court. Further, the United States Supreme Court has banned the use of polygraph tests by employers except under special circumstances (Aronson, Wilson, & Akert, 1999).

How can we improve the use of eyewitness testimony? Four measures offer hope for reducing errors in eyewitness testimony (Myers, 1999). First, social psychologists recommend that police follow specific guidelines (see Table 1) to make lineup identifications as accurate as possible (Aronson, Wilson, & Akert, 1999).

Table 1 *How to Avoid Mistaken Identification by Eyewitnesses in a Lineup*

1. Make sure everyone in the lineup resembles the witness's description of the suspect.
2. Tell the witness that the suspect may or may not be in the lineup.
3. Do not always include the suspect in the initial lineup.
4. Present people in the lineup sequentially instead of simultaneously.
5. Present witnesses with photographs of lineup people *and* audio recordings of their voices.

From Aronson, Wilson, & Akert, 1999, p. 615.

Second, police and investigators who conduct lineups or interview eyewitnesses should take care to give as little information as possible to eyewitnesses. In one study, when an interviewer gave feedback that confirmed or disconfirmed witnesses' identification, witnesses who received confirming feedback felt much more confident in their choice (Wells & Bradfield, 1998). Even a casual comment by an interviewer may greatly influence the confidence of a witness—even if the witness believes that the comment had no effect (Wells & Bradfield, 1998).

Third, interviewers can improve eyewitness accuracy by conducting *cognitive interviews* (Fisher, Geiselman, & Amador, 1989). During this process, eyewitnesses tell what happened in their own words, without interruptions. Then, the interviewer encourages the witness to remember more by helping him or her to mentally reconstruct the crime setting (e.g., visualize the scene, remember his or her thoughts and feelings at the time, etc.). These steps prompt memories of the situation that otherwise may have been forgotten (Cutler & Penrod, 1988). Finally, the interviewer may ask evocative questions, such as "Was there anything unusual about the person's appearance or clothing," to fill in details. Clearly, interviewers must take care not to suggest or add specific details through their questions (Loftus & Zanni, 1975). In one

study, interviewers trained in this way were able to help eyewitnesses remember 50 percent more information, without increasing the false memory rate (Fisher, Geiselman, & Amador, 1989; Fisher, McCauley, & Geiselman, 1994).

Fourth, jurors can be educated to think more critically about eyewitness testimony. Studies show that jurors are unaware of most of what we have been discussing in this section: that the circumstances of a lineup determine the reliability of an identification, confident eyewitness are not necessarily accurate, and memory can be influenced by misleading questions or by stress at the time of the incident (Cutler, Penrod, & Stuve, 1988). Table 2 lists the findings that jurors should know (Kassin, Ellsworth, & Smith, 1989).

Table 2 *What Jurors Should Know About Eyewitness Testimony*

An eyewitness's testimony about an event can be affected by the wording of questions.
Police instructions can affect an eyewitness's willingness to make an identification.
Police instructions can affect the likelihood that an eyewitness will feel obligated to identify somebody.
Eyewitness testimony about an event often reflects not only what the witness actually saw but information he or she obtained later.
Jurors should disregard the confidence with which an eyewitness offers testimony.
An eyewitness's perception and memory of an event may be affected by his or her attitudes and expectations.
Eyewitnesses often perceive events selectively.
Witnesses often choose the wrong person from a lineup.
Witnesses are especially prone to error when trying to identify someone of another race.

From Kassin, Ellsworth, & Smith, 1989, as cited in Myers, 1999, pp. 611-112.

Juries: Group Process in Action. Ultimately, the judgment of guilt or innocence of a defendant lies in the hands of jurors: 12 individuals chosen to represent the defendant's peers. As individuals, they are subject to personal biases, attitudes toward the death penalty, and misunderstandings of instructions—all of which can affect the outcome of a trial. As a group, they are also subject to group influences, including persuading (informational social influence) and pressuring (normative social influence).

The deliberation process. To understand the group processes that affect juries, we must first grasp how a jury operates. After hearing the evidence and arguments in a case, the jury is instructed by the judge about the kind of decision that must be reached. Once they start their deliberation, juries pass through three stages (Hastie, Penrod, & Pennington, 1983). First is the relaxed *orientation* period, during which the 12 jurors set an agenda, explore the facts, and raise questions. At some point, they take the first vote. Differences of opinions are revealed, and the jurors now divide into factions. Here they move into the second stage, called *open conflict*. They take a closer look at the evidence and reconsider the judge's instructions (Pennington & Hastie, 1992). If they reach an agreement, then a verdict is returned. The third stage, *reconciliation*, occurs if the jurors smooth over conflicts and affirm the group's decision. However, if the group cannot reach consensus, then they must continue with deliberation or open conflict. If jurors find that they are still not making progress toward a consensus, then they may declare a hung jury.

Majority wins. Both laboratory studies using mock juries and real criminal trials with actual juries reveal that a jury's first vote is highly predictive of the final vote (Kalven & Zeisel, 1966; Sandys & Dillehay, 1995). If this is the case, you might wonder why juries need to deliberate further. Research shows that forcing a jury to make a unanimous decision makes them consider the evidence more carefully (Hastie, Penrod, & Pennington, 1983). In addition, even though those holding the minority opinion may not persuade those holding the majority opinion to change their vote, the minority often does convince the majority about the ultimate verdict (Pennington & Hastie, 1990). For example, rather than convincing the majority that a defendant is innocent, minority opinions may convince the others that the defendant is guilty of a lesser offense, such as manslaughter rather than first-degree murder.

Leniency. Interestingly, some studies have found that jurors are more likely to vote "guilty" on their own than in a group, and become more lenient after deliberating with others (MacCoun & Kerr, 1988). Indeed, another study demonstrated that judges agreed with juries' decisions about 78 percent of the time. But when they disagreed, it was because the jury returned a more lenient decision than the judge would (often acquitting a defendant whom the judge thought to be guilty) (Kalven & Zeisel, 1966). However, yet another study found that jurors became more harsh after deliberation, suggesting a polarization effect of the jury-deliberation process (Hastie, Penrod, & Pennington, 1983). Clearly, more information is needed to fully understand the impact of deliberation on juror's decisions.

Jury size. Why do U.S. juries consist of 12 persons? The practice derives from a the British tradition. For a time, courts in the United States experimented with smaller juries in order to save time and money during criminal trials. In 1978 the U.S. Supreme Court rejected the use of five-person juries but allowed the use of six-person juries in some cases, such as criminal trials. However, there are some important differences between six- and 12-person juries that suggest that 12-person juries indeed ensure more justice.

In a line-length study on conformity (Asch, 1956), the researcher found that a lone dissenter had a difficult time opposing the majority. However, acquiring even one ally greatly reduced participants' tendency to conform.

Psychologically, it is more difficult to be the lone dissenter against five than to be one of two dissenters against 10, even though the ratio of majority to minority (83-to-17 percent) is the same in both cases. Many psychologists argue, therefore, that a 12-person jury eases conformity pressure and makes it more likely that a minority opinion will be heard. Thus the defendant has a better chance at a fair trial (Saks, 1974). Other studies confirm that a 12-person jury is more likely to represent various segments of the population (Saks & Marti, 1997). In addition, six-person juries spend less time deliberating the case and are more likely to reach a unanimous verdict than 12-person juries are (Davis, Au, Hulbert, Chen, & Zarnoth, 1997).

The Supreme Court's ruling to allow the use of six-person juries in some cases is ironic, for several reasons. First, the court misapplied Asch's research when it made this decision (Ellsworth & Mauro, 1998). Essentially, the judges reasoned that because the *ratios* were equal, the *situations* were equal. As you know, the two situations are *not* equal. Second, many of the court's criticisms of five-person juries apply to six-person juries as well (Ellsworth & Mauro, 1998). Not surprisingly, most social psychologists who do research in this area advocate a 12-person jury (Aronson, Wilson, & Akert, 1999).

⚘ SOCIAL PSYCHOLOGY AND HEALTH

Many of us would agree that good health is not merely a physical state. Surely part of staying healthy has to do with one's attitude and outlook. The field of health psychology—drawing on theory and research from social psychology—uses a model in which health or illness is determined by a complex interaction of biological, psychological, and social factors (Taylor, 1982; Taylor, Peplau, & Sears, 2000). Biological factors may include a genetic predisposition to certain diseases, or physical exposure to a flu virus. Psychological factors may include feelings of stress or depression. Social factors may include the amount of support we have from family and friends. Below we explore the impact of these three factors on health and illness, with a special emphasis on psychological and social elements.

Health Behaviors. In the United States today, many infectious diseases such as influenza, pneumonia, and tuberculosis are no longer the threat they once were. The biggest dangers to our health are largely preventable through lifestyle changes and behavior modification (Taylor, Peplau, & Sears, 2000). Think about how lung cancer can be controlled through avoiding smoking, and how heart attacks can be prevented through diet and stress management (Taylor, Peplau, & Sears, 2000). Health behaviors are the things we can do while healthy to maintain our good health, such as avoiding alcohol, smoking, and drug use; getting sufficient sleep; using seat belts and sun screen; getting inoculated; and being screened for certain illnesses like heart disease and breast cancer (Taylor, 1999). But how can we help each other actually adopt these behaviors? That's where social psychology comes in.

Table 3 *Attitudes and Beliefs Leading to the Practice of Health Behaviors*

General health values, including interest in and concern about health

The perception that the threat to health posed by a disorder or disease is severe

A belief in personal vulnerability to a disorder or disease

A belief that one is able to perform the response necessary to reduce the threat

A belief that the response will be effective in overcoming the threat.

From Taylor, Peplau, & Sears, 2000, pp. 422-423.

People are more likely to practice healthy behaviors if they hold the attitudes and beliefs presented in Table 3. These beliefs predict a wide range of specific behaviors, including smoking cessation (Kaufert, Rabkin, Syroutuik, Boyko, & Shane, 1986), exercise (Wurtele & Maddux, 1987), teeth brushing and flossing (Tedesco, Keffer, & Fleck-Kandath, 1991), sunscreen use (Leary & Jones, 1993), breast self-examination (Champion & Huster, 1995), safer sex (Aspinwall, Kemeny, Taylor, Schneider, & Dudley, 1991), condom use (Goldman & Harlow, 1993), and dieting (Uzark, Becker, Dielman, & Rocchini, 1987).

But these positive attitudes are often not enough to change people's unhealthy behaviors. As psychologists have suggested, people must also progress through certain stages when trying to change their behaviors. Knowing what stage a person is in can help others identify the most effective form of influence (Taylor, Peplau, & Sears, 2000; see Table 4).

For example, someone who is in the *pre-contemplation* stage makes a very poor target for intervention, because he or she has no intention of changing or is unaware of the problem. However, providing people with information about their problem may get them to move into the *contemplation* stage.

People in that stage may be prodded into the *preparation* stage by interventions aimed at changing their attitudes; for example, public service messages in the media advocating seat belt use or smoking cessation. People in the preparation stage may then be motivated to take *action* through interventions that help them make explicit commitments to change. Once individuals have advanced into the *maintenance* stage, then teaching them coping skills and providing them with social support help them keep their new, healthy lifestyle.

Stress. Stress is a negative emotional experience accompanied by physiological, biochemical, and behavioral changes (Baum, 1990). We can't totally avoid stress. However, coping with it ineffectively can cause us harm, while effective coping can help us maintain good health (Brehm, Kassin, & Fein, 1999).

When we are faced with a threat, the body springs into action to confront the danger (Selye, 1936). Our heart rate, blood pressure, and breathing all increase. Functions not immediately needed—such as growth, digestion, and the immune system— slow. While these kinds of reactions help the body cope with the threat in the short term, they compromise our health in the long term (Selye, 1936). Stress eventually weakens our immune system, causing us to become vulnerable to disease and even death (Barthrop, Lazarus, Luckhurst, Kiloh, & Penny, 1977; Cohen, Tyrrell, & Smith, 1993).

Our evaluation of a potentially stressful situation determines how we will respond to it (Lazarus & Folkman, 1984). For example, one person might be devastated over a divorce, while another might view it as an escape. In this case, the former person will experience far more psychological distress and have a harder time adjusting to his or her new status than the latter person. We can also take steps to keep a potentially stressful event from happening (Aspinwall & Taylor, 1997). For example, some people manage exam stress by studying a little each day well in advance of the exam rather than waiting until the last minute and pulling an all-nighter.

Moreover, stress comes in many forms. You might have wondered which is worse: everyday hassles like an arduous commute in heavy traffic, or major life events such as the death of a loved one. While there are many ways of defining

Table 4 *Stages of Change Model*

Pre-contemplation	No awareness of a problem OR
	No intention to change a problem behavior
Contemplation	Awareness of the problem
Preparation	Intention to change the behavior (but no actual changes implemented)
Action	Commitment of time and energy to change the behavior
	Action to change the behavior
Maintenance	Work to prevent relapse
	Consolidation of gains

From Taylor, Peplau, & Sears, 2000, p. 426-427.

and measuring stress (Cohen, Kessler, & Gordon, 1995), we can divide it roughly into three categories: crises and catastrophes, major life events, and everyday hassles (Brehm, Kassin, & Fein, 1999). Psychologists have discovered that *all* kinds of stressors have the potential to do us harm if we do not handle them in a healthy manner.

Crises and catastrophes. Traumatic effects in the aftermath of severe floods, hurricanes, tornadoes, plane crashes, car accidents, sexual and violent crimes, divorce, and the death of a parent, child, or spouse are all examples of catastrophic stressors (Brehm, Kassin, & Fein, 1999). These kinds of stressors corrode our health long after the event has passed (e.g., Baum & Fleming, 1993). After a major catastrophe, such as a natural disaster, statistics show an increase in medical emergencies and in reported cases of domestic abuse and alcohol abuse (Adams & Adams, 1984). Psychological disorders, including anxiety, phobias, depression, alcohol abuse, and suicide, also rise (Krug et al., 1998; Rubonis & Bickman, 1991).

In particular, people may experience what's known as posttraumatic stress disorder (PTSD) long after particularly vivid and traumatic experiences (Kessler, Sonnega, Bromet, Hughes, & Nelson, 1995). PTSD may consist of anxiety, sleeplessness, nightmares, flashbacks, intrusive thoughts, problems in paying attention, and social withdrawal (Brehm, Kassin, & Fein, 1999). Depending on the severity of the initial event, some symptoms can recur up to 20 years or more after the initial event (Goldberg, True, Eisen, & Henderson, 1990; Kessler et al., 1995).

Major life events. What could be more exciting than getting married, starting a new job, or having a baby? Try going through a divorce, losing your job, or having your grown child leave home. At one time, psychologists thought that *any* major life event could cause stress (Holmes & Rahe, 1967). We now know that negative life events put far more strain on our health than positive life events (Sarason & Sarason, 1984). While there are long-term health consequences of negative life events (Taylor, 1991), there appears to be no such lasting negative impact of positive life events (Stewart, Sokol, Healy, & Chester, 1986).

Everyday hassles. The most common kind of stress in most of our lives comes in the form of *microstressors,* or the everyday hassles of life (Kohn, Lafreniere, & Gurevich, 1991). The accumulation of tension from things like noise, cigarette smoke, crowding, extreme heat or cold, heavy traffic, long lines, hassles with colleagues, housework, etc. damage our health and well-being more than major life events do (Kohn, Lafreniere, & Gurevich, 1991). In fact, one study revealed that interpersonal conflicts are the most upsetting of all microstressors (Bolger, DeLongis, Kessler, & Schilling, 1989).

Coping. We try to "master and manage" stressful life events through coping (Taylor, Peplau, & Sears, 2000, p. 432), which is the process of managing demands that we perceive as stressful (Lazarus & Folkman, 1984). In coping with stress, we have various strategies and resources available to us.

Problem-focused vs. emotion-focused. Psychologists distinguish between *problem-focused coping* and *emotion-focused coping* (Lazarus & Folkman, 1984). Problem-focused coping, or *active coping,* consists of cognitive or behavioral attempts to eradicate the *source* of the stress—such as through negotiating or working harder. By contrast, emotion-focused coping involves trying to manage emotional *reactions* to the stressful event, such as through positive reinterpretation, acceptance, or a reliance on religion (Park, Cohen, & Herb, 1990). Generally, problem-focused coping is better (Aspinwall & Taylor, 1992), especially with situations that in fact *can* be changed. Emotion-focused coping works better with situations that cannot be changed (Vitaliano, DeWolfe, Maiuro, Russo, & Katon, 1990).

Moreover, people can do things in order to *prevent* stress from even occurring, or to lessen its impact (Aspinwall & Taylor, 1997). This *proactive coping* may involve strategies such as accumulating resources in the form of money or health insurance, cultivating supportive friendships, or getting involved in relaxing or engaging hobbies and activities.

Shutting down vs. opening up. There are two general ways to deal with the emotional aspects of stress: suppressing unwanted thoughts (shutting down), or confronting the stressor (opening up) (Brehm, Kassin, & Fein, 1999).

Denying or suppressing unpleasant thoughts or feelings can prove an effective way of coping in situations where we have little control over reality (Auerbach, Kiesler, Strentz, Schmidt, & Serio, 1994). Even distraction can help in such situations. Yet telling yourself *not* to think about something can only make the unwanted thought more salient or vivid in your mind (Wegner, 1994). To keep the thought at bay, you can practice *focused distraction,* whereby you purposely think of something else. In one study, people who did this recovered from pain more quickly than people who tried to suppress their pain (Cioffi & Holloway, 1993). Distraction ("think about lying on the beach") is a better coping strategy than suppression ("don't think about the pain") (Brehm, Kassin, & Fein, 1999, p. 522). Similarly, keeping secrets and holding in strong emotions is physiologically taxing and may even compromise our health (Cole, Kemeny, Taylor, Visscher, & Fahey, 1996; Gross & Levenson, 1997).

The opposite of suppression—confiding in someone, sharing thoughts and feelings, and talking freely about troubles—may also have psychological and physical benefits (Pennebaker, 1997; Smyth, 1998). These activities can help us sort out our thoughts, understand the problem, and perhaps even gain valuable new insights (Pennebaker, 1990). However, merely ruminating on our troubles is not an effective coping strategy (Nolen-Hoeksema & Girgus, 1994); nor is confiding in an untrustworthy or nonsupportive individual (Kelly & McKillop, 1996).

Social support. Having people to confide in—through psychotherapy, self-help groups, or religious rituals—helps us gain sympathy and support, which, as we have just seen, facilitates coping (Pennebaker, 1990). Social support in the form of many social contacts, a few intimate others, or even just the perceived availability of others is vital to coping with stress and is far superior than trying to handle hard times alone (Brehm, Kassin, & Fein, 1999). Supportive relationships can actually *lessen* stress, enhance both problem- and emotion-focused coping, and improve psychological and physical health (Sarason, Sarason, & Gurung, 1997; Taylor, 1999; Uchino, Cacioppo, & Kiecolt-Glaser, 1996; Wills, 1990). For example, studies show that people who live with others, have many close friends and relatives, and participate in community groups live longer than people who lack these social connections, regardless of gender, race, or socioeconomic status (Berkman & Syme, 1979). People in married or committed relationships also fight cancer or AIDS better than people who must go it alone (Schneider, Taylor, Hammen, Kemeny, & Dudley, 1991; Taylor, 1990). Even pets provide a kind of nonjudgmental support that can calm and comfort us (Allen, Blascovich, Tomaka, & Kelsey, 1991). Finally, friends provide encouragement, sympathy, and reassurance; listen; help sort out problems; and boost our confidence, self-esteem, and security (Brehm, Kassin, & Fein, 1999).

Stress management. Sometimes people have difficulty dealing with a particularly stressful event. Stress-management programs can help (Taylor, Peplau, & Sears, 2000). In such programs, participants monitor their own behavior, identifying events that trigger stress reactions. For example, a student may become anxious at the thought of having to give a presentation in class, or a worker may get nervous while interacting with the boss. Participants are taught to then recognize and examine negative self-talk they might engage in as a result of their anxiety. For example, the student might think "I'm so stupid" when tongue-tied in class. Or the worker might think "I'm no good at this job" when facing the boss. Such negative thoughts only intensify anxiety and undermine people's confidence enough that they can't take action.

Next, participants identify problem behaviors that they would like to change. They also set realistic goals, such as making a comment in class or asking the boss for clarification on a task. At the same time, participants may learn relaxation techniques, such as breathing deeply or taking a break, so as to control their physiological reactions to the stressful event. Participants learn many cognitive and behavioral coping techniques as well. Not every technique will work for each person, but through the program, individuals learn which techniques work best for them (Taylor, Peplau, & Sears, 2000).

This brief overview of the applications of social psychological theory and research to the environment, the law, and health is just a beginning of what can be an exciting, valuable field of study. There are many other areas in which social psychologists are working to improve the human condition, including business and politics. This introduction sets you on the path to explore these areas.

REFERENCES

THE SOCIAL ENVIRONMENT

Altman, I. (1975). *The environment and social behavior.* Monterey, CA: Brooks/Cole.

Aronson, E., Wilson, T. D., & Akert, R. M. (1999). *Social psychology* (3rd ed.). New York: Addison Wesley.

Baron, R. M., Mandel, D. R., Adams, C. A., & Griffen, L. M. (1976). Effects of social density in university residential environments. *Journal of Personality and Social Psychology, 34,* 434–446.

Cialdini, R. B., Reno, R. R., & Kallgren, C. A. (1990). A focus theory of normative conduct: Recycling the concept of norms to reduce littering in public places. *Journal of Personality and Social Psychology, 58,* 1015–1026.

Dickerson, C., Thibodeau, R., Aronson, E., & Miller, D. (1992). Using cognitive dissonance to encourage water conservation. *Journal of Applied Social Psychology, 22,* 841–854.

Edwards, J. N., Fuller, T. D., Sermsri, S., & Vorakitphokatorn, S. (1994). Why people feel crowded: An examination of objective and subjective crowding. *Population & Environment: A Journal of Interdisciplinary Studies, 16,* 149–173.

Elmstahl, S., Annerstedt, L., & Ahlund, O. (1997). How should a group living unit for demented elderly be designed to decrease psychiatric symptoms? *Alzheimer Disease and Associated Disorders, 11*(1), 47–52.

Evans, G. W. (1974). An examination of the information overload mechanism of personal space. *Man-Environment Systems, 4,* 61.

Evans, G. W. (1980). Environmental cognition. *Psychological Bulletin, 88,* 259–287.

Evans, G. W., & Lepore, S. J. (1992). Conceptual and analytic issues in crowding research. *Journal of Environmental Psychology, 12,* 163–173.

Feldman, R. S. (1998). *Social psychology* (2nd ed.). Upper Saddle River, NJ: Prentice Hall.

Festinger, L., Schachter, S., & Back, K. (1950). *Social pressures in informal groups: A study of a housing community.* New York: Harper.

Gillis, A. R., Richard, M. A., & Hagan, J. (1986). Ethnic susceptibility to crowding: An empirical analysis. *Environment & Behavior, 18,* 683–706.

Gonzales, M. H., Aronson, E., & Costanzo, M. (1988). Using social cognition and persuasion to promote energy conservation: A quasi-experiment. *Journal of Applied Social Psychology, 18*, 1049–1066.

Guagnano, G. A., Stern, P. C., & Dietz, T. (1995). Influences on attitude-behavior relationships: A natural experiment with curbside recycling. *Environment & Behavior, 27*, 699–718.

Hall, E. T. (1966). *The hidden dimension*. Garden City, NY: Doubleday.

Hayduk, L. A. (1978). Personal space: An evaluative and orienting overview. *Psychological Bulletin, 85*, 117–134.

Paulus, P. B., McCain, G., & Cox, V. (1981). Prison standards: Some pertinent data on crowding. *Federal Probation, 15*, 48–54.

Reno, R. R., Cialdini, R. B., & Kallgren, C. A. (1993). The transsituational influence of social norms. *Journal of Personality and Social Psychology, 64*, 104–112.

Sommer, R., & Becker, F. D. (1969). Territorial defense and the good neighbor. *Journal of Personality and Social Psychology, 11*, 85–92.

Watson, O. M., & Graves, T. D. (1966). Quantitative research in proxemic behavior. *American Anthropologist, 68*, 971–985.

Williams, R. H., & Ross, M. H. (1980, March/April). Drilling for oil and gas in our houses. *Technology Review*, 24–36.

Yates, S. M., & Aronson, E. (1983). A social psychological perspective on energy conservation in residential buildings. *American Psychologist, 38*, 435–444.

LAW

Aronson, E., Wilson, T. D., & Akert, R. M. (1999). *Social psychology* (3rd ed.). New York: Addison Wesley.

Asch, S. E. (1956). Studies of independence and conformity: A minority of one against a unanimous majority. *Psychological Monographs, 70*(9, Whole No. 416).

Buckhout, R. (1974). Eyewitness testimony. *Scientific American, 231*, 23–31.

Cutler, B. L., & Penrod, S. D. (1988). Context reinstatement and eyewitness identification. In G. M. Davies & D. M. Thomson (Eds.), *Context reinstatement and eyewitness identification*. New York: Wiley.

Cutler, B. L., Penrod, S. D., & Stuve, T. E. (1988). Juror decision making in eyewitness identification cases. *Law and Human Behavior, 12*, 41–55.

Davis, J. H., Au, W. T., Hulbert, L., Chen, X., & Zarnoth, P. (1997). Effects of group size and procedural influence on consensual judgments of quantity: The example of damage award and mock civil juries. *Journal of Personality and Social Psychology, 73*, 703–718.

DePaulo, B. M., & Pfeiffer, R. L. (1986). On-the-job experience and skill at detecting deception. *Journal of Applied Social Psychology, 16*, 249–267.

Dunning, D., & Stern, L. B. (1994). Distinguishing accurate from inaccurate eyewitness identification via inquiries about decision processes. *Journal of Personality and Social Psychology, 67*, 818–835.

Ekman, P. (1992). *Telling lies: Clues to deceit in the marketplace, politics, and marriage* (Rev. ed.). New York: Norton.

Ekman, P., & O'Sullivan, M. (1991). Who can catch a liar? *American Psychologist, 46*, 913–920.

Ellsworth, P. C., & Mauro, R. (1998). Psychology and law. In D. Gilbert, S. Fiske, & G. Lindzey (Eds.), *The handbook of social psychology* (4th ed., Vol. 2, pp. 684-732). New York: McGraw-Hill.

Fisher, R. P., Geiselman, R. E., & Amador, M. (1989). Field test of the cognitive interview: Enhancing the recollection of actual victims and witnesses of crimes. *Journal of Applied Psychology, 74*, 722–727.

Fisher, R. P., McCauley, M. R., & Geiselman, R. E. (1994). Improving eyewitness testimony with the cognitive interview. In D. F. Ross, J. D. Read, & M. P. Toglia (Eds.), *Adult eyewitness testimony: Current trends and developments*. New York: Cambridge University Press.

Fiske, S. T., Bersoff, D. N., Borgida, E., Deaux, K., & Heilman, M. E. (1991). Social science research on trial: Use of sex stereotyping research in *Price Waterhouse v. Hopkins. American Psychologist, 46*, 1049—1060.

Hastie, R., Penrod, S. D., & Pennington, N. (1983). *Inside the jury*. Cambridge, MA: Harvard University Press.

Kalven, H., & Zeisel, H. (1966). *The American jury*. Boston, MA: Little, Brown.

Kassin, S. M., Ellsworth, P. C., & Smith, V. L. (1989). The "general acceptance" of psychological research on eyewitness testimony: A survey of the experts. *American Psychologist, 44*, 1089–1098.

Koehnken, G., Malpass, R. S., & Wogalter, M. S. (1996). Forensic application of line-up research. In S. L. Sporer, R. S. Malpass, & G. Koehnken (Eds.), *Psychological issues in eyewitness identification* (pp. 205–231). Mawah, NJ: Erlbaum.

Leippe, M. R. (1985). The influence of eyewitness nonidentification on mock-jurors. *Journal of Applied Social Psychology, 15*, 656–672.

Lindsay, D. S., & Johnson, M. K. (1989). The eyewitness suggestibility effect and memory for source. *Memory and Cognition, 17*, 349–358.

Loftus, E. F. (1974, December). Reconstructing memory: The incredible eyewitness. *Psychology Today*, 117–119.

Loftus, E. F. (1979a). *Eyewitness testimony*. Cambridge, MA: Harvard University Press.

Loftus, E. F. (1979b). The malleability of human memory. *American Scientist, 67*, 312–320.

Loftus, E. F. (1997). Creating false memories. *Scientific American*, 70–75.

Loftus, E. F., Loftus, G. R., & Messo, J. (1987). Some facts about "weapons focus." *Law and Human Behavior, 11*, 55–62.

Loftus, E. F., & Zanni, G. (1975). Eyewitness testimony: The influence of the wording in a question. *Bulletin of the Psychonomic Society, 5*, 86–88.

Lykken, D. T. (1984). Polygraphic interpretation. *Nature, 307*, 681–684.

MacCoun, R. J., & Kerr, N. L. (1988). Asymmetric influence in mock jury deliberation: Jurors' bias for leniency. *Journal of Personality and Social Psychology, 54*, 21–33.

Myers, D. G. (1999). *Social psychology* (6th ed.). Boston: McGraw-Hill.

Pennington, N., & Hastie, R. (1990). Practical implications of psychological research on juror and jury decision making. *Personality and Social Psychology Bulletin, 16,* 90–105.

Pennington, N., & Hastie, R. (1992). Explaining the evidence: Tests of the story model for jury decision making. *Journal of Personality and Social Psychology, 62,* 189–206.

Raskin, D. C. (1986). The polygraph in 1986: Scientific, professional, and legal issues surrounding applications and acceptance of polygraph evidence. *Utah Law Review,* 29–74.

Saks, M. J. (1974). Ignorance of science is no excuse. *Trial, 10,* 18–20.

Saks, M. J., & Marti, M. W. (1997). A meta-analysis of the effects of jury size. *Law and Human Behavior, 21,* 451–468.

Sandys, M., & Dillehay, R. C. (1995). First-ballot votes, predeliberation dispositions, and final verdicts in jury trials. *Law and Human Behavior, 19,* 175–195.

Schacter, D. L. (1999). The seven sins of memory. *American Psychologist, 54,* 182–203.

Smith, V. L., Kassin, S. M., & Ellsworth, P. C. (1989). Eyewitness accuracy and confidence: Within- versus between-subjects correlations. *Journal of Applied Psychology, 74,* 356–359.

Tollestrup, P. A., Turtle, J. W., & Yuille, J. C., (1994). Expectations of eyewitness performance: Jurors' verdicts do not follow from their beliefs. In D. F. Ross, J. D. Read, & M. P. Toglia (Eds.), *Adult eyewitness testimony: Current trends and developments.* New York: Cambridge University Press.

Visher, C. A. (1987). Juror decision making: The importance of evidence. *Law and Human Behavior, 11,* 1–17.

Wells, G. L. (1983). What do we know about eyewitness identification? *American Psychologist, 48,* 553–571.

Wells, G. L., & Bradfield, A. L. (1998). "Good, you identified the suspect": Feedback to eyewitnesses distorts their reports of the witnessing experience. *Journal of Applied Psychology, 83,* 360–376.

Wells, G. L., & Murray, D. M. (1983). What can psychology say about the *Neil v. Biggers* criteria for judging eyewitness accuracy? *Journal of Applied Psychology, 68,* 347–362.

HEALTH

Adams, P. R., & Adams, G. R. (1984). Mount Saint Helen's ashfall: Evidence for a disaster stress reaction. *American Psychologist, 39,* 252–260.

Allen, K. M., Blascovich, J., Tomaka, J., & Kelsey, R. M. (1991). Presence of human friends and pet dogs as moderators of autonomic responses to stress in women. *Journal of Personality and Social Psychology, 61,* 582–589.

Aspinwall, L. G., Kemeny, M. E., Taylor, S. E., Schneider, S. G., & Dudley, J. P. (1991). Psychosocial predictors of gay men's AIDS risk-reduction behavior. *Health Psychology, 10,* 432–444.

Aspinwall, L. G., & Taylor, S. E. (1992). Modeling cognitive adaptation: A longitudinal investigation of the impact of individual differences and coping on college adjustment

and performance. *Journal of Personality and Social Psychology, 63,* 989–1003.

Aspinwall, L. G., & Taylor, S. E. (1997). A stitch in time: Self-regulation and proactive coping. *Psychological Bulletin, 121,* 417–436.

Auerbach, S. M., Kiesler, D. J., Strentz, T., Schmidt, J. A., & Serio, C. D. (1994). Interpersonal impacts and adjustment to the stress of simulated captivity: An empirical test of the Stockholm Syndrome. *Journal of Social and Clinical Psychology, 13,* 207–221.

Barthrop, R. W., Lazarus, L., Luckhurst, E., Kiloh, L. G., & Penny, R. (1977). Depressed lymphocyte function after bereavement. *Lancet, 1,* 834–839.

Baum, A. (1990). Stress, intrusive imagery, and chronic distress. *Health Psychology, 9,* 653–675.

Baum, A., & Fleming, I. (1993). Implications of psychological research on stress and technological accidents. *American Psychologist, 48,* 665–672.

Berkman, L., & Syme, S. L. (1979). Social networks, host resistance, and mortality: A nine-year follow-up study of Alameda County residents. *American Journal of Epidemiology, 109,* 186–204.

Bolger, N., DeLongis, A., Kessler, R. C., & Schilling, E. A. (1989). Effects of daily stress and negative mood. *Journal of Personality and Social Psychology, 57,* 808–818.

Brehm, S. S., Kassin, S. M., & Fein, S. (1999). *Social psychology* (4th ed.). Boston: Houghton Mifflin.

Champion, V. L., & Huster, G. (1995). Effect of interventions on stage of mammography adoption. *Journal of Behavioral Medicine, 18,* 169–188.

Cioffi, D., & Holloway, J. (1993). Delayed costs of suppressed pain. *Journal of Personality and Social Psychology, 64,* 274–282.

Cohen, S., Kessler, R. C., & Gordon, L. U. (1995). Measuring stress: A guide for health and social scientists. New York: Oxford University Press.

Cohen, S., Tyrrell, D. A. J., & Smith, A. P. (1993). Negative life events, perceived stress, negative affect, and susceptibility to the common cold. *Journal of Personality and Social Psychology, 64,* 131–140.

Cole, S. W., Kemeny, M. E., Taylor, S. E., Visscher, B. R., & Fahey, J. L. (1996). Accelerated course of human immunodeficiency virus infection in gay men who conceal their homosexual identity. *Psychosomatic Medicine, 58,* 219–231.

Goldberg, J., True, W. R., Eisen, S. A., & Henderson, W. G. (1990). A twin study of the effects of the Vietnam War on posttraumatic stress disorder. *Journal of the American Medical Association, 263,* 1227–1232.

Goldman, J. A., & Harlow, L. L. (1993). Self-perception variables that mediate AIDS-preventive behavior in college students. *Health Psychology, 12,* 489–498.

Gross, J. J., & Levenson, R. W., (1997). Hiding feelings: The acute effects of inhibiting negative and positive emotion. *Journal of Abnormal Psychology, 106,* 95–103.

Holmes, T. H., & Rahe, R. H. (1967). The Social Readjustment Rating Scale. *Journal of Psychosomatic Research, 11,* 213–218.

Kaufert, J. M., Rabkin, S. W., Syroutuik, J., Boyko, E., & Shane, F. (1986). Health beliefs as predictors of success of alternate modalities of smoking cessation: Results of a control trial. *Journal of Behavioral Medicine, 9*, 475–489.

Kelly, A. E., & McKillop, K. J. (1996). Consequences of revealing personal secrets. *Psychological Bulletin, 120*, 450–465.

Kessler, R. C., Sonnega, A., Bromet, E., Hughes, M., & Nelson, C. B. (1995). Posttraumatic stress disorder in the National Comorbidity Survey. *Archives of General Psychiatry, 52*, 1048 1060.

Kohn, P. M., Lafreniere, K., & Gurevich, M. (1991). Hassles, health, and personality. *Journal of Personality and Social Psychology, 61*, 478–482.

Krug, E. G., Kresnow, M., Peddicord, J. P., Dahlberg, L. L., Powell, K. E., Crosby, A. E., & Annest, J. L. (1998). Suicide after natural disasters. *New England Journal of Medicine, 338*, 373–378.

Lazarus, R. S., & Folkman, S. (1984). *Stress, appraisal, and coping.* New York: Springer.

Leary, M. R., & Jones, J. L. (1993). The social psychology of tanning and sunscreen use: Self-presentational motives as predictors of health risk. *Journal of Applied Social Psychology, 23*, 1390–1406.

Nolen-Hoeksema, S., & Girgus, J. S. (1994). The emergence of gender differences in depression during adolescence. *Psychological Bulletin, 115*, 424–443.

Park, C., Cohen, L. H., & Herb, L. (1990). Intrinsic religiousness and religious coping as life stress moderators for Catholics versus Protestants. *Journal of Personality and Social Psychology, 59*, 562–574.

Pennebaker, J. W. (1990). *Opening up.* New York: Morrow.

Pennebaker, J. W. (1997). Writing about emotional experiences as a therapeutic process. *Psychological Science, 8*, 162–166.

Rubonis, A. V., & Bickman, L. (1991). Psychological impairment in the wake of disaster: The disaster-psychopathology relationship. *Psychological Bulletin, 109*, 384–399.

Sarason, B. R., Sarason, I. G., & Gurung, R. A. R. (1997). Close personal relationships and health outcomes: A key to the role of social support. In S. Duck (Ed.), *Handbook of personal relationships* (pp. 547–573). New York: Wiley.

Sarason, I. G., & Sarason, B. R. (1984). Life changes, moderators of stress, and health. In A. Baum, S. E. Taylor, & J. E. Singer (Eds.), *Handbook of psychology and health: Social psychological aspects of health* (Vol. 4, pp. 279–299). Hillsdale, NJ: Erlbaum.

Schneider, S. G., Taylor, S. E., Hammen, C., Kemeny, M. E., & Dudley, J. (1991). Factors influencing suicide intent in gay and bisexual suicide ideators: Differing models for men with and without human immunodeficiency virus. *Journal of Personality and Social Psychology, 61*, 776–778.

Selye, H. (1936). A syndrome produced by diverse nocuous agents. *Nature, 138*, 32.

Smyth, J. M. (1998). Written emotional expression: Effect sizes, outcome types, and moderating variables. *Journal of Consulting and Clinical Psychology, 66*, 174–184.

Taylor, S. E. (1982). Social cognition and health. *Personality and Social Psychology Bulletin, 8*, 549–562.

Taylor, S. E. (1991). Asymmetrical effects of positive and negative events: The mobilization-minimization hypothesis. *Psychological Bulletin, 110*, 67–85.

Taylor, S. E. (1999). *Health psychology* (4th ed.). New York: McGraw Hill.

Taylor, S. E., Peplau, L. A., & Sears, D. O. (2000). *Social psychology* (10th ed.). Upper Saddle River, NJ: Prentice-Hall.

Tedesco, L. A., Keffer, M. A., & Fleck-Kandath, C. (1991). Self-efficacy, reasoned action, and oral health behavior reports: A social cognitive approach to compliance. *Journal of Behavioral Medicine, 14*, 341–356.

Uchino, B. N., Cacioppo, J. T., & Kiecolt-Glaser, J. K. (1996). The relationship between social support and psychological processes: A review with emphasis on underlying mechanisms and implications for health. *Psychological Bulletin, 119*, 488–531.

Uzark, K. C., Becker, M. H., Dielman, T. W., & Rocchini, A. P. (1987). Psychosocial predictors of compliance with a weight control intervention for obese children and adolescents. *Journal of Compliance in Health Care, 2*, 167–178.

Vitaliano, P. P., DeWolfe, D. J., Maiuro, R. D., Russo, J., & Katon, W. (1990). Appraised changeability of a stress as a modifier of the relationship between coping and depression: A test of the hypothesis of fit. *Journal of Personality and Social Psychology, 59*, 582–592.

Wegner, D. M. (1994). Ironic processes of mental control. *Psychological Review, 101*, 34–52.

Wills, T. A. (Ed.). (1990). Social support in social and clinical psychology [Special issue]. *Journal of Social and Clinical Psychology, 9*.

Wurtele, S. K., & Maddux, J. E. (1987). Relative contributions of protection motivation theory components in predicting exercise intentions and behavior. *Health Psychology, 6*, 453–466.

Suggested Readings

The Social Environment

Hall, E. T. (1966). *The hidden dimension.* Garden City, NY: Doubleday.

Sommer, R. (1969). *Personal space.* Englewood Cliffs, NJ: Prentice Hall.

Winter, D. D. H. (1996). *Ecological psychology: Healing the split between planet and self.* New York: Addison Wesley.

Law

Abramson, J. (1995). *We, the jury: The jury system and the ideal of democracy.* New York: Basic Books.

Bedau, H. A. (Ed.). (1997). *The death penalty in America: Current controversies.* New York: Oxford University Press.

Ross, D. F., Read, D. J., Toiglia, M. P. (Eds.). (1994). *Adult eyewitness testimony: Current trends and developments.* New York: Cambridge University Press.

HEALTH

Pennebaker, J. W. (1990). *Opening up: The healing powers of confiding in others.* New York: William Morrow.

Salovey, P., Rothman, A. J., & Rodin, J. (1998). Social psychology and health behavior. In D. Gilbert, S. Fiske, & G. Lindzey (Eds.), *The handbook of social psychology* (4th ed., Vol. 2, pp. 633-683). New York: McGraw-Hill.

Taylor, S. E. (1999). *Health psychology* (4th ed.). New York: McGraw-Hill.

Stop Blaming Yourself:
How You Explain Unfortunate Events to Yourself May Influence Your Achievements as Well as Your Health

Robert J. Trotter

What started out as a failed experiment—laboratory dogs wouldn't jump over a barrier to escape a shock—turned out to reveal a new phenomenon in psychology: learned helplessness. According to Martin Seligman, the way that we think about the causes of a bad occurrence, like failing a test or losing a job, can either set us up for further psychological and physical troubles or can buffer us against stress and hard times. In this article, writer Robert Trotter explains Seligman's theory of learned helplessness and describes the research that Seligman and his students have done in applying this work to understanding depression in humans. Seligman identifies two ways of explaining things that can make some people fall apart under stress and others come out on top.

Martin E. P. Seligman is a gambler: bridge, volleyball, high-stakes poker—even his career. In 1966 he went against the odds and prevailing thought by arguing that animals could learn to be helpless. Now after 20 years of supporting research he is betting that the way we explain the things that happen to us may be more important than what actually happens. The way we explain bad things, he says, can affect our future behavior and can have some serious implications for our mental and physical health.

Seligman got his first clue to this as a young graduate student at the University of Pennsylvania, when he saw a group of dogs that had failed a learning experiment. Usually, when an animal in such an experiment receives a shock it runs around until it accidentally jumps over a barrier and escapes the shock. The next time, the dog knows just what to do. It has learned how to escape. But the animals in this experiment didn't try to escape. They sat there as if they were helpless. Seligman found out that these dogs had previously been exposed to a shock from which they could not escape and suggested that they had learned that efforts to escape were fruitless. It was not the shock that interfered with the animals' response, says Seligman, but the expectation that they would have no control over it.

Collaborating with fellow graduates students Steven F Maier and Bruce Overmier (now at the University of Colorado and the University of Minnesota, respectively),

Seligman worked for the next five years to document this learned helplessness phenomenon and link it to depression in humans. "When I first saw the helpless animals," he explains, "I thought it might be a model of human helplessness that would aid us in understanding the kind of helplessness seen in people suffering from depression." The idea of helping people was what made Seligman decide to become a psychologist in the first place, rather than a philosopher or a professional bridge player. He still likes to talk philosophy and is an excellent bridge player, but he says, "Psychology seemed just perfect for me. It combined enough serious intellectual challenge with a real opportunity to do something that might help people."

After earning his Ph.D. in 1967, Seligman taught for three years at Cornell University, exploring what he saw as obvious parallels between learned helplessness and the major symptoms of human depression. His students convinced him, however, that he just didn't know enough about depression. So he grew a beard and took a year of psychiatric residency at the University of Pennsylvania to learn about depression firsthand.

Seligman still sees a few clients as a licensed therapist but feels that he is more suited to research than therapy. "As a therapist," he says, "I might help 200 or 300 people during my life, but I think I can make a better contribution by trying to uncover general laws of psychology that might help many more people." That's why he stayed with the learned helplessness theory. "I want to follow it to the bitter end. I like low-probability/high-payoff science," he explains. "It is hard work, but it might make a difference." And that is what

"Stop Blaming Yourself," by Robert J. Trotter, reprinted from *Psychology Today,* February 1987, pp. 31–39.

Seligman has been trying to do since he joined the psychology department at the University of Pennsylvania in 1971.

After getting his clinical training, Seligman wrote his first paper on depression and began experimenting with human helplessness. He says he was amazed to find that people reacted just like the animals when he exposed them to the same things, such as an inescapable loud noise. They acted as if they were helpless and didn't even try to turn off the noise. "This was counterintuitive," Seligman says. "Learning theory said that if you give inescapable events to humans or animals it would energize them, not make them passive." (See "Fall into Helplessness," *Psychology Today,* June 1973).

Seligman continued to document the parallels between helplessness and depression for several years. Then, just as the bet was beginning to pay off, people (especially his students Lyn Abramson, Lauren Alloy and Judy Garber) began to have second thoughts. Seligman, just back from a year as a Guggenheim Fellow at the Institute of Psychiatry at Maudsley Hospital in London, was greeted with arguments that his theory of helplessness was wrong on several counts. For one thing, exposure to uncontrollable bad events does not always lead to helplessness and depression. Furthermore, the helplessness theory did not explain the loss of self-esteem often seen in depressed people. Why should people blame themselves for events over which they have no control?

Seligman and his colleagues, worked for several years revising the theory to meet these objections. The revised theory emphasizes what they call explanatory style. The reason uncontrollable bad events don't always lead to helplessness and depression is that people don't simply accept these events uncritically. They ask why. The answer, or explanation for the event, affects what they expect about the future and determines the extent to which they will be helpless or depressed.

Some bad events are truly uncontrollable—my house burned to the ground because it was struck by lightning—and a person's explanations for them are simple statements of fact. But in many instances, reality is ambiguous—my lover accepted a job in another city because it paid a lot more money or, possibly, to get out of our relationship. The revised helplessness theory says that people have a characteristic way of explaining events when reality is ambiguous. They explain the event as being caused by something stable or unstable, global or specific, internal or external. If your relationship breaks up, for example, you can come up with a variety of reasons. If you explain it as something that it stable over time (I always screw up my personal relationships), you will expect it to happen again and will show signs of helplessness in future relationships. If you explain it as global rather than specific (I'm incapable of doing anything right), you will expect bad things to happen in all areas of your life and feel even more helpless. If you explain it as internal rather than external (It was all my fault; my lover did everything possible to keep the relationship going), you are likely to show signs of lowered self-esteem.

According to Seligman's revised helplessness theory, a person who tends to explain the bad things in stable, global and internal terms (It's going to last forever, it's going to affect everything I do and it's all my fault) is most at risk for depression when bad events occur. To test this, Seligman and his colleagues first developed a method of measuring explanatory style. The Attributional Style Questionnaire (ASQ) consists of six bad and six good hypothetical events. People taking the test are asked to imagine themselves in each of these situations and to decide what they feel would be the major cause of the situation if it happened to them. Then they are asked to rate each cause on a scale of 1 to 7 for instability versus stability, specificity versus globality, and internality versus externality.

In the first test of the revised theory, Seligman and his colleagues administered the ASQ to 143 college students and had them fill out a short form of the Beck Depression Inventory, a 13-item questionnaire that is highly reliable in detecting symptoms of depression. As expected, depression could be predicted by the kinds of explanations offered. Students who gave mainly stable, global and internal explanations for bad events were consistently more depressed than those who offered unstable, specific and external reasons. The researchers had similar findings with women on welfare, maximum-security prisoners, grade school children who showed signs of depression, college students who did poorly on a midterm exam and patients hospitalized for depression.

Since the first tests of Seligman's theory, there have been at least 104 experiments involving nearly 15,000 subjects, almost all showing that a pessimistic explanatory style is related to depression.

Seligman's most recent research goes beyond depression. He believes that explanatory style should be able to predict achievement as well as illness and death. It seems logical that people who habitually provide stable, global and internal explanations (such as stupidity) for their failures should be less likely to persist, take chances or rise above their potential than those who explain failure in unstable, specific and external terms (such as luck). This link between learned helplessness and achievement has been demonstrated in work with children. Several researchers have found that the way children explain their performance strongly influences whether they give up following a failure (helpless children) or persist (mastery-oriented children).

When Leslie Kamen and Seligman gave the ASQ to 289 freshmen and 175 upperclassmen at the University of Pennsylvania they found that using explanatory style plus measures such as the Scholastic Aptitude Test and high school grades predicted a student's grade point average more accurately than using the more traditional measures alone. Students with the best explanatory style (unstable, specific, external) got better grades than the traditional methods predicted.

Explanatory style also predicts performance on the job. Seligman and Peter Schulman administered the ASQ to 101 insurance sales representatives right after they had been hired; a year later, those with a positive explanatory style were twice as likely as those with a negative style to be among the 42 agents still on the job. Furthermore, the agents with the positive style had sold 25 percent more insurance, on average, than the others.

The insurance company executives were so impressed with these results that they agreed to a second experiment in which both the ASQ and the usual screening tests were given to thousands of applicants. One thousand were hired on the basis of the usual test. A special force of 100 who failed the industry test but had an optimistic explanatory style were also hired and compared with a group who passed the industry test but had a pessimistic explanatory style. The optimists are out-selling the pessimists among the regularly hired agents, Seligman says and the special force is outselling everybody. "I think we've got a test for who can face a stressful, challenging job and who can't," he says. "My guess is that this test could save the insurance company millions of dollars a year in training alone since it costs about $30,000 each to train new people, and half of them quit."

Seligman plans to take the test into other industries as well. "I think you can order jobs on this dimension—how a person deals with challenge and failure," he says. "It would be a much more humane way to hire people and place them in jobs, jobs that they are up to emotionally." Even defense departments, he says, could make use of such a test. "Some people are better able to cope with going out on the front line, while others are better at operating computers in the back room because they can't cope with failure and give up."

Explanatory style also plays an important role in physical health. Evidence is mounting that stressful life events, such as bereavement and school and family pressures, lead to increased vulnerability to infection and disease. But not everyone reacts in the same way. Some fight against stressors while others see them as uncontrollable and react with helplessness and passivity, characteristics that can be detected in their explanatory style. Seligman believes that people with a poor explanatory style are more likely to go on to have bad health than those with an optimistic outlook.

He cites a study that supports this prediction. Three months following a simple mastectomy for breast cancer, 69 women were asked how they viewed the nature and serious-ness of the disease and how it had affected their lives. Five years later, 75 percent of the women who had reacted to the disease with a fighting spirit or who denied they had cancer were still alive and had no recurrence of the cancer. Only 35 percent of the women who had stoically or helplessly accepted the disease were still alive with no recurrence. A feeling of helplessness appears to impair the body's ability to combat disease.

The immune system, the body's defense mechanism, is the obvious place to look for evidence that such psychological states can affect physical health. Kamen and Seligman, working with Judith Rodin of Yale University, have found that explanatory style does seem to be related to immune functioning. They took blood samples from a group of older people who had been interviewed regarding life changes, stress and health changes. The ones whose interviews indi-cated a pessimistic or depressive explanatory style had a larger percentage of suppressor cells. Since these cells are thought to undermine the body's ability to fight tumor growth, Seligman says, the findings suggest a link between explanatory style and susceptibility to diseases, including cancer.

Explanatory style can also predict actual illness. Seligman's colleague, Christopher Peterson of the University of Michigan, measured the explanatory style of 172 under-graduates and then questioned them one month later about how many days they had been sick and one year later about how often they had been to the doctor. He found a strong cor-relation between helpless explanatory styles and subsequent illness. To see if this relationship holds over the long term, Peterson and Seligman worked with psychiatrist George Vaillant, who has been keeping track of members of the Harvard classes of 1939 through 1944. In 1946, the men had responded to the questionnaires about their experiences in World War II. Seligman analyzed their responses (see "Time Machine Psychology," this article) to see if their explanatory style for negative events was related to later physical health, which was assessed in 1980. The results are preliminary, he says, but they suggest that a person's explanatory style is a reliable predictor of physical health 20 to 35 years later.

He cautions, however, that psychology plays only a minor role in physical illness. "If a crane falls on you," he explains, "it doesn't mater what you think. If the magnitude of your cancer is overwhelming, your psychological outlook counts for zero. On the other hand, if your cancer is marginal or if an illness is just beginning, your psychological state may be critical."

"Some of the studies I'm involved in are long shots," Seligman admits, "but that's part of the intellectual adventure I enjoy. I'm not afraid to be wrong. It keeps me from getting bored and from being boring. My style is to follow an idea doggedly, to repeat each study until I am sure the results are reliable. This can be tedious, but if after all the work the long shot comes in and I am right, these are the studies that can really make a difference in terms of helping people."

If Seligman is right about the physical and psychological importance of explanatory style, then the way to help people is to find out how explanatory style originates and how it can be changed. Seligman, Joan Girgus and Susan Nolen-Hoeksema have identified several possible factors that might influence the development of explanatory style in children. The timing of a child's first trauma or serious loss, for instance, could have a major influence on later explanatory style. One study, for example, found that middle- and work-ing-class women in London were more likely to be depressed if before the age of 11 they had lost their mothers. In terms of Seligman's theory, the loss of a mother at an early age is a seriously negative agent that has both stable and global implications: The mother will never return, and almost every aspect of the child's life will be affected. In addition, young children often blame themselves (internal) when bad events occur. Such a loss at an early age, Seligman says, could set a pattern for the interpretation of future losses or major difficulties.

He also thinks that children may adopt or imitate the explanatory style of their parents. One of his studies found a strong correlation between the way mothers, but not fathers, and children explain bad events.

Teachers are another model, of explanatory style. There is considerable evidence that girls exhibit more helpless behavior than boys in school, and research suggests that this might be explained by the different way teachers treat children. When teachers criticize girls they tend to use stable and global terms commenting, for instance, on their intelligence. When they criticize boys they are likely to use more unstable and specific explanations accusing them of not concentrating. And the kids seem to get the message. In a study in which fourth-graders were presented with unsolvable problems, the boys were less likely than girls to give helpless answers. They said things like "I wasn't trying hard," or "I don't care about your problem." Girls more often attributed their failure to incompetence or stupidity and said, "I just can't do it."

If children continually receive feedback indicating that they lack ability, they may begin to explain their failures in helpless terms. This could be prevented by teaching children to think differently about what happens to them. Seligman says. We might be able to immunize them against helplessness and depression. "I'd like to try that for 10 years and see if the rates of childhood disease, depression and suicide go

down. The history of prevention has been much better than the history of cure," he says.

There is, however, a cure for bad explanatory style. "If you learned it," Seligman says, "you can unlearn it." This was shown rather dramatically when Seligman and Peterson asked psychiatrist Mardi Horowitz of the University of California, San Francisco, to send them excerpts from 12 therapy sessions with depressed patients who had recently suffered a severe loss. The idea was to read the excerpts as if they contained answers to the ASQ and make some conclusions about the patients based on their explanatory style. They did this and sent the 12 evaluations back to Horowitz.

"His response both surprised us and gratified us," say Seligman and Peterson, who thought the statement had come from 12 patients. Instead, Horowitz informed them, they had come from four patients at the beginning, middle and end of successful therapy. For each statement, the ranking of good versus bad explanatory style identified where the patient had been in the process of therapy. And the patient with the worst style at the beginning of therapy had been judged by Horowitz as suicidal.

Explanatory style, Seligman concludes, can change in response to the important events in one's life, including psychotherapy. And he believes that cognitive therapy is the best approach, since it assumes that depression is a result of distorted thinking about the world (global), the future (stable) and oneself (internal). "Cognitive therapy works directly on explanations. You get people to look at what causes they are evoking when they feel depressed," he explains, "and then get them to think about new kinds of causes. It helps people. I'd bet on it."

ⓢ TIME MACHINE PSYCHOLOGY

The economic hardships of the 1930s produced lasting psychological effects, both good and bad. Sociologist Glen Elder of the University of North Carolina, who has been studying people who grew up during the Great Depression, has found, for example, that women whose middle-class families suffered a major financial loss were better off emotionally 40 years later than were similar women whose families had not suffered a major loss. But women whose working-class families suffered large losses during the 1930s were more likely to be helpless and passive later in life.

One reason for these differences is that the Depression served as a training ground for dealing with future losses. Middle-class women who generally had enough financial and educational resources to overcome their problems were strengthened by the struggle and were more resilient in meeting challenges later in life. Middle-class women who did not

go through this experience rank lower on measures of emotional well-being 40 years later.

The story was different for women from working-class families, who had fewer resources for dealing with the challenges of the 1930s and little chance of financial recovery. For them the Depression seemed an uncontrollable force—both stable and global. This perception might have led them to develop a depressive explanatory style that made them feel helpless in the face of later losses.

Discussing these ideas with Seligman, Elder said, "Marty, it's too bad we don't have a time machine so we could go back and look at their explanatory style."

"Maybe we do," Seligman said. "Give me something these women wrote and we can analyze it." Using writing samples taken from interviews conducted with 28 of the women in 1943 and again in 1970, Seligman and his colleagues found that the women's explanatory styles had not changed much over the years, and that each woman's explanatory style was a good predictor of her psychological health 40 years later.

The method Seligman uses for analyzing such material is called the Content Analysis of Verbatim Explanations (CAVE) technique, which he developed with his colleague Christopher Peterson. With the CAVE technique, they say, "subjects famous, quick, dead, uninterested or otherwise unavailable can be studied as easily as introductory psychology students as long as they have left some verbal record."

First, they take a 500-to-1,000-word sample of verbatim material (diary, letter, newspaper quote, therapy transcript) and extract statements in which the person explains an event. The researchers then treat the statements as if they were answers to the ASQ and rate them on a seven-point scale for stability, globality and internality.

During the past several years, Seligman and his colleagues have applied the CAVE technique in a variety of ways, including a study of members of the Baseball Hall of Fame who had played ball between 1990 and 1950. They chose these men because they had been quoted in sports page articles. The idea was to see if their explanatory styles at an early age were related to their later health and life span.

Seligman and his colleagues read the complete sports pages of *The New York Times* and *The Philadelphia Inquirer* for September and early October between 1900 and 1950 and found enough quotes to rate the explanatory style of 30 players. Those men with a generally optimistic style ("Nothing but the breaks beat me in that game. . . . but I'll get my share next time") tended to live longer than those with a pessimistic style ("My aim is still good, but I know I haven't got the stuff I used to have").

All of Seligman's bets don't pay off, however. He and his colleagues reasoned that if explanatory style predicts future performance, then quotes from basketball players following a loss should predict how they would play in the next game. They read the sports pages of *The Boston Globe* (for the Celtics), *The Washington Post* (for the Bullets), *The Philadelphia Inquirer* (for the 76ers) and *The New York Times* and the *New York Daily News* (for the Knicks and Nets) for the entire 1982–83 season and extracted explanations made by coaches and players for losses or other bad events. These were used to rate the explanatory style of each team.

The next step was to see how the teams performed against the point spread in the 1983–84 season in games following a loss. In testing the theory, Seligman explains, it was important to use the point spread, a reliable estimate of how many points a team is expected to win by, rather than simply whether the team wins or loses. You wouldn't expect a strong team, like the Celtics, to lose to a poor team just because its member had a negative explanatory style for why they lost the previous game. But they might win by less than expected.

The Celtics, who had the best explanatory style, beat the point spread 68 percent of the time in games following a defeat. The Knicks, with the next-best style, beat the spread 58 percent of the time. The Bullets beat it 50 percent of the time. The 76ers and Nets, who had the worst explanatory styles, beat it only 40 percent and 37 percent of the time, respectively.

From a bettor's point of view the theory looked like a real money-maker. During the 1983–84 season, there were 134 games following defeats. If you had bet $100 on the two teams with the best style to beat the spread and $100 against the two teams with the worst style, you would have won 83 times (62 percent) and made $3,200. The theory worked again in the 1984–85 season, but unfortunately, it proved to be a two-year wonder. If you had used the same system in the 1985–86 season you would have lost money.

"It's been real frustrating," Seligman says. "We spent about 3,000 hours going through newspaper replicating the study every year for three years before we finally convinced ourselves that the theory just wasn't holding up. I wouldn't bet on it."

department's National Institute of Justice asked Mr. Wells and five fellow scholars to join a panel of law-enforcement officials, criminal-defense lawyers, and prosecutors created to write guidelines for handling eyewitness testimony.

The guide, published in October, gave scholars the opportunity to show that human memory is not a highly reliable tool for determining guilt in the courtroom. For example, contrary to popular belief, people under stress remember events no better than, and often less well than, they do under ordinary circumstances. Witnesses also perceive time as moving more slowly during traumatic events. That, in turn, leads them to overestimate how much time they had to notice details, a key factor of their credibility in court. And studies have found that witnesses to a crime are so distracted by the presence of a weapon—a phenomenon called "weapon focus"—that they remember little else with accuracy.

Researchers cannot ethically recreate the trauma of real crimes. But plenty of field research suggests that witnesses are apt to misidentify people.

For example, many studies have tested the ability of convenience-store clerks and bank tellers to recall customers they encountered in non-stressful situations. Around a third of the time, the employees wrongly identified faces from "lineups" that did not include the person they had actually met.

✑ THE DETERIORATION OF MEMORY

In addition, all sorts of factors inhibit our ability to recognize and recall facial detail. For instance, psychologists have established that most of us have more difficulty recognizing people of a different race. And memory deteriorates very quickly over time.

Elizabeth F. Loftus, a psychologist at the University of Washington and a pioneer in research on false memory, has discovered that it's remarkably easy to alter one's recollection without realizing it. Human beings are highly susceptible to incorporating "post-event information" newspaper articles, comments by police, conversations with other witnesses—into their recollections.

Witnesses also have been known to identify as criminals people they recognized from some other encounter, a process called "transference." In one bizarre example, an Australian psychologist and memory researcher named Donald Thomson was himself once identified by a rape victim as her attacker. Not only was his alibi airtight—he was being interviewed on live television at the time—but she had mistaken him for the rapist because she had seen his face on her television screen during the assault.

✑ IMPROVING POLICE PROCEDURES

Of course, policymakers can't do much to improve the flaws in our memories. So scholars like Mr. Wells, who wanted to reduce eyewitness mistakes, began to focus on things that the justice system can control—particularly police procedures.

One of the biggest problems with eyewitness identification, researchers have found, is that uncertain witnesses are often prompted to finger the person whom police have detained, even when the suspect is not the same person they spotted at the scene. Witnesses viewing a lineup tend to assume that police have caught the person they saw. So they think their job is to find the face that most resembles the description they gave to police.

The police sometimes exacerbate that tendency by designing lineups poorly. Imagine a witness to a liquor-store robbery who says the robber was white, stocky, and bearded. Based on that description, the police identify a suspect and ask the witness to look at a lineup of live individuals or at a spread of photos (known as a "six-pack").

Too often, say researchers, the "distractor" faces used by police do not match the witness's description, or the suspect's photo looks different from the others. If the suspect stands out in any way, if his is the only color photo in the six-pack, for instance, the witness is far more likely to say, "That's the guy."

Lineups are also fraught with the possibility of mistaken identity, researchers report, because of our tendency to overlook differences in facial appearance among people not of our race. Not only are white witnesses, say, more likely to mistake one black suspect for another (and vice versa), but police officers may overestimate the degree to which the distractors they choose match the suspect's description.

Recently, Mr. Wells has raised the alarm about the way a witness's confidence can be manipulated. Witnesses are easily influenced during and after the lineup—by talking with other witnesses or police interviewers—to be more certain of their choice than their recall warrants. Police investigators, for example, may praise a witness for "picking the right guy" out of the lineup.

That taint frequently makes its way to the jury box. Understandably, jurors put a lot of stock in a witness who can point to the defendant and say, "He's the one. I'll never forget his face." But scholars have learned that the degree of confidence during trial is a poor predictor of a witness's accuracy. And, they warn, jurors ought to be particularly skeptical if they learn that a witness professed more confidence on the witness stand than in the squad room. Recall, they say, doesn't improve over time.

⋑ ASKING THE RIGHT QUESTIONS

Until recently, the criminal-justice system made little use of those findings. Defense lawyers, of course, have embraced and exploited them at least since the 1980's. But according to Brian L. Cutler, a psychologist at Florida International University, they have rarely been able to use the research to cross-examine eyewitnesses or police.

"Defense lawyers have no special training—they don't know what questions to ask," says Mr. Cutler. "If they do ask the right questions, how well equipped are jurors to evaluate the questions?" Unfortunately, jurors cling to a belief that "the way memory works is a matter of common sense," he says. "It just isn't so."

"People expect it's like videotape, that we attend equally well to everything out there," says Roy S. Malpass, a psychologist at the University of Texas at El Paso who served on the Justice Department panel. In fact, he says, "we're highly selective."

No one knows how often eyewitness error leads to false convictions, but some scholars have taken a stab at the question. In their book *Mistaken Identification: The Eyewitness, Psychology, and the Law* (Cambridge University Press, 1995), Mr. Cutler and Steven D. Penrod, of the University of Nebraska at Lincoln, do some courtroom calculations: If just 0.5 percent of America's yearly 1.5 million convictions for serious crimes are erroneous—a rate suggested by some studies—then other research allows the authors to infer that well over half of those defendants, or around 4,500 innocent people, are convicted on false eyewitness testimony.

All that may change now that the nation's top law-enforcement officials have created new guidelines for police conduct. The Justice Department report, "Eyewitness Evidence: A Guide for Law Enforcement," reads like a primer on eyewitness research. Among other things, it instructs investigators who assemble a lineup to:

- Select "distractors" that match the witness's description, even simulating tattoos or other unusual features if necessary.

- Remind the witness that the suspect they saw may not even be in the lineup, and that the lineup is intended to clear the innocent as much as it is to identify the guilty.

- Avoid any comments that might influence the witness's selection.

- Ask for and record the witness's degree of certainty immediately.

- Photograph or film lineups to make the police more accountable to the defense.

Before they can take their new influence for granted, psychologists say, there is more to be done. For one thing,

police officers and prosecutors need to be educated about the guidelines, which do not have the force of law. But Mr. Wells and others believe that both groups will embrace them once defense lawyers in the courtroom begin to hold the guidelines up as the gold standard of diligent police work.

⋑ NO DOUBLE-BLIND LINEUPS

The social scientists didn't win every battle. Despite their urgings, law-enforcement officials on the Justice Department panel batted down two key suggestions for improving police lineups. Research suggests that lineups are more accurate when they are double-blind—in other words, when the investigator in charge doesn't know which person is the suspect—and sequential—when the witness sees faces one at a time.

According to participants, police representatives nixed the former idea, because logistically it would be difficult to round up investigators who didn't know who the suspect was. More important, they said, it would be a tough sell to their fellow cops, because it smacks of mistrust and requires them to cede control of an investigation to someone else.

After scholars lost the battle to include double-blind procedures, participants say, they gave up on demanding sequential line-ups. Without the first precaution, they explained, sequential lineups might be even more vulnerable to manipulation than simultaneous lineups are.

John Turtle, a panel member and psychologist at the Ryerson Polytechnic Institute, in Toronto, believes that he has a high-tech solution to all those concerns. He has developed computer software that purports to take the bias out of the photo-spread lineups, which constitute about 80 percent of those in the United States and virtually all of those in Canada.

All a police investigator would need to do is scan a photo of the suspect into a computer and sit the witness down in front of the screen. The machine would then automatically choose photos of others who match the witness's description from a large database, and offer standardized, neutral instructions that wouldn't nudge the witness toward a particular response.

Psychologists deny they are imputing bad faith to police investigators. It's human nature, they say, to want your results to match your expectations. The scholars are simply urging police officers to treat their procedures for handling witnesses with all the care of scientific experiments. "Human memory is a form of trace evidence, like blood or semen or hair, except the trace exists inside the witness's head," says Mr. Wells. "How you go about collecting that evidence and preserving it and analyzing it is absolutely vital."

⁊ Questions

1. In the article, psychologist Gary Wells asks, "Why should people make good eyewitnesses?" Are people good eyewitnesses? Why or why not? What factors, often present during a crime, make it difficult for people to be good eyewitnesses?

2. In what ways are the memories of eyewitnesses flawed?

3. In what ways do police procedures inadvertently foster misidentification by an eyewitness?

4. What has the criminal justice system done to apply the research discussed in this article in order to improve the fairness and accuracy of verdicts in criminal trials? How else could the criminal justice system use the findings discussed in this article to improve accuracy of verdicts?